Exam Ref 70-414
Implementing an
Advanced Server
Infrastructure

Steve Suehring

PUBLISHED BY
Microsoft Press
A Division of Microsoft Corporation
One Microsoft Way
Redmond, Washington 98052-6399

Library of Congress Control Number: 2014940676
ISBN: 978-0-7356-7407-3

Printed and bound in the United States of America.

Second Printing

Microsoft Press books are available through booksellers and distributors worldwide. If you need support related to this book, email Microsoft Press Book Support at mspinput@microsoft.com. Please tell us what you think of this book at http://www.microsoft.com/learning/booksurvey.

The example companies, organizations, products, domain names, email addresses, logos, people, places, and events depicted herein are fictitious. No association with any real company, organization, product, domain name, email address, logo, person, place, or event is intended or should be inferred.

Acquisitions Editor: Anne Hamilton
Developmental Editor: Karen Szall
Editorial Production: Box Twelve Communications
Technical Reviewer: Brian Svidergol
Cover: Twist Creative • Seattle

Contents at a glance

Contents

What do you think of this book? We want to hear from you!

Microsoft is interested in hearing your feedback so we can continually improve our
books and learning resources for you. To participate in a brief online survey, please visit:

www.microsoft.com/learning/booksurvey/

Chapter 3   Plan and implement a server virtualization
infrastructure   117

What do you think of this book? We want to hear from you!

Microsoft is interested in hearing your feedback so we can continually improve our
books and learning resources for you. To participate in a brief online survey, please visit:

www.microsoft.com/learning/booksurvey/

Introduction

This book covers the 70-414 certification exam, "Implementing an Advanced Server Infrastructure." More specifically, the book examines the second revision, or "R2," edition of the exam objectives. The book is written for IT professionals who already have experience with Windows networks.

The 70-414 exam covers advanced topics that IT professionals encounter in the enterprise environment. Topics such as monitoring, virtualization, and high availability are emphasized in the exam objectives. You should have a thorough understanding of a basic server infrastructure as a prerequisite for this book and the 70-414 exam.

There are four main objective areas on the 70-414 exam and each area is covered to a differing level:

- Manage and maintain a server infrastructure: 25 to 30 percent
- Plan and implement a highly available enterprise infrastructure: 25 to 30 percent
- Plan and implement a server virtualization infrastructure: 20 to 30 percent
- Design and implement identity and access solutions: 20 to 25 percent

As you can see from the broad objective areas, there is coverage of both planning and implementation as well as management and design. This level of coverage means that you'll likely need to be able to choose an appropriate solution given a specific scenario or set of technologies for that scenario. Once chosen, you'll then need to be able to determine the most successful path for implementation.

This book covers every exam objective, but it does not cover every exam question. Only the Microsoft exam team has access to the exam questions, and Microsoft regularly adds new questions to the exam, making it impossible to cover specific questions. You should consider this book a supplement to your relevant real-world experience and other study materials. If you encounter a topic in this book that you do not feel completely comfortable with, use the links you'll find in the text to find more information and take the time to research and study the topic. Great information is available on MSDN, TechNet, and in blogs and forums.

Microsoft certifications

Microsoft certifications distinguish you by proving your command of a broad set of skills and experience with current Microsoft products and technologies. The exams and corresponding certifications are developed to validate your mastery of critical competencies as you design and develop, or implement and support, solutions with Microsoft products and technologies both on-premises and in the cloud. Certification brings a variety of benefits to the individual and to employers and organizations.

> **MORE INFO** **ALL MICROSOFT CERTIFICATIONS**
>
> For information about Microsoft certifications, including a full list of available certifications, go to *http://www.microsoft.com/learning/en/us/certification/cert-default.aspx*.

Acknowledgments

Thanks to Karen Szall and the Microsoft Press team, as well as Jeff Riley. It's been a pleasure working with you all, as always.

Free ebooks from Microsoft Press

From technical overviews to in-depth information on special topics, the free ebooks from Microsoft Press cover a wide range of topics. These ebooks are available in PDF, EPUB, and Mobi for Kindle formats, ready for you to download at:

> *http://aka.ms/mspressfree*

Check back often to see what is new!

Errata, updates, & book support

We've made every effort to ensure the accuracy of this book and its companion content. You can access updates to this book—in the form of a list of submitted errata and their related corrections—at:

> *http://aka.ms/ER414R2*

If you discover an error that is not already listed, please submit it to us at the same page.

If you need additional support, email Microsoft Press Book Support at mspinput@microsoft.com.

Please note that product support for Microsoft software and hardware is not offered through the previous addresses. For help with Microsoft software or hardware, go to *http://support.microsoft.com*.

We want to hear from you

At Microsoft Press, your satisfaction is our top priority, and your feedback our most valuable asset. Please tell us what you think of this book at:

http://aka.ms/tellpress

The survey is short, and we read every one of your comments and ideas. Thanks in advance for your input!

Stay in touch

Let's keep the conversation going! We're on Twitter: http://twitter.com/MicrosoftPress.

Preparing for the exam

Microsoft certification exams are a great way to build your resume and let the world know about your level of expertise. Certification exams validate your on-the-job experience and product knowledge. While there is no substitution for on-the-job experience, preparation through study and hands-on practice can help you prepare for the exam. We recommend that you round out your exam preparation plan by using a combination of available study materials and courses. For example, you might use this Exam Ref and another study guide for your "at home" preparation and take a Microsoft Official Curriculum course for the classroom experience. Choose the combination that you think works best for you.

Note that this Exam Ref is based on publicly available information about the exam and the author's experience. To safeguard the integrity of the exam, authors do not have access to the live exam.

CHAPTER 1

Manage and maintain a server infrastructure

The 70-414 exam looks to stretch your understanding of planning, implementation, and management of an advanced Microsoft-based infrastructure. The tools and products included in the exam are used in enterprise-level networks and emphasize automation, high availability, and self-service. The first chapter of this book discusses objectives surrounding server infrastructure management. Within this chapter and indeed the entire book, you'll find hands-on examples that directly tie to the exam objectives, and you'll find numerous links to more information on TechNet.

> **IMPORTANT**
> ### Have you read page xv?
> It contains valuable information regarding the skills you need to pass the exam.

Objectives in this chapter:

- Objective 1.1: Design an administrative model
- Objective 1.2: Design a monitoring strategy
- Objective 1.3: Plan and implement automated remediation

Objective 1.1: Design an administrative model

Designing an administrative model for an enterprise network involves a large amount of planning, especially in complex or highly structured enterprises. A good administrative model will enable delegation of authority while also enforcing the principle of least privilege. Many organizations have unique needs, but the overall administrative model can follow a common pattern. For example, an organization that's geographically dispersed may allow personnel at remote locations to change passwords for users at that remote site.

Understanding administrative model design considerations

Typical enterprise administrative and privilege models use groups to assign and delegate permissions. Groups save time and administration overhead by combining similar users and computers into one entity that can then be assigned permissions.

> **MORE INFO** **DESIGN STRATEGIES FOR ACTIVE DIRECTORY DOMAIN SERVICES (AD DS)**
>
> This section examines user rights and built-in groups. If you're unfamiliar with design strategies for Active Directory Domain Services (AD DS), you can find more information in the AD DS Design Guide at *http://technet.microsoft.com/library/cc754678.aspx*.

Groups can have users and computers and are created as a security group or a distribution group. The security group type is covered in this chapter; distribution groups are typically used to create email distribution lists and aren't covered in this book. Groups are also scoped, which means that they can apply locally to a computer, to a domain, or to an entire forest. Table 1-1 describes the three types of group scopes available in AD DS.

TABLE 1-1 Active Directory Domain Services group scope

Group Scope	Description
Domain Local	Members in a Domain Local scoped group can have permissions within the same domain where the Domain Local group is located and can contain any combination of groups with domain local, global, or universal scope.
Global	Members of groups with a Global scope can have permissions in any domain within a forest, but members can come from only the domain within which the group is defined.
Universal	Members of groups with Universal scope can have permissions in any domain or forest and can originate from any domain or forest.

User rights

Before looking at user rights, it's important to agree on the definition of a user right. You can find a definition all the way back to Windows NT Server 4.0 in the "NT Server 4.0 Concepts and Planning Manual" on TechNet, where a *right* is defined as something that "authorized a user to perform certain actions on a computer system." See *http://technet.microsoft.com/en-us/library/cc751446.aspx* for more discussion on the definition.

What's important to realize is the distinction between a right and a permission. A *right* defines what a user can do on a computer system, whereas *permissions* apply to objects. Rights can override permissions in certain instances. For example, if a user is a member of a group that has the right to back up a computer or has the Back Up Files and Directories right, that user inherently has read access to the files on the computer, even if permissions would normally deny such access. More specifically, the Back Up Files and Directories right has the following permissions:

- Traverse Folder/Execute File
- List Folder/Read Data
- Read Attributes
- Read Extended Attributes
- Read Permissions

The Back Up Files and Directories right is just one example of this concept. Table 1-2 shows several other security-related user rights available with Windows Server 2012. An abbreviated constant name applies to each of the rights described in Table 1-2. The constant names are used for logging and can also be used for Windows PowerShell, as discussed later in this section.

TABLE 1-2 Additional security-related user rights

User Right	Description	Constant Name
Access Credential Manager as a trusted caller	Applies to Credential Manager during backup-related processes. This privilege is assigned to the Winlogon service only and should not be assigned to the account.	SeTrustedCredManAccessPrivilege
Access this computer from the network	Determines whether a user can utilize protocols related to accessing a given computer, such as Service Message Block (SMB), NetBIOS, Common Internet File System (CIFS), and Component Object Model Plus (COM+).	SeNetworkLogonRight
Act as part of the operating system	Applies to processes to determine whether they can use a user's identity to gain access to the privileges granted to that user.	SeTcbPrivilege

User Right	Description	Constant Name
Add workstations to domain	Enables a user to add a computer to a domain.	SeMachineAccountPrivilege
Adjust memory quotas for a process	Enables a user to change the memory used by a process.	SeIncreaseQuotaPrivilege
Allow logon locally	Enables a user to start an interactive session.	SeInteractiveLogonRight
Allow logon through Remote Desktop Services	Enables a user to log on using Remote Desktop Services.	SeRemoteInteractiveLogonRight
Back up files and directories	Enables an account to bypass permissions for backup purposes.	SeBackupPrivilege
Bypass traverse checking	Enables an account to traverse an NTFS file system without needing to check the Traverse Folder permission.	SeChangeNotifyPrivilege
Change the system time	Enables a user to change the time on the local computer.	SeSystemtimePrivilege
Change the time zone	Enables a user to change the time zone on the local computer.	SeTimeZonePrivilege
Create a pagefile	Enables a user to change settings around the pagefile, including its size.	SeCreatePagefilePrivilege
Create a token object	Enables a process to create a token using the privileged account.	SeCreateTokenPrivilege
Create global objects	Enables creation of global objects.	SeCreateGlobalPrivilege
Create permanent shared objects	Enables creation of directory objects.	SeCreatePermanentPrivilege
Create symbolic links	Enables an account to create a file system symbolic link.	SeCreateSymbolicLinkPrivilege
Debug programs	Enables a user to attach to a process for debugging.	SeDebugPrivilege
Deny access to this computer from the network	Prevents users from accessing the computer.	SeDenyNetworkLogonRight
Deny logon as a batch job	Prevents an account from logging on using batch-related methods.	SeDenyBatchLogonRight
Deny logon as a service	Prevents an account from logging on as a service.	SeDenyServiceLogonRight
Deny logon locally	Prevents an account from logging on locally at a computer console.	SeDenyInteractiveLogonRight
Deny logon through Remote Desktop Services	Prevents users from logging on to a computer using Remote Desktop Services.	SeDenyRemoteInteractiveLogonRight

User Right	Description	Constant Name
Enable computer and user accounts to be trusted for delegation	Enables a user to set the Trusted for Delegation setting.	SeEnableDelegationPrivilege
Force shutdown from a remote system	Allows a user to shut down a computer when connected remotely.	SeRemoteShutdownPrivilege
Generate security audits	Enables an account to generate audit records in the security log.	SeAuditPrivilege
Impersonate a client after authentication	Enables a program to impersonate a user or account and act on behalf of that user or account.	SeImpersonatePrivilege
Increase a process working set	Enables a user to increase the size of a working set of a process.	SeIncreaseWorkingSetPrivilege
Increase scheduling priority	Enables a user to increase the base priority of a process.	SeIncreaseBasePriorityPrivilege
Load and unload device drivers	Enables a user to dynamically load or unload device drivers.	SeLoadDriverPackage
Lock pages in memory	Enables an account to keep data from a process in physical memory.	SeLockMemoryPrivilege
Log on as a batch job	Enables an account to log on using batch-related methods, including Task Scheduler.	SeBatchLogonRight
Log on as a service	Enables a service account to register a process.	SeServiceLogonRight
Manage auditing and security log	Enables a user to work with auditing and security log.	SeSecurityPrivilege
Modify an object label	Enables an account to modify integrity labels used by Windows Integrity Controls (WIC).	SeRelabelPrivilege
Modify firmware environment values	Enables a user to modify non-volatile RAM (NVRAM) settings.	SeSystemEnvironmentPrivilege
Perform volume maintenance tasks	Enables a user to do volume- and disk management–related tasks.	SeManageVolumePrivilege
Profile single process	Enables a user to view performance aspects of a process.	SeProfileSingleProcessPrivilege
Profile system performance	Enables a user to use the Windows Performance Monitor tools.	SeSystemProfilePrivilege
Remove computer from docking station	Enables a user to undock a computer without logging on.	SeUndockPrivilege
Replace a process level token	Enables a process to replace an access token of a child process.	SeAssignPrimaryTokenPrivilege
Restore files and directories	Enables a user to bypass the normal permission checks when restoring.	SeRestorePrivilege

User Right	Description	Constant Name
Shut down the system	Enables a local user to shut down the system.	SeShutdownPrivilege
Synchronize directory service data	Enables a user to synchronize service data, such as LDAP directory synchronization.	SeSyncAgentPrivilege
Take ownership of files or other objects	Enables an account to take ownership of objects in the computer.	SeTakeOwnershipPrivilege

The constant name described in Table 1-2 can be used with Windows PowerShell cmdlets related to privileges:

- Get-Privilege
- Grant-Privilege
- Revoke-Privilege
- Test-Privilege

As described in Table 1-2, user rights generally shouldn't be applied to accounts directly, but rather should be granted through the use of groups.

> **MORE INFO** USER RIGHTS ASSIGNMENT
>
> See *http://technet.microsoft.com/library/dn221963* for more information on user rights assignment.

Built-in groups

Built-in groups, also called *default groups*, are added with the operating system. Many of the default groups have user rights assigned already. Certain rights also apply depending on the type of computer on which the right is being exercised. For example, the Allow Logon Locally right is granted to the following groups for logging on to workstations and servers:

- Administrators
- Backup Operators
- Users

By contrast, the following groups have the Allow Logon Locally right for domain controllers:

- Account Operators
- Administrators
- Backup Operators
- Print Operators
- Server Operators

Table 1-3 shows the local groups for a computer and the user rights granted to them by default.

TABLE 1-3 User rights for local groups

Group	User Rights
Administrators	Access this computer from the network Adjust memory quotas for a process Allow logon locally Allow logon through Remote Desktop Services Back up files and directories Bypass traverse checking Change the system time Change the time zone Create a page file Create global objects Create symbolic links Debug programs Force shutdown from a remote system Impersonate a client after authentication Increase scheduling priority Load and unload device drivers Log on as a batch job Manage auditing and security log Modify firmware environment variables Perform volume maintenance tasks Profile system performance Remove computer from docking station Restore files and directories Shut down the system Take ownership of files or other objects
Backup Operators	Access this computer from the network Allow logon locally Back up files and directories Bypass traverse checking Log on as a batch job Restore file and directories Shut down the system
Cryptographic Operators	No user rights granted by default
Distributed COM Users	No user rights granted by default
Guests	No user rights granted by default
IIS_IUSRS	No user rights granted by default
Network Configuration Operators	No user rights granted by default
Performance Log Users	No user rights granted by default
Performance Monitor Users	No user rights granted by default
Power Users	No user rights granted by default
Remote Desktop Users	Allow logon through Remote Desktop Services
Replicators	No user rights granted by default

Group	User Rights
Users	Access this computer from the network Allow logon locally Bypass traverse checking Change the time zone Increase a process working set Remove the computer from a docking station Shut down the system
Offer Remote Assistance Helpers	No user rights granted by default

MORE INFO **DEFAULT LOCAL GROUPS**

See *http://technet.microsoft.com/library/cc771990.aspx* for more information on default local groups.

AD DS also contains default groups. These groups are placed into either the Builtin or Users container.

Table 1-4 describes the groups in the Builtin container.

TABLE 1-4 Groups in the Builtin container

Group	User Rights
Account Operators	Allow logon locally Shut down the system
Administrator	Access this computer from the network Adjust memory quotas for a process Back up files and directories Bypass traverse checking Change the system time Create a pagefile Debug programs Enable computer and user accounts to be trusted for delegation Force a shutdown from a remote system Increase scheduling priority Load and unload device drivers Allow logon locally Manage auditing and security log Modify firmware environment values Profile single process Profile system performance Remove computer from docking station Restore files and directories Shut down the system Take ownership of files or other objects
Backup Operators	Back up files and directories Allow logon locally Restore files and directories Shut down the system
Guests	No user rights granted by default

Group	User Rights
Incoming Forest Trust Builders	No user rights granted by default; applicable to forest root domain only
Network Configuration Operators	No user rights granted by default
Performance Monitor Users	No user rights granted by default
Performance Log Users	No user rights granted by default
Pre-Windows 2000 Compatible Access	Access this computer from the network Bypass traverse checking
Print Operators	Allow logon locally Shut down the system
Remote Desktop Users	No user rights granted by default
Replicator	No user rights granted by default
Server Operators	Back up files and directories Change the system time Force shutdown from a remote system Allow logon locally Restore files and directories Shut down the system
Users	No user rights granted by default

Table 1-5 describes the groups in the Users container.

TABLE 1-5 Groups in the Users container

Group	User Rights
Cert Publishers	No user rights granted by default
DnsAdmins	No user rights granted by default; installed as part of DNS
DnsUpdateProxy	No user rights granted by default; installed as part of DNS
Domain Admins	Access this computer from the network Adjust memory quotas for a process Back up files and directories Bypass traverse checking Change the system time Create a pagefile Debug programs Enable computer and user accounts to be trusted for delegation Force a shutdown from a remote system Increase scheduling priority Load and unload device drivers Allow logon locally Manage auditing and security log Modify firmware environment values Profile single process Profile system performance Remove computer from docking station Restore files and directories Shut down the system Take ownership of files or other objects

Group	User Rights
Domain Computers	No user rights granted by default
Domain Controllers	No user rights granted by default
Domain Guests	No user rights granted by default
Domain Users	No user rights granted by default
Enterprise Admins	Note: Permissions are applicable to forest root domain only Access this computer from the network Adjust memory quotas for a process Back up files and directories Bypass traverse checking Change the system time Create a pagefile Debug programs Enable computer and user accounts to be trusted for delegation Force a shutdown from a remote system Increase scheduling priority Load and unload device drivers Allow logon locally Manage auditing and security log Modify firmware environment values Profile single process Profile system performance Remove computer from docking station Restore files and directories Shut down the system Take ownership of files or other objects
Group Policy Creator Owners	No user rights granted by default
IIS_WPG	No user rights granted by default; installed with IIS
RAS and IAS Servers	No user rights granted by default
Schema Admins	No user rights granted by default; applicable to forest root domain only

Built-in groups are different from special identities. A special identity is a group for which membership cannot be modified, such as the Everyone group. Special identities include those in Table 1-6.

TABLE 1-6 Special identities

Identity	Description
Anonymous Logon	Used for anonymous access to services and resources
Everyone	All network users, with the exception of the Anonymous Logon group
Interactive	Users who are logged on locally to the computer
Network	Users who are accessing a computer's resources over the network

Understanding delegation in System Center 2012 R2

Microsoft System Center 2012 R2 consists of several products, including Configuration Manager, Operations Manager, Data Protection Manager, Service Manager, AppController, and Virtual Machine Manager (VMM). The products used in the organization determine the delegation structure. For example, certain roles are only applicable for Virtual Machine Manager and others are applicable for Configuration Manager. If the organization doesn't use VMM, then those roles wouldn't be used. However, the concepts of delegated authority and role-based administration are applicable no matter what products are being used. This section examines delegation for Configuration Manager and Operations Manager. Other products such as Virtual Machine Manager and Data Protection Manager are covered in other objectives in this chapter.

Role-based administration

System Center 2012 R2 uses role-based administration to facilitate the structure needed in many organizations. Using role-based administration you can limit the authority and scope of permissions to the least amount necessary in order to complete a task. For example, an organization may grant the ability to change passwords for normal users to help desk staff. This scenario can be accomplished by granting the limited privileges to the help desk personnel. An important concept surrounding role-based administration in System Center is administrative scope. Administrative scope defines the permissions that a given user has on objects within the scope's control. Administrative scopes consist of:

- Security roles
- Collections
- Security scopes

SECURITY ROLES

Security roles, which you might think of like a group in Active Directory, are used to grant sets of permissions to users based on their role. For example, the Asset Analyst role is granted certain permissions to view Asset Intelligence and inventory information. Users can then be given the Asset Analyst role to do their job.

Each security role is granted specific permissions, such as Approve, Create, Delete, Modify, and so on. The permissions apply to specific object types within System Center. There are several built-in security roles that come with Configuration Manager and with other System Center products. The permissions granted to these roles can't be changed. However, the roles can be copied, and a new role can be built and modified as needed.

The general steps for planning security roles are:

1. Identify tasks. Examine the responsibilities for administrators. For example, you might have administrators that are responsible for client security while others are responsible for software updates.

2. Map tasks to roles. Determine how the responsibilities connect to built-in security roles.

3. Assign roles. Assign roles to users. If a user has responsibilities across multiple roles, assign that user to multiple roles.

4. Create new roles (optional). Create new roles if the responsibilities don't map to one or more of the built-in roles.

COLLECTIONS

Computers and users are grouped into collections in Configuration Manager. Collections are important in the hierarchical delegation of administration for Configuration Manager. Collections can be created to meet the needs of the organization. For example, you might create a collection for each physical location in an organization, or you might create a functional collection that includes all servers or all client computers. Like security roles, there are several built-in collections that can't be modified. Collections become very useful when you want to distribute software, provide reporting, or ensure configuration changes are consistent across the devices within the collection.

> **MORE INFO COLLECTIONS**
>
> See *http://technet.microsoft.com/en-us/library/gg682177* for more information on collections.

SECURITY SCOPES

Security scopes can be used to grant access to securable objects by type. Security scopes provide granular access control. However, security scopes can't be nested or used in a hierarchical manner. Security scopes are useful for segregating objects of the same type so that different levels of access can be granted to them. For instance, if a set of administrators should be granted full access only to non-production servers, the servers can be scoped to separate production from development servers.

There are two built-in security scopes:

- **All**   Includes all scopes. Objects cannot be added to this scope.
- **Default**   Installed with Configuration Manager, the default scope also includes all objects.

EXAM TIP

Security scopes are configured within Configuration Manager in the Set Security Scopes dialog box found in the Classify group.

Certain objects can't be secured by security scopes. Instead, access to these objects is granted using security roles. Objects that can't be included in security scopes are:

- Active Directory forests
- Administrative users
- Alerts
- Boundaries
- Computer associations
- Default client settings
- Deployment templates
- Device drivers
- Exchange server connectors
- Migration site-to-site mappings
- Mobile device enrollment profiles
- Security roles
- Security scopes
- Site addresses
- Site system roles
- Software titles
- Software updates
- Status messages
- User device affinities

Delegation design

Hierarchical structure is important for designing a delegated administration for System Center. When it is properly structured, you can delegate responsibilities merely by using scopes and security roles. However, as the organization's needs change, so too will the needs for delegated administration. For example, if a merger takes place, the newly merged company may need to manage its own site.

Designing delegation involves determining the following:

- **Who** Who is responsible for managing a given client computer or server? Determine the various tasks involved in administration, whether that's software updates, security, or anything else that System Center can do. These tasks will map to security roles.

- **Which and Where** Which computers, servers, or other objects will those people manage, based on their roles? Where are those objects located, both physically and logically? For instance, there may be different responsibilities based on physical location or logical location (production versus test). Collections are used to group the objects together in Configuration Manager, and security scopes can be used to provide more granular control over the objects.

- **What** What permissions do administrators need on a given object? Permissions can be changed within the security roles, and their scope can be limited through security scopes.

Configuration Manager

System Center 2012 R2 Configuration Manager is an important piece of enterprise IT management. Configuration Manager provides a unified solution for management of operating systems, devices, software updates, asset inventory, and more. Using Configuration Manager, an enterprise can deliver software to devices within the organization and ensure consistency of updates and configurations. Configuration Manager also integrates with other System Center products and with other services like Windows Intune.

Configuration Manager can be configured as a standalone set of services or in a hierarchy, known as primary site and central administration site, respectively. The primary site-only scenario is useful for small implementations or small networks, whereas the central administration site scenario is useful for larger enterprises, especially those that need hierarchical or delegated management.

Site system roles

Within Configuration Manager, site system roles are used to define what tasks the various servers perform within a site. Site system roles shouldn't be confused with role-based administration, which is also covered in this section. Table 1-7 describes some of the typical site system roles.

TABLE 1-7 Core site system roles

Role	Description
Component server	A basic service that is responsible for running Configuration Manager services. This role is automatically installed for all roles except the distribution point role.
Site database server	The server that runs the SQL Server database and is used to store information and data related to the Configuration Manager deployment.
Site server	The server from which the core functionality of Configuration Manager is provided.
Site system	The site system role is a basic role installed on any computer hosting a site system.
SMS Provider	Provides the interface between the Configuration Manager console and the site database. Note that the SMS Provider role can be used only on computers that are in the same domain as the site server.

Multiple site system roles typically run on a single server, especially in new or small implementations of Configuration Manager. Additional servers can be deployed as distribution points to ensure availability of software packages and related files or to provide those files at strategic locations. For example, you might place a distribution point close to a large number of client computers.

Aside from the core site system roles, other site system roles may be used. Table 1-8 describes some other site system roles.

TABLE 1-8 Additional site system roles

Role	Description
Application Catalog web service point	Responsible for providing information from the Software Library to the Application Catalog website.
Application Catalog website point	A website that displays available software from the Application Catalog.
Asset Intelligence synchronization point	Exchanges Asset Intelligence information with Microsoft.
Certificate registration point	New for System Center 2012 R2, this role provides for communication for devices using Simple Certificate Enrollment Protocol (SCEP) with Network Device Enrollment Service. This role cannot exist on the same server as the computer running Network Device Enrollment Service.
Distribution point	A role that holds software packages, updates, system images, and other files for clients to download.
Endpoint Protection point	Accepts Endpoint Protection license terms and configures default membership for Microsoft Active Protection Service.
Enrollment point	Enrolls mobile devices and Mac computers using public key infrastructure and also provisions Intel Active Management Technology computers.
Enrollment point proxy	Manages enrollment requests for mobile devices and Mac computers.

Role	Description
Fallback status point	Monitors client installation and identifies clients that can't communicate with their management point.
Management point	A role that interacts with client computers to receive configuration data and send policy and service location information.
Out of band service point	Configures Intel AMT computers for out of band management.
Reporting services point	A role that creates and manages Configuration Manager reports. This role works with SQL Server Reporting Services.
Software update point	Together with Windows Software Update Services (WSUS), this role provides software updates to clients.
State migration point	Holds client user state data during migration to a new operating system.
System Health Validator point	Validates Network Access Protection (NAP) policies. The role must be installed on a NAP health policy server.
Windows Intune connector	Manages mobile devices with Windows Intune through the Configuration Manager console. This role is available with Service Pack 1 (SP1).

> *MORE INFO* **ROLE-BASED ADMINISTRATION IN CONFIGURATION MANAGER**
>
> See *http://blogs.technet.com/b/hhoy/archive/2012/03/07/role-based-administration-in-system-center-2012-configuration-manager.aspx* for more information on Role-Based Administration in Configuration Manager.

Operations Manager

System Center 2012 R2 Operations Manager provides monitoring capabilities to computers across an enterprise. The roles necessary within Operations Manager include those to create monitoring configurations, view and edit reports, and provide overall administration, among others.

Operations Manager uses many of the same concepts as other System Center products for rights delegation. Operations Manager uses user roles and role profiles which are then combined with a scope to produce the user role. For example, Operations Manager has several built-in user roles, called *profiles* in Operations Manager:

- Administrator
- Advanced Operator
- Application Monitoring Operator
- Author
- Operator
- Read-only Operator
- Report Operator
- Report Security Administrator

Each of these built-in user roles can be changed through its properties settings. The scopes can be changed, as can the tasks and dashboards and views available to the user role. This is illustrated in Figure 1-1.

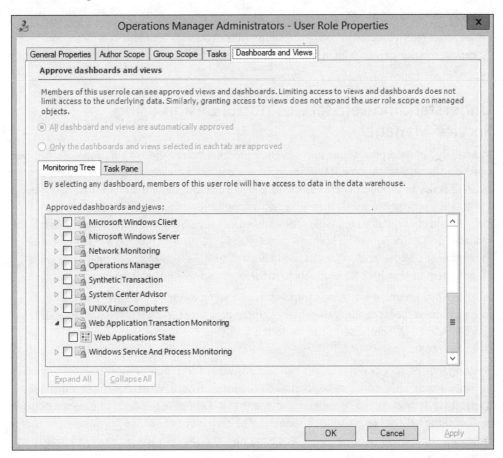

FIGURE 1-1 Changing the dashboards and views available to one of the built-in user roles in Operations Manager

Each of the built-in user roles can contain one or more local or Active Directory–based groups or users. For example, the Operations Manager Administrators user role (shown in Figure 1-1) contains the BUILTIN\Administrators group.

You can also create user roles within Operations Manager by using the Create User Role Wizard. When creating a new user role you first choose the type of user role on which the new user role will be based from among these choices:

- Operator
- Read-Only Operator
- Author
- Advanced Operator

Each of these profiles provides certain privileges that are connected to that profile. For example, the Author profile contains privileges specific to creating monitoring configurations.

MORE INFO **USER ROLES**

See *http://technet.microsoft.com/en-us/library/hh230728.aspx* for more information on implementation of user roles in Operations Manager.

Understanding self-service portal design using Service Manager

Maintaining an enterprise server infrastructure can be accomplished in a number of ways, but when considering management solutions that scale to large environments, the System Center 2012 R2 family of products comes to the forefront. For example, with Service Manager, you can create a self-service portal for end users, among other things. Service Manager provides incident and configuration management while enabling visibility into current issues. Service Manager uses a Configuration Management Database (CMDB) to provide a master location for all changes, issues, and requests for an infrastructure. Service Manager integrates with other System Center 2012 R2 products to provide an end-to-end solution.

At a minimum, there are three components to a Service Manager implementation: a management server, a configuration management database server, and the management console. Additional components can be added for things like data warehousing, which then facilitates reporting.

Using the self-service portal, users can find answers to common support questions, change their passwords, create help-desk tickets, and request software. When designing a management structure, you should consider deployment of the self-service portal to ease the burden on IT and the help desk for common requests. The end-user self-service portal requires a Silverlight component to run on the client computer and thus is applicable only to those platforms that can run Silverlight through the browser.

MORE INFO **SELF-SERVICE PORTAL**

See *http://technet.microsoft.com/library/hh667344.aspx* for more information on the self-service portal in Service Manager.

Delegating rights for the private cloud

System Center 2012 Virtual Machine Manager provides a centralized management console for virtual machines, such as those managed by Hyper-V. VMM manages virtual machines, networks, and storage as resources, which are then configured within the organization. A VMM deployment consists of a management server, database, library (and library server), and console.

Another component of managing the private cloud is App Controller. App Controller looks at service provision from a service-oriented view rather than from a server or software view. In other words, using App Controller you can connect the components that make up a service to facilitate management.

User roles can be created to manage various aspects of private cloud-based virtualization infrastructure. Virtual Machine Manager can be used to create such a delegation, and then App Controller can be used to manage the private cloud.

Rights are managed within the User Roles area of the Security section in the Settings area of Virtual Machine Manager. User roles can be created using individual user accounts or using Active Directory groups. The scope of the user role can then be assigned to the private cloud, as shown in Figure 1-2.

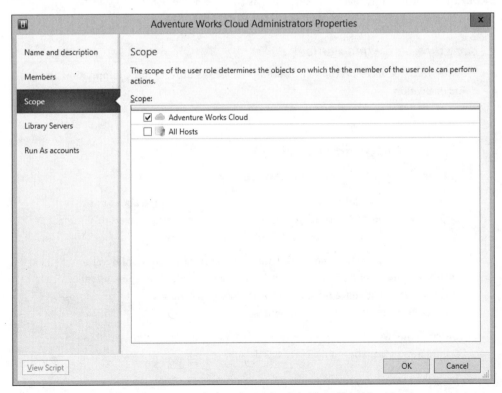

FIGURE 1-2 Assigning a scope to a user role for private clouds in Virtual Machine Manager

Members that have been assigned to the new user role will be able to log on to App Controller and manage private clouds within the user role scope.

An alternate method to assign access is by clicking Assign Cloud from the VMs and Services section in Virtual Machine Manager. Doing so enables you to select the user role to be assigned privileges for a given cloud or to create a new user role for the private cloud, as shown in Figure 1-3.

FIGURE 1-3 Assigning a user role to a cloud in the Assign Cloud dialog box

---

MORE INFO **DELEGATING RIGHTS**

See *http://technet.microsoft.com/en-us/library/hh221343.aspx* for more information on rights delegation.

 Thought experiment

Delegating administrative authority

In the following thought experiment, apply what you've learned about this objective to predict what steps you need to take. You can find answers to these questions in the "Answers" section at the end of this chapter.

You're working on delegating administrative authority for your Configuration Manager deployment. You need to enable certain individuals to apply updates to test computers and, once tested, enable another set of individuals to apply those updates in the production environment.

Describe the overall concepts and types of configuration items that you'll use in Configuration Manager to facilitate this design.

Objective summary

- User rights and built-in groups can be used to provide a robust administrative model.
- Certain user rights shouldn't be assigned to users or groups but are instead used by system processes and functions.
- Built-in groups have certain user rights inherently assigned to them.
- System Center 2012 R2 can utilize a delegated administration structure that enables separation of responsibilities within an infrastructure.
- Security roles, security scopes, and collections are all used to facilitate the delegated administration structure necessary.
- Determining who, which and where, and what can be helpful for designing a delegation of role structure.
- Service Manager is used to provide end-user self service.
- Service Manager requires at least three servers to run including a management server, configuration management database server, and console.

Objective review

Answer the following questions to test your knowledge of the information in this objective. You can find the answers to these questions and explanations of why each answer choice is correct or incorrect in the "Answers" section at the end of this chapter.

1. Which of the following permissions allows the currently logged on user to shut the computer down?

   A. SeShutdownComputer

   B. SeShutdownPrivilege

   C. SePrivilegeShutdown

   D. En_ShutdownComputerPermission

2. Which of the following is not a privilege of the built-in Backup Operators group?

   A. Shut down the system

   B. Create symbolic links

   C. Back up files and directories

   D. Allow logon locally

3. Which of the following roles provides the core functionality for System Center?

   A. Site server

   B. Component server

   C. Core server

   D. Site Core server

4. Which of the following are not built-in security scopes in Configuration Manager?

   A. All

   B. System

   C. Administrator

   D. Default

Objective 1.2: Design a monitoring strategy

As it pertains to the exam, Operations Manager is the primary tool used for enterprise monitoring. Operations Manager provides security logging (through Audit Collection Services) and performance monitoring and meets the criteria for centralized monitoring and reporting, which are all part of the objectives for this section.

> **This objective covers how to:**
>
> - Understand monitoring servers using Audit Collection Services (ACS) and System Center Global Service Monitor, performance monitoring, application monitoring, centralized monitoring, and centralized reporting
> - Implement and optimize System Center 2012 R2 Operations Manager management packs
> - Plan for monitoring Active Directory

Enabling Audit Collection Services (ACS)

Part of Operations Manager, Audit Collection Services (ACS) collects audit policy records for analysis and reporting. When used as part of an overall monitoring design strategy, ACS is responsible for collecting security-related events. This effectively means that you can gather security audit logs from multiple sources, including Linux and Unix–based computers, and access them from that centralized console for reporting and further action, as necessary.

ACS consists of the following:

- **ACS forwarders** The ACS forwarder is included, but not enabled, as part of the Operations Manager agent installation. Once enabled, security events are sent to the ACS collector and the local security event log.

- **ACS collector** The ACS collector is responsible for processing events from ACS forwarders so that the event can be entered into the database.

- **ACS database** The ACS database relies on SQL Server as its backend database and is responsible for holding the events sent to it from the ACS collector.

Each of these components can exist on the same server, though you'll install ACS forwarders on each computer to be monitored. When considering performance and as the deployment grows, the collector and ACS database servers can be split onto separate servers. For many enterprise deployments, SQL Server will exist on a separate server as part of the initial rollout of Operations Manager.

> **MORE INFO ACS SYSTEM REQUIREMENTS**
>
> See *http://technet.microsoft.com/en-us/library/hh212908.aspx* for more information on ACS system requirements.

ACS forwarders are not enabled as part of the normal health-monitoring agent in Operators Manager. Instead, ACS forwarders are enabled through the Monitoring, Operations Manager, Agent Health State section of the Operations Manager console. Within the details pane of this area, selecting the computers (agents) and then selecting Enable Audit Collection within the Health Service Tasks section of the Actions pane enables ACS to begin collecting from that computer.

> **EXAM TIP**
>
> If necessary, a firewall exception for TCP port 51909 should be added to allow an ACS forwarder to communicate with the ACS collector.

When designing ACS-based solutions, the number of events sent by forwarders can overwhelm the ACS collector. Additionally, the ACS collector queues events when the ACS database server is offline, such as for maintenance. The collector queue has settings that can be adjusted for performance. These settings are in the registry at HKEY_LOCAL_MACHINE\ SYSTEM\CurrentControlSet\Services\AdtServer\Parameters. The settings are described in Table 1-9.

> **NOTE MANAGING DOWNTIME**
>
> The Enterprise version of SQL Server can be deployed to prevent maintenance-related downtime.

TABLE 1-9 ACS collector queue settings

Setting	Description	Default
MaximumQueueLength	The maximum number of events that can be held in the ACS collector queue if the database is offline.	0x40000
BackOffThreshold	The maximum number of queued events before the ACS collector denies new connections. The value is a percentage of the MaximumQueueLength.	75
DisconnectThreshold	The maximum number of queued events before the ACS collector begins disconnecting ACS forwarders. Like BackOffThreshold, this value is a percentage of the MaximumQueueLength.	90

ACS collects every Windows Security Event for each forwarder involved in the deployment. This can be a large amount of data and, in many instances, isn't necessary. One approach is to create a filter to prevent unnecessary events from being logged to the ACS database. Combining a filter with a policy for archiving ACS events ensures that compliance is met while at the same time not overwhelming the ACS implementation (or the administrators responsible for it).

Management of ACS is accomplished using the AdtAdmin.exe command-line tool found in %WINDIR%\System32\Security\AdtServer. Using AdtAdmin, you can create groups, show information about forwarders, and filter audit event data.

You might filter event data if the ACS collector queue is becoming full. ACS event filters are defined using Windows Management Instrumentation Query Language (WQL), which is a subset of standard SQL.

Table 1-10 describes some of the parameters available for AdtAdmin.

TABLE 1-10 AdtAdmin parameters

Parameter	Description
/AddGroup	Creates a group of ACS forwarders.
/DelGroup	Deletes a group of ACD forwarders.
/Disconnect	Disconnects an ACS forwarder or group.
/GetDBAuth	Shows information regarding the connection between the collector and database.
/GetQuery	Shows the current WQL queries being used by the ACS collector.
/ListForwarders	Shows information about forwarders.
/ListGroups	Shows the groups available on the collector.
/SetDBAuth	Sets the authentication method (SQL or Windows authentication) between the collector and the database.
/SetQuery	Configures a WQL query for filtering audit events.
/Stats	Shows statistics about the forwarders.
/UpdForwarder	Makes changes to a forwarder, including its name or the group to which the forwarder belongs.
/UpdGroup	Renames a group.

As described in Table 1-10, the current value of the WQL query can be obtained using the command:

```
AdtAdmin /getquery
```

By default, the WQL query for events is:

```
select * from AdtsEvent
```

The performance of ACS can be monitored through the Operations Manager console. Several counters are included by default and can be used to help diagnose and monitor performance of ACS itself.

Understanding Global Service Monitor

Global Service Monitor is provided as a management pack for Operations Manager and as part of an online offering such as a cloud-based service. Global Service Monitor provides an external view of websites for an organization. Global Service Monitor has two primary components: an online component managed by Microsoft and an Operations Manager component, which is handled as a management pack.

It's important to understand how Global Service Monitor fits within an enterprise scenario. Global Service Monitor is used for monitoring externally facing websites, such as those hosted through Microsoft Azure; as such, it fits within but isn't intended to be a replacement for Operations Manager but rather an enhancement to an Operations Manager installation. Global Service Monitor facilitates and makes easy the process of setting up multiple, globally dispersed monitoring locations for web applications.

The next section describes importing management packs as well as additional monitoring scenarios discussed in the objective domain for the 70-414 exam. Once a management pack is imported and a subscription started, you can configure monitoring through Operations Manager. Tests run with Global Service Monitor can be executed from multiple locations around the world so that you can have a complete view into your web application.

The simplest of tests is the Web Application Availability Monitoring test, which performs a basic HTTP request from an external location. If you need a more complex test, such as when you need to view multistep transactions or provide authentication details, then the Visual Studio Web Test Monitoring scenario is the correct choice. Finally, Web Application Transaction Monitoring provides monitoring for internal web applications that aren't available from external locations.

When configuring a test, you can set several parameters, such as the length of time that a request can take, the interval between requests, whether to look for specific text on the resulting page, and many additional settings, as shown in Figure 1-4.

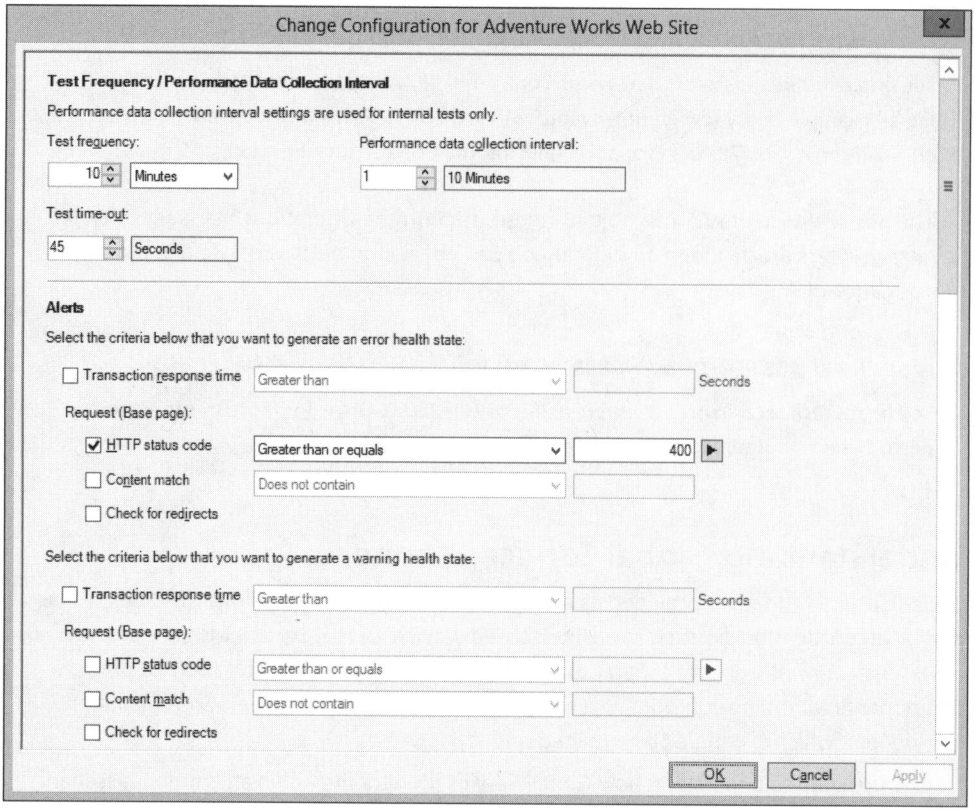

FIGURE 1-4 Configuring parameters related to a web availability test in Global Service Monitor

These settings are useful when you need to ensure specific behavior of a webpage or ensure that the page is served in less than a certain number of seconds. You can even check portions of the request, such as the time it takes to receive the first byte, the time it takes for DNS resolution, and so on.

When integrating Global Service Monitor into a monitoring design, consider the areas from which your customers will most likely access your website. Choose external monitoring locations close to your customer base.

> **MORE INFO CONFIGURING GLOBAL SERVICE MONITOR**
>
> Because this is a design-based objective, the actual configuration steps aren't covered in this text. Instead, see *http://technet.microsoft.com/en-us/library/jj860370.aspx* and *http://technet.microsoft.com/en-us/library/jj860376.aspx* for specific information on configuration in Global Service Monitor.

Implementing and optimizing Operations Manager management packs

Looking beyond performance monitoring of ACS, Operations Manager can provide performance monitoring, application monitoring, and reporting for Windows computers and the network as a whole. To do so, a System Center management pack can be installed. The management pack contains additional information about monitoring points for Windows Server.

Management packs provide information about how to monitor servers, applications, and services on a network. Management packs can also provide reports, tasks, and other components as defined by the management pack. For example, a management pack for a Windows Server might contain information on how to monitor disk performance. Management packs can be created by third parties to provide an integrated monitoring solution within Operations Manager.

> **MORE INFO** **MANAGEMENT PACKS**
>
> If you're unfamiliar with management packs, see "What Is in an Operations Manager Management Pack?" at *http://technet.microsoft.com/en-us/library/hh212794.aspx* for additional details.

The management pack lifecycle includes the following stages:

- Install the management pack in a nonproduction environment to ensure that the management pack is compatible and provides the desired functionality.

- Customize the management pack. Create overrides, add knowledge, and make other changes to the management pack for your environment.

- Deploy the management pack. Install the management pack and any changes in the production environment.

- Maintain the management pack. As your environment changes, you may need to make changes to the management pack. For example, you may require additional monitoring, or the application being monitored may change.

IMPLEMENTING A MANAGEMENT PACK

Management packs are added through the Administration area of the Operations Manager console by clicking Import Management Packs. The Import Management Packs Wizard will begin and enable you to choose the location from which the management pack should be installed. You can choose an existing catalog or add from a file. Alternately, the Import-SCOMManagementPack cmdlet is used to import a management pack using Windows PowerShell.

MORE INFO IMPORTING MANAGEMENT PACKS

Importing management packs is covered in depth at *http://technet.microsoft.com/en-us/ library/hh212691.aspx*.

Monitoring Windows servers requires the Windows Server Operating System Library, the Windows Server 2012 Operating System (Discovery), and the Windows Server 2012 Operating System (Monitoring) management packs. The Import Management Packs tool, shown in Figure 1-5, can resolve dependencies. For example, selecting the Windows Server 2012 Operating System (Monitoring) management pack requires that the additional management packs mentioned earlier be installed as well. The Import Management Packs tool can install those prerequisites.

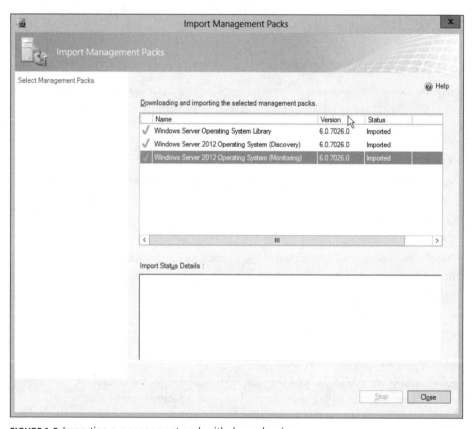

FIGURE 1-5 Importing a management pack with dependencies

MANAGEMENT PACK OPTIMIZATION

An important step in deploying management packs is optimizing them for your environment. When first installed, management packs perform discovery to find applicable objects for monitoring. Those objects are then monitored according to the rules set forth in the management pack. The default management pack rules may not be appropriate for your environment and should therefore be changed as necessary.

> **NOTE** **CREATE A NEW MANAGEMENT PACK**
>
> When making changes to a management pack, it is recommended that you create a new management pack for the changes, rather than changing the default.

The overall process for optimizing a management pack is to examine the highest severity alerts first and then proceed to the lowest severity. Alerts should be examined to ensure that they are both valid and actionable. In other words, if you don't need to react when an event occurs, then it's probably not worth alerting. That's not to say that the event isn't noteworthy, so it may need to be logged but not alerted. Related to alerting is ensuring that only one alert is generated for a given event.

Management packs are customized through overrides. Overrides change the configuration of a monitor or diagnostic. When configuring an override, you choose whether the override will apply to all objects of the current class (such as all Windows Server 2012 computers), to a group, to a specific object of the current class, or to all objects of another class. This gives you the flexibility to gather objects for which you don't need alerts, such as nonproduction Windows servers.

Classes, sometimes called *targets*, are used to help define the items that can be discovered and managed. Groups are sets of objects that help define the scope of an override.

> **NOTE** **CLASSES AND GROUPS**
>
> Classes can be applied for monitors, rules, discoveries, overrides, and tasks. Groups can define scope for overrides, views, user roles, and notifications.

> **MORE INFO** **USING CLASSES AND GROUPS**
>
> See *http://technet.microsoft.com/en-us/library/hh212771.aspx* for more information on classes and groups for overrides, and see *http://technet.microsoft.com/en-us/library/hh212869.aspx* for information on creating an override.

Another optimization for management packs is achieved through knowledge. Knowledge is used to provide notes and other information about a monitor or rule. Adding knowledge is accomplished in the Authoring workspace of the Operations Manager console within the properties settings for a given monitor or rule. However, as of this writing, adding or editing knowledge requires the Operations Manager console on a 32-bit operating system with the 32-bit version of Microsoft Word 2010 and other prerequisites as described at *http://technet.microsoft.com/en-us/library/hh212900.aspx*. Adding or editing knowledge requires the Author or Administrator role.

Planning for Active Directory monitoring

The AD DS management pack for System Center enables monitoring of several aspects of an AD DS environment. Several key monitoring scenarios for Active Directory monitoring are identified at *http://technet.microsoft.com/library/dd262116.aspx* and described in Table 1-11.

TABLE 1-11 Active Directory monitoring scenarios

Scenario	Description
Multi-forest monitoring	Gather health and performance data from remote forests through two workflows, Microsoft.AD.Topology.Discovery and Microsoft.AD.Remote.Topology.Discovery. Note that AgentProxySetting must be enabled on all domain controllers for this scenario.
Replication	Gather health of data replication between domain controllers. You can monitor both health and performance of replication. See *http://technet.microsoft.com/en-us/library/dd262066.aspx* and *http://technet.microsoft.com/en-us/library/ee662305.aspx* for more information on each of these aspects of replication monitoring.
Essential services	Gather health information on the following services, which are vital to the operation of Active Directory: NT File Replication Service (NTFRS) Distributed File System Replication (DFSR) Windows Time Service (W32Time) Intersite Messaging (ISM) Key Distribution Center (KDC) NT Directory Services (NTDS) Net Logon (NetLogon) Active Directory Web Service (ADWS)
Trust monitoring	Gather trust information using the TrustMon WMI provider.
Directory service availability	Gather various metrics on the availability of Active Directory, including: GC Response - The time it takes to load the global catalog GC Search Time - The time it takes to return a search result from a global catalog Lost & Found Count - The number of Lost and Found objects DNS Verification - Verify DNS records AD General Response - The time it takes to do a serverless bind
Active Directory database monitoring	Verify the health of the Active Directory database, including its size, consistency, and that there is sufficient space available for the database to grow.
Time skew monitoring	Gather information on the time skew or difference between computers taking part in authentication. The authoritative time source is chosen as follows: The primary domain control (PDC) for the root domain is authoritative in all instances. If a computer is a PDC for a nonroot domain, the PDC for the root domain is authoritative. If a computer is not a PDC then its own local PDC is authoritative.
Operations Master monitoring	Gather information on availability of the following Operations Master roles: Schema Operations Master Domain Naming Operations Master Infrastructure Operations Master Relative ID (RID) Operations Master PDC Emulator Operations Master

Thought experiment

Managing Active Directory performance

In the following thought experiment, apply what you've learned about this objective to predict what steps you need to take. You can find answers to these questions in the "Answers" section at the end of this chapter.

You've set up the Active Directory management pack. After receiving reports of slow logons, you investigate.

1. What are some of the performance indicators and alerts you can examine?

2. Where are those performance indicators and alerts located?

Objective summary

- Management packs are configured using overrides, which include customizations for your infrastructure.
- ACS is composed of one or more forwarders, an ACS collector, and an ACS database.
- The AdtAdmin.exe program can be used to configure ACS.
- The Active Directory management pack enables advanced performance monitoring and alerting for an Active Directory domain.
- Global Service Manager provides an external view of web application performance from multiple geographically dispersed locations.

Objective review

Answer the following questions to test your knowledge of the information in this objective. You can find the answers to these questions and explanations of why each answer choice is correct or incorrect in the "Answers" section at the end of this chapter.

1. Which of the following commands would be used to change the audit event filter for ACS?

    A. AdtAdmin /setquery

    B. AdtAdmin /addFilter

    C. AcsAdmin /addFilter

    D. AcsFilter /add

2. Which of the following roles is required to add or edit company knowledge for a management pack?

   A. Operator

   B. Knowledge Administrator

   C. Author

   D. Management Pack Administrator

3. Which of the following is not an essential service for Active Directory monitoring?

   A. NTDS

   B. NetLogon

   C. DFSR

   D. ADMon

4. What is the correct registry path for collector queue settings?

   A. HKEY_LOCAL_MACHINE\SYSTEM\CurrentControlSet\Services\ADT \Parameters

   B. HKEY_LOCAL_MACHINE\SYSTEM\CurrentControlSet\Services\AdtServer\Parameters

   C. HKEY_LOCAL_MACHINE\User\CurrentWindowsServices\AdtServicer\Parameters

   D. HKEY_LOCAL_MACHINE\SYSTEM\CurrentControlSet\Services\AdtSvc\Parameters

Objective 1.3: Plan and implement automated remediation

This objective covers how to:

- Create an update baseline in Virtual Machine Manager
- Implement a Desired Configuration Management (DCM) baseline
- Implement Virtual Machine Manager integration with Operations Manager
- Configure Virtual Machine Manager to move a VM dynamically based on policy
- Integrate System Center 2012 R2 for automatic remediation into your existing enterprise infrastructure
- Design and implement a Windows PowerShell Desired State Configuration (DSC) solution

Creating an update baseline in VMM

Update baselines are used to manage updates within a VMM fabric. For example, a virtual machine can be compared to the update baseline and, if found to be out of compliance with that baseline, the virtual machine can be remediated and brought into compliance.

When VMM is configured with a WSUS server and synchronization is complete, two sample update baselines will be created. These samples can be found within the Update Catalog And Baselines area of the Library workspace, shown in Figure 1-6.

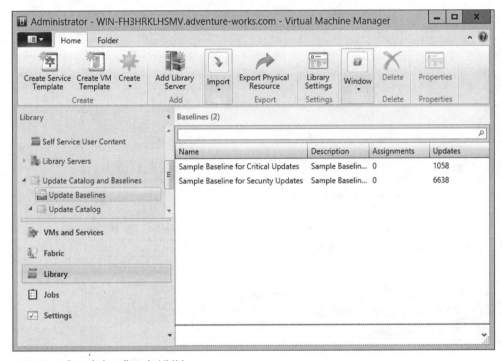

FIGURE 1-6 Sample baselines in VMM

When working with baselines, you can use one of the existing sample baselines or create a new one. This section looks at creating a new baseline in VMM.

An update baseline is created in the Update Baselines area of the Library workspace. Within that area, selecting Baseline from the Create group opens the Update Baseline Wizard. In the Update Baseline Wizard, you first specify a name and optionally a description, as shown in Figure 1-7.

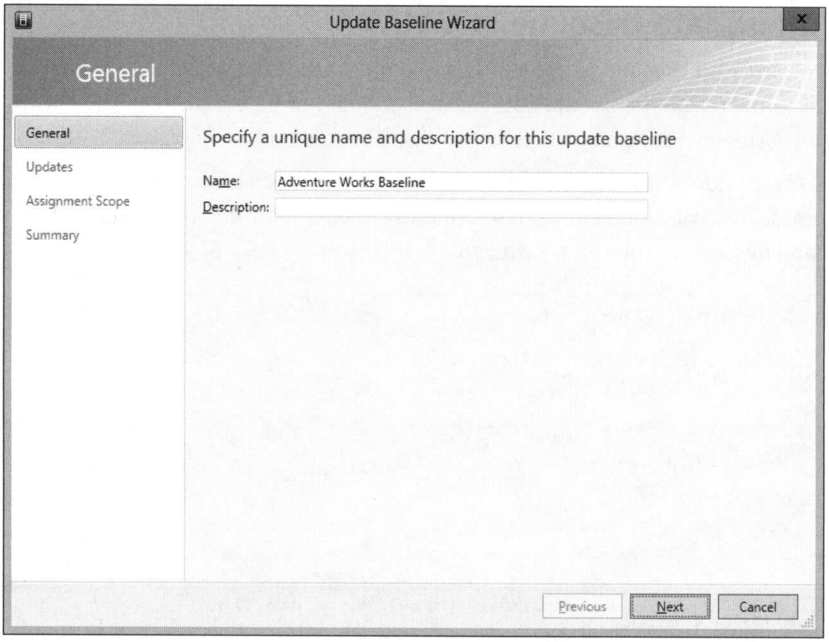

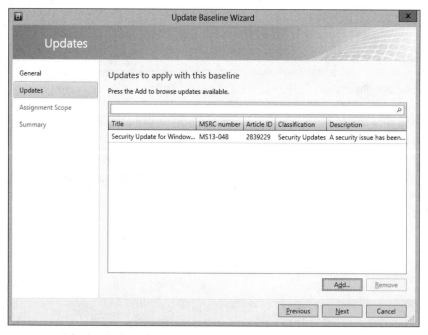

FIGURE 1-7 Entering a name to create a new baseline

Next, you select the updates that will be included in this baseline. For this example, a single update has been selected, as shown in Figure 1-8, but you could select more updates by clicking Add.

FIGURE 1-8 Selecting updates for the baseline

Finally, you select the scope to which the baseline will apply. This is accomplished within the Assignment Scope page, shown in Figure 1-9, where All Hosts has been selected.

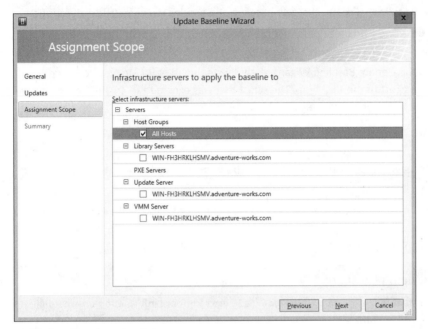

FIGURE 1-9 Choosing an assignment scope

Once complete, the summary page will display, and clicking Finish will start the jobs for baseline creation. The newly created baseline will be shown in the VMM console, as depicted in Figure 1-10.

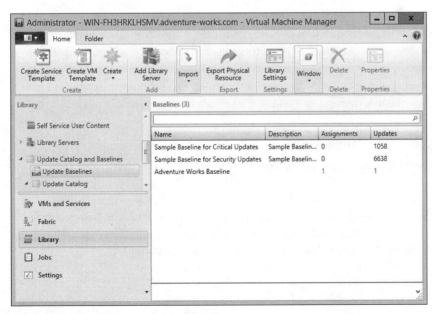

FIGURE 1-10 The newly created update baseline

You also have the option to create a baseline using Windows PowerShell. The relevant cmdlets include:

- **New-SCBaseline**   Creates the new baseline and assigns it a name and a description
- **Set-SCBaseline**   Changes parameters such as the host group and update list to the baseline

When using the Update Baseline Wizard, the final step enables you to view the scripts that will be run as part of the VMM job. The script that was executed to create the Adventure Works Baseline example is shown here:

```
$baseline = New-SCBaseline -Name "Adventure Works Baseline" -Description ""
$addedUpdateList = @()
$addedUpdateList += Get-SCUpdate -ID "7254a3fc-98db-4ca6-ad3f-3bf095de0bc8"
$scope = Get-SCVMHostGroup -Name "All Hosts" -ID "0e3ba228-a059-46be-aa41-2f5cf0f4b96e"
Set-SCBaseline -Baseline $baseline -AddAssignmentScope $scope -JobGroup
"c1477221-a4a0-4c4f-82ef-e502b46a517f" -RunAsynchronously
Set-SCBaseline -Baseline $baseline -RunAsynchronously -AddUpdates $addedUpdateList
-JobGroup
"c1477221-a4a0-4c4f-82ef-e502b46a517f" -StartNow
```

> **MORE INFO UPDATE BASELINES**
>
> See *http://technet.microsoft.com/library/gg675110.aspx* for more information on creating update baselines in VMM.

Implementing a Desired Configuration Management (DCM) baseline and automatic remediation

DCM baselines are used in Configuration Manager to ensure compliance for a variety of configuration settings. This section focuses primarily on the exam objective of implementing DCM. DCM provides assessment of managed computers against desired or known-good configurations, for example, whether an update has been applied. This section looks at both the implementing DCM subobjective as well as the automatic remediation subobjective contained within the overall "Implement Automated Remediation" exam objective.

> **MORE INFO   UNDERSTANDING DCM**
>
> See *http://technet.microsoft.com/en-us/library/bb680553.aspx* for an overview of DCM.

DCM baselines are configured within the Assets and Compliance workspace within Compliance Settings, Configuration Baselines. Clicking Create Configuration Baseline opens the Create Configuration Baseline dialog box. Within the Create Configuration Baseline dialog box, you enter details of the baseline to be created, as shown in Figure 1-11.

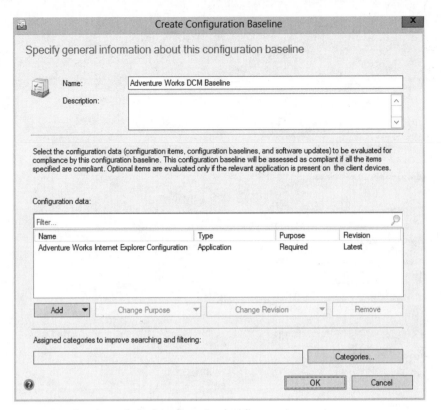

FIGURE 1-11 Creating a desired configuration baseline

A configuration baseline applies one or more configuration items, other configuration baselines, or software updates. The example shown in Figure 1-11 uses a previously defined configuration item, which was added through the Configuration Items page of the Compliance Settings area in Configuration Manager.

Once a configuration baseline is created, it needs to be deployed. This is accomplished by selecting Deploy within the Configuration Baselines area. Clicking Deploy opens the Deploy Configuration Baselines dialog box shown in Figure 1-12. You can select the Remediate Noncompliant Rules When Supported option, select the Generate An Alert option, and specify a schedule for the baseline to be deployed. The deployment will apply to the collection that you select within this dialog box.

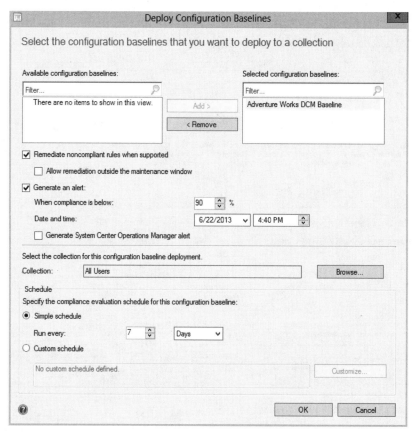

FIGURE 1-12 Preparing to deploy a configuration baseline

In addition to configuring automatic remediation through host groups, you can also configure automatic remediation within a configuration item or within the deployment of a configuration baseline. For example, Figure 1-13 shows the Edit Rule dialog box for a configuration item on the Compliance Rules tab. Note the Remediate Noncompliant Rules When Supported option is selected.

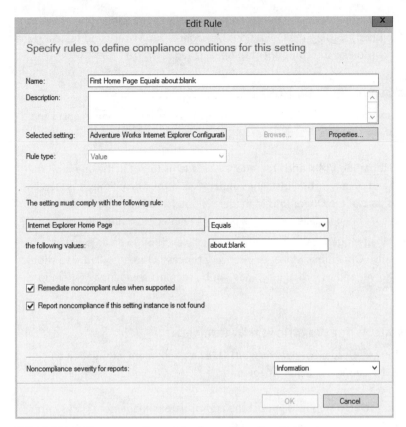

FIGURE 1-13 Editing a compliance rule of a configuration item

Implementing VMM integration with Operations Manager

Virtual Machine Manager can be integrated with Operations Manager. Integrating VMM and Operations Manager involves configuring both the Operations Manager server and the server running VMM.

EXAM TIP

Windows PowerShell 2.0 is required for System Center 2012, and Windows PowerShell 3.0 is required for System Center 2012 SP1 and System Center 2012 R2.

The first step in integration is to install the Operations Manager console on the VMM server. This is accomplished by using the Operations Manager Setup Wizard and selecting the Operations Manager console as the component to be installed.

> **MORE INFO** **INSTALLING THE OPERATIONS MANAGER CONSOLE**
>
> See *http://technet.microsoft.com/en-us/library/hh298607.aspx* for information on installing the Operations Manager console.

The next step in integrating VMM and Operations Manager is to install the agent on the server running VMM and on any virtual machines under its control. Many times this step has already been done as part of the Operations Manager rollout. However, if the Operations Manager agent hasn't yet been installed, do so as part of the integration implementation.

The Operations Manager agent can be installed manually or through an automated means, such as the native Operations Manager discovery process. Once installed, you should verify that the VMM server and its virtual machines can be seen from within the Operations Manager console.

> **MORE INFO** **INSTALLING THE OPERATIONS MANAGER AGENT**
>
> See *http://technet.microsoft.com/en-us/library/hh551142.aspx* for more information on methods to install the Operations Manager agent.

The next installation-related step is to import the appropriate management packs into Operations Manager. The necessary management packs include:

- Windows Server Internet Information Services 2003
- Windows Server 2008 Internet Information Services 7, including Windows Server 2008 Operating System (Discovery) and the Windows Server Operating System Library, which are prerequisites
- Windows Server Internet Information Services Library
- SQL Server Core Library

> **NOTE** **ABOUT THE PREREQUISITES**
>
> These seemingly outdated prerequisites are still necessary even though the Operations Manager and VMM servers are running Windows Server 2012 with Internet Information Services 8.0.

Integration of VMM and Operations Manager is accomplished from the VMM server, specifically in the Settings workspace of the VMM console. Within the Settings workspace, selecting System Center Settings reveals the Operations Manager Server, as shown in Figure 1-14.

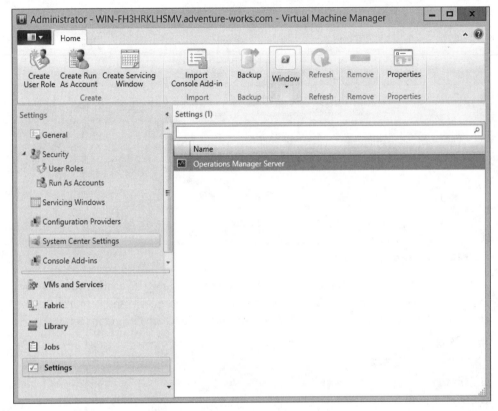

FIGURE 1-14 Viewing System Center settings

With Operations Manager Server selected, click Properties to start the Add Operations Manager Wizard, shown in Figure 1-15.

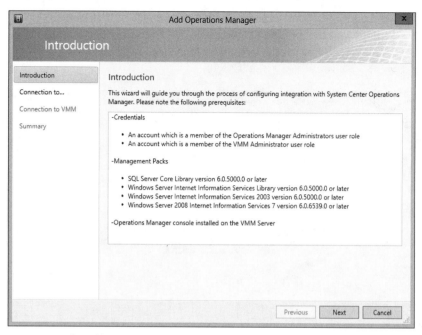

FIGURE 1-15 The Add Operations Manager Wizard

The Connection to Operations Manager page, shown in Figure 1-16, enables you to enter the server name and credentials, and to select the Enable Performance And Resource Optimization (PRO) and Enable Maintenance Mode Integration With Operations Manager options.

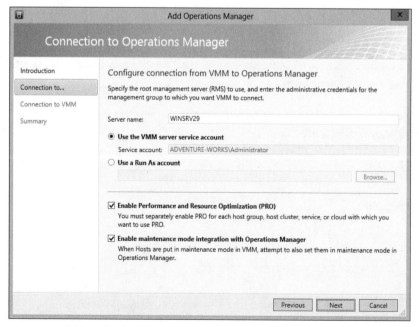

FIGURE 1-16 Adding details of the integration

The Connection to VMM page, shown in Figure 1-17, is where you specify credentials to be used by Operations Manager when connecting to VMM.

FIGURE 1-17 Specifying Operations Manager credentials

A summary page shows a summary of the configuration about to take place. When you click Finish, a job will begin the integration by installing the VMM management pack on the Operations Manager server.

Like other operations, integrating with Operations Manager can be accomplished through PowerShell. The New-SCOpsMgrConnection cmdlet can be used to add the connection.

> **MORE INFO** **THE NEW-SCOPSMGRCONNECTION CMDLET**
>
> See *http://technet.microsoft.com/en-us/library/hh801397.aspx* for more information on the New-SCOpsMgrConnection cmdlet.

Configuring VMM to move a virtual machine dynamically based on policy

This section provides a brief overview of automated migration of virtual machines using dynamic optimization.

Dynamic optimization enables virtual machines to be migrated between hosts in a host group based on load and other factors. Figure 1-18 shows the Dynamic Optimization page for a host group.

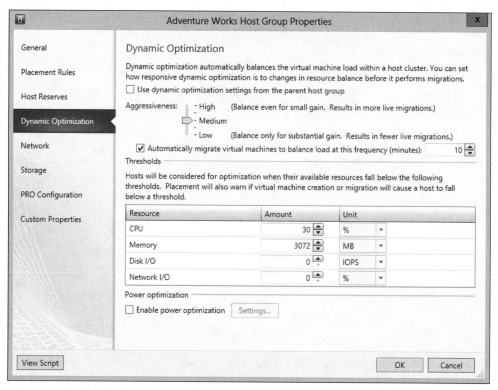

FIGURE 1-18 Configuring dynamic optimization in Virtual Machine Manager

By default, dynamic optimization rules will be inherited from the parent host group. (This option is not selected in Figure 1-18 to better illustrate the available options.) Dynamic optimization can be configured for manual migrations or automatic, as is depicted in Figure 1-18. Manual migrations are the default option, but when configured for automatic migrations, 10 minutes is the default frequency for dynamic optimization.

> **MORE INFO DYNAMIC OPTIMIZATION**
>
> See *http://technet.microsoft.com/en-us/library/gg675109.aspx* for more information on dynamic optimization.

Designing and implementing a Windows PowerShell Desired State Configuration solution

Desired State Configuration (DSC) is a new feature found in Windows PowerShell that enables scripting of configuration data. This configuration data can then be shared across servers to ensure consistency and promote ease of administration. For example, with DSC you can create a script that assists in deployment of web servers or other servers within the organization.

EXAM TIP

DSC is new with Windows Server 2012 R2.

The DSC service enables a server to act as a centralized repository for configuration scripts. When designing a DSC implementation for the enterprise, consider placing the DSC service server geographically close to the computers that will pull from it. Even though the configuration scripts themselves are small, you can store additional resources on the DSC service server, which could place a measurable load on resources.

DSC scripts are defined with the Configuration keyword and frequently written using Windows PowerShell Integrated Scripting Environment (ISE), as shown in Figure 1-19.

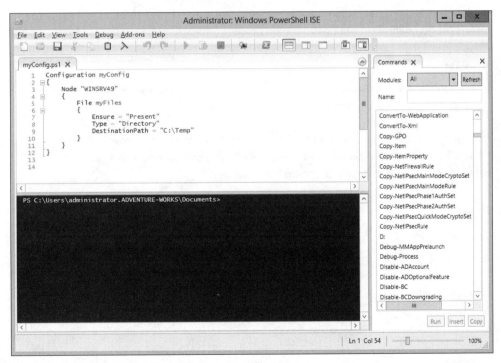

FIGURE 1-19 Creating a DSC script in Windows PowerShell ISE

Once created, the script is run from within the ISE and then enacted from within the ISE command prompt by typing the script name. Doing so creates Microsoft Operations Framework (MOF) files for each node identified in the script. For example, the following script (also shown in Figure 1-19) ensures that there's a directory called C:\Temp on the server named WINSRV49.

```
Configuration myConfig
{
    Node "WINSRV49"
    {
        File myFiles
        {
            Ensure = "Present"
            Type = "Directory"
            DestinationPath = "C:\Temp"
        }
    }
}
```

The MOF file is placed within a directory with the same name as the configuration script. From there, the desired configuration for a configuration named myConfig would be invoked with the command Start-DscConfiguration -Wait -Verbose -Path .\myConfig.

Once invoked, the command will run and apply the desired configuration to each of the servers (nodes) defined in the Configuration block.

EXAM TIP

You can also check to ensure that configuration changes are still applied to a given node using the Test-DscConfiguration cmdlet.

Parameters can be used within DSC scripts. Therefore, rather than repeating the same configuration within several hundred node blocks, you could instead use a parameter to define node programmatically, as shown here:

```
Configuration myConfig
{
    param ($nodeName)
    Node $nodeName
    {
        File myFiles
        {
            Ensure = "Present"
            Type = "Directory"
            DestinationPath = "C:\Temp"

        }
    }

}
```

MORE INFO **DESIRED STATE CONFIGURATION**

See *http://technet.microsoft.com/en-us/library/dn249918.aspx* for more information on getting started with DSC.

Thought experiment
Understanding update baselines

In the following thought experiment, apply what you've learned about this objective to predict what steps you need to take. You can find answers to these questions in the "Answers" section at the end of this chapter.

The infrastructure at your organization has shown remarkable growth over the past year. Unfortunately, the staff to maintain that infrastructure has not grown. Therefore, you're looking at ways to automate as many tasks as possible. You've been asked to brief the management team on some of the solutions available for automating the infrastructure.

- Describe update baselines and Desired Configuration Management.

Objective summary

- Update baselines provide an automated means by which virtual machines in a VMM deployment can have updates deployed automatically.
- DCM enables advanced configuration settings to be deployed across clients managed by Configuration Manager.
- System Center can be integrated for automatic remediation of various issues.

Objective review

Answer the following questions to test your knowledge of the information in this objective. You can find the answers to these questions and explanations of why each answer choice is correct or incorrect in the "Answers" section at the end of this chapter.

1. Which command creates an update baseline in VMM?

   A. New-SCBaseline

   B. Create-SCBaseline

   C. SCBaseline /new

   D. New-VMMBaseline

2. Which of the following is not a setting that can be used when creating a configuration management baseline?

   A. Configuration Item

   B. Software Update

   C. Configuration Agent

   D. Configuration Baseline

3. What's the default frequency for automatic dynamic optimization?

   A. One day

   B. One hour

   C. 10 minutes

   D. 24 hours

Answers

This section contains the solutions to the thought experiments and answers to the lesson review questions in this chapter.

Objective 1.1: Thought experiment

You'll likely use security roles to enable the administrators to apply those updates to a security scope of each type of server, test, and production. The key elements for this answer are the security roles and the security scopes.

Objective 1.1: Review

1. **Correct answer:** B

    A. **Incorrect:** SeShutdownComputer is not a valid privilege.

    B. **Correct:** SeShutdownPrivilege is the correct privilege.

    C. **Incorrect:** SePrivilegeShutdown is not a valid privilege.

    D. **Incorrect:** En_ShutdownComputerPermission is not a valid privilege.

2. **Correct answer:** B

    A. **Incorrect:** Shut down the system is a privilege for the Backup Operators group.

    B. **Correct:** Create symbolic links is not a privilege of the Backup Operators group.

    C. **Incorrect:** Back up files and directories is a privilege for the Backup Operators group.

    D. **Incorrect:** Allow logon locally is a privilege for the Backup Operators group.

3. **Correct answer:** A

    A. **Correct:** Site server is the core functionality for System Center.

    B. **Incorrect:** Component server is not the core functionality for System Center.

    C. **Incorrect:** Core server is not a valid functionality.

    D. **Incorrect:** Site Core server is not a valid functionality.

4. **Correct answers:** B, C

    A. **Incorrect:** All is a built-in scope.

    B. **Correct:** System is not a built-in scope.

    C. **Correct:** Administrator is not a built-in scope.

    D. **Incorrect:** Default is a built-in scope.

Objective 1.2: Thought experiment

1. There are several performance indicators that can be examined, including the GC Response time, as well as GC Search Time and AD General Response.

2. Operations Manager contains the performance monitoring and alerts for this scenario.

Objective 1.2: Review

1. **Correct answer:** A

    A. **Correct:** AdtAdmin /setquery is the correct command to change the audit event filter.

    B. **Incorrect:** AdtAdmin /addFilter doesn't perform the requested action.

    C. **Incorrect:** AcsAdmin is not a valid command.

    D. **Incorrect:** AcsFilter /add is not a valid command.

2. **Correct answer:** C

    A. **Incorrect:** Operator does not have this privilege.

    B. **Incorrect:** Knowledge Administrator is not a valid role.

    C. **Correct:** Author has this privilege.

    D. **Incorrect:** Management Pack Administrator is not a valid role.

3. **Correct answer:** D

    A. **Incorrect:** NTDS should be monitored.

    B. **Incorrect:** NetLogon should be monitored.

    C. **Incorrect:** DFSR should be monitored.

    D. **Correct:** ADMon is not a valid service.

4. **Correct answer:** B

    A. **Incorrect:** HKEY_LOCAL_MACHINE\SYSTEM\CurrentControlSet\Services\ADT \ Parameters is not a valid path.

    B. **Correct:** HKEY_LOCAL_MACHINE\SYSTEM\CurrentControlSet\Services\AdtServer\ Parameters is the correct path.

    C. **Incorrect:** HKEY_LOCAL_MACHINE\User\CurrentWindowsServices\AdtServicer\ Parameters does not exist.

    D. **Incorrect:** HKEY_LOCAL_MACHINE\SYSTEM\CurrentControlSet\Services\AdtSvc\ Parameters is not a valid path.

Objective 1.3: Thought experiment

Update baselines are used to maintain updates on virtual machines. Update baselines are coordinated with a WSUS server, and an administrator chooses the appropriate updates for a given baseline. Sample baselines are included to provide a starting point.

DCM enables advanced configuration items to be tracked across a Configuration Manager deployment. For example, a registry setting can be monitored and changed (remediated) automatically using DCM.

Objective 1.3: Review

1. **Correct answer:** B

   A. **Incorrect:** New-SCBaseline is not a valid command.

   B. **Correct:** Create-SCBaseline is the correct command for this question.

   C. **Incorrect:** SCBaseline /new is not a valid command.

   D. **Incorrect:** New-VMMBaseline is not a valid command.

2. **Correct answer:** C

   A. **Incorrect:** Configuration Item can be used as a setting for DCM.

   B. **Incorrect:** Software Update can be used as a setting for DCM.

   C. **Correct:** Configuration Agent is not a setting used with DCM.

   D. **Incorrect:** Configuration Baseline can be used with DCM.

3. **Correct answer:** C

   A. **Incorrect:** One day is not the default frequency.

   B. **Incorrect:** One hour is not the default frequency.

   C. **Correct:** 10 minutes is the default direct optimization frequency.

   D. **Incorrect:** 24 hours is not the correct frequency.

CHAPTER 2

Plan and implement a highly available enterprise infrastructure

The second set of exam objectives looks at the skills necessary to ensure an infrastructure is always available. This typically means scaling out horizontally to provide redundancy not only in the event of failure, but also under heavy workloads. Microsoft has made great improvements in high availability and disaster recovery options. From robust failover clustering to highly available storage to disaster recovery, you can use Microsoft products and technologies to ensure an always-on, always-available infrastructure.

Objectives in this chapter:

- Objective 2.1: Plan and implement failover clustering
- Objective 2.2: Plan and implement highly available network services
- Objective 2.3: Plan and implement highly available storage solutions
- Objective 2.4: Plan and implement highly available server roles
- Objective 2.5: Plan and implement a business continuity and disaster recovery solution

Objective 2.1: Plan and implement failover clustering

Clustering refers to the use of multiple servers, known as nodes, to provide a redundant and scalable application or service. With a clustered service, the service or application being clustered will remain available even if one of the servers involved becomes unavailable. Therefore, it's important that single points of failure are eliminated as much as possible.

The failover clustering provided by Microsoft enables certain roles to be clustered and then managed through a central console called the Failover Cluster Manager. Shared storage, called cluster-shared volumes (CSV), can be used for providing shared storage among the clustered nodes.

This objective covers how to:

- Plan for and implement multi-node and multi-site clustering, including the use of networking storage, name resolution, and Global Update Manager (GUM)
- Understand design considerations, including redundant networks, network priority settings, resource failover and failback, heartbeat and DNS settings, Quorum configuration, storage placement and replication, and Cluster Aware Updating (CAU)

Planning for and implementing failover clustering

Cluster planning involves first determining what the goals are for the cluster. For example, the business need might simply be to provide high availability for certain services. Alternatively, the cluster might be used for disaster recovery between multiple sites. This section focuses on high-level design and planning considerations. Recommendations for specific services and applications are included throughout the chapter where appropriate for each exam objective.

Windows Server 2012 R2 adds several new features to failover clustering, including the ability to deploy an Active Directory–detached cluster. This new cluster scenario doesn't create computer objects in Active Directory Domain Services (AD DS) for the cluster nodes or the cluster itself. This also means that you no longer need to have permissions to add objects to AD DS to create a cluster. It's worth noting that the cluster nodes will need to be joined to an Active Directory domain.

When planning a cluster, certain prerequisites must be met. Among these requirements are that the hardware involved meets the Certified for Windows Server 2012 logo criteria and that the hardware configuration passes the Validate a Configuration Wizard for clustering. The Validate a Configuration Wizard examines several aspects of the server's hardware and software configuration to determine its suitability for taking part in a cluster. When completed successfully, as shown in Figure 2-1, a Failover Cluster Validation Report will be created.

When possible, the server hardware in a cluster should match. This helps to alleviate some management overhead in trying to balance different performance levels on different hardware. Multi-site clusters should have an even number of nodes and should use the Node and File Share Majority option for the cluster.

> **MORE INFO** **NETWORK AND STORAGE FOR CLUSTERS**
>
> See *http://technet.microsoft.com/en-us/library/jj612869.aspx* for more information on network and storage options for clusters.

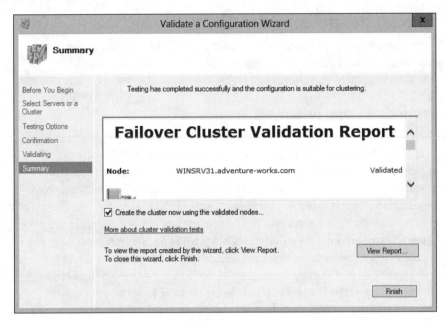

FIGURE 2-1 Viewing a Failover Cluster Validation Report

Global Update Manager (GUM) is used to communicate updates about a cluster to the cluster nodes. In Windows Server 2012, GUM uses an All (write) and Local (read) mode, which requires that all cluster nodes receive and process an update in order for the change to be committed. However, as of Windows Server 2012 R2, you can also configure a mode called Majority (read and write), which requires that a majority of clusters receive and process the update rather than all nodes. Hyper-V failover clusters use this mode as the default in Windows Server 2012 R2. Another mode called Majority (write) and Local (read) is also available; it uses the majority receive and process, but on database reads the local node doesn't compare the timestamp.

EXAM TIP

The DatabaseReadWriteMode property of the Get-Cluster cmdlet is available to set and view the current value for the GUM mode. A value of 0 corresponds to All (write) and Local (read), a value of 1 indicates Majority (read and write), and a value of 2 indicates Majority (write) and Local (read) mode.

Microsoft recommends using All (write) and Local (read) for clusters that require consistency, such as when running a clustered Exchange server.

Understanding design considerations

Many design considerations for clusters are simply best practices for network redundancy, such as eliminating single points of failure and so on. This section examines design considerations related to planning clustering.

Network redundancy and priority

Planning for network redundancy is a vital issue when providing a clustered service or application. The network layer can be made redundant by including multiple network adapters that are connected to separate networks or by building the redundancy at the network layer with multiple switches, routers, and so on. Most organizations will likely have some level of redundancy at the network layer already, so when analyzing solutions for providing network redundancy, it's important to consider each and every point where failure might occur. Having two or more network adapters will provide minimum redundancy, and cluster nodes connected to the same network will also pass the redundancy check in the Cluster Configuration Wizard. However, for true redundancy, not only should the network adapters be made redundant and connected to different network hardware, but other adapters, such as those used for iSCSI connections, should also be made redundant.

Clusters can use multiple networks, including those dedicated for cluster traffic. This is configured within the properties of a given network, as shown in Figure 2-2.

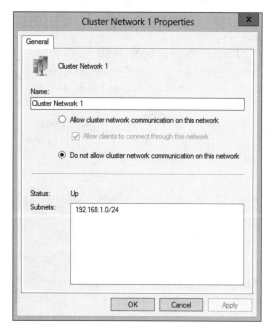

FIGURE 2-2 Network properties within a cluster

You can configure the priority of the network to use for Hyper-V live migrations. This is accomplished in the Live Migration Settings dialog box, which is found within the Networks area of the Failover Cluster Manager (see Figure 2-3).

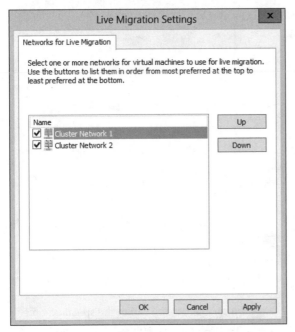

FIGURE 2-3 Live migration network settings

MORE INFO FURTHER TUNING

See *http://blogs.msdn.com/b/clustering/archive/2012/11/21/10370765.aspx* for more tuning information for cluster networking.

Resource failover and failback

Resource failover and failback are configured within the core Cluster Group Properties dialog box, shown in Figure 2-4.

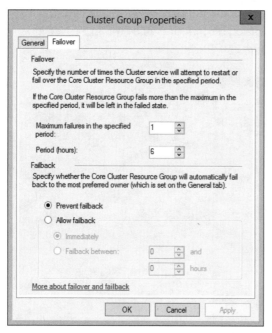

FIGURE 2-4 Configuration settings for failover and failback

Failover settings determine how many times the service can fail within the specified time period. For example, Figure 2-4 shows a configuration where the service can fail only once within a six-hour period. If the service fails a second time, it won't be restarted.

Failback determines when the service will transfer to its preferred owner after a failure, with the default being to prevent failback, as shown in Figure 2-4.

Heartbeat and DNS settings

Heartbeat and DNS settings for a cluster are configured with Windows PowerShell cmdlets. You can view current settings using the following command:

```
Get-Cluster | Format-List -Property *
```

When you run that cmdlet, you'll get several lines of output. Within the output, the settings related to heartbeat include:

- SameSubnetDelay
- SameSubnetThreshold
- CrossSubnetDelay
- CrossSubnetThreshold

Setting these parameters affects the amount of delay and the time limits for heartbeat communication between cluster nodes. The default behavior is five missed heartbeats before a failover occurs.

Additional parameters can be found with the Get-ClusterResource and Get-ClusterParameter combination, like so:

```
Get-ClusterResource | Get-ClusterParameter
```

Many of the cluster properties can be changed. For example, the HostRecordTTL property can be changed from its default, 1200, to a lower value, such as 60. You'd do this so that a change in the hostname to IP address would propagate faster. Here's an example of changing that value:

```
Get-ClusterResource | Set-ClusterParameter -Name HostRecordTTL -Value 60
```

EXAM TIP

The HostRecordTTL value can then be verified with the previously shown command to retrieve the DNS-related parameters.

MORE INFO **WINDOWS POWERSHELL CMDLETS**

See *http://technet.microsoft.com/en-us/library/ee461009.aspx* for information on the cluster-related Windows PowerShell cmdlets.

Quorum configuration

Quorum defines the voting nodes or elements that need to be active for the cluster to continue operations (or start). You can add a witness that also gets a Quorum vote, and you can configure the voting properties for nodes. You configure the Quorum based on the number of nodes and the site topology, but you should also consider the available network bandwidth and reliability between nodes, as well as the available resources and the priority of each node in the cluster. Ideally, there will be an odd number of voting nodes for a cluster. If you'll be using an even number of nodes in the cluster, you can configure a witness, either disk or file share, as long as the nodes can access the witness, and a Quorum witness should always be configured with Windows Server 2012 R2 clusters.

For dynamic Quorum clusters in Windows Server 2012 R2, the witness vote is changed based on the number of voting nodes in the cluster. If the number of voting nodes is even, then the witness has a vote.

Table 2-1 contains considerations for witness configuration.

TABLE 2-1 Witness configuration

Type	Description and Requirements
Disk	Logical Unit Number (LUN) that's at least 512 MB that is visible by all nodes. The LUN should be NTFS or ReFS formatted but can't be part of a CSV.
File Share	SMB file share with at least 5 MB of free space. Must be visible to all nodes, and the cluster name computer object requires write permissions on the share to keep cluster information in the witness.log file.

Disk witness types are typically found in single site clusters, while file share witness types are helpful for multi-site clusters. Also, a disk witness will store a copy of the cluster database while a file share witness will not.

Quorum configuration is automatically done based on the number of nodes and shared storage available at the time of cluster creation. However, you may want to change the Quorum configuration in certain circumstances, such as:

- Long-term node or witness failure
- Addition or removal of nodes
- Addition or removal of storage
- Multi-site cluster recovery

Quorum can be configured through the Configure Cluster Quorum Wizard. When configuring Quorum you can choose from three methods as shown in Figure 2-5.

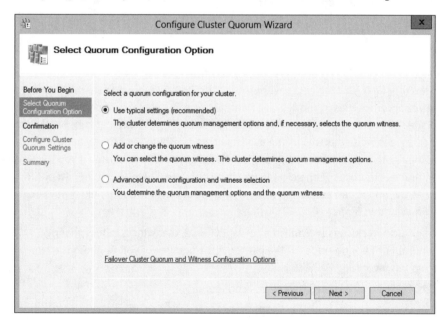

FIGURE 2-5 Configuring Quorum

Selecting either of the options other than Use Typical Settings (Recommended) enables you to change the configuration. For example, you can add a disk or file share witness, as shown in Figure 2-6. Using the Advanced Quorum Configuration and Witness Selection option, you can configure voting configuration and Quorum management and add a disk or file share witness.

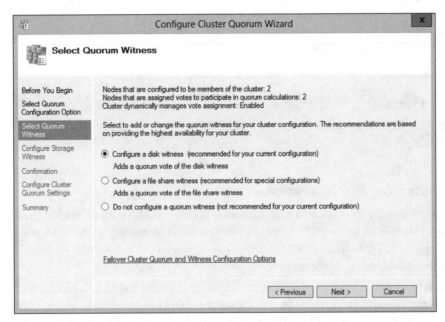

FIGURE 2-6 Configuring witness settings for a cluster

Quorum is configured in three modes, as described in Table 2-2.

TABLE 2-2 Quorum configuration

Type	Description
Node majority	No Quorum witness is configured. The majority of voting nodes is the Quorum. This type is used for clusters with an odd number of nodes.
Node majority with witness	Both the nodes and the witness have votes. The majority of voting nodes plus the witness is the Quorum. This type of Quorum is used for clusters with an even number of nodes.
No majority (disk witness only)	Only the disk witness has a vote, nodes do not. The disk witness determines the state of the cluster. This mode creates a potential single point of failure and is not recommended.

Windows Server 2012 enables dynamic Quorum management, which manages the voting rights for a node based on its status. When a node leaves the active cluster, dynamic Quorum management removes its vote.

The current voting status of a cluster node can be verified by looking for a value of 1 for the DynamicWeight property when running Get-ClusterNode through Windows PowerShell. Other Windows PowerShell cmdlets are helpful for cluster management, including using the Get-ClusterQuorum cmdlet and running Test-Cluster to perform the Validate Quorum Configuration test.

Another new feature of Windows Server 2012 R2 is forced Quorum resiliency. The /fq switch, when added to the start parameters of the cluster service, is useful for partitioned or "split brain" clusters. Quorum resiliency causes detection of cluster partitions as they're brought back online.

> **MORE INFO** **QUORUM CONFIGURATION**
>
> See *http://technet.microsoft.com/en-us/library/jj612870.aspx* for more information on Quorum configuration.

Storage placement and replication

There are several options for storage in a cluster scenario. However, the storage needs to be compatible with Windows Server 2012. Storage should be Serial Attached SCSI (SAS), Fibre Channel, FCoE, or iSCSI. When using iSCSI, a network adapter should be dedicated to the iSCSI traffic, and teaming is not supported for iSCSI (though MPIO is).

When directly attached, storage should be configured on multiple disks (LUNs), including the disk witness if one is used. Additionally, basic disks should be used, and they should be formatted as NTFS. Or, if they are configured as CSV, then the volume needs to be NTFS-formatted.

Replication is especially important in a multi-site cluster. Some organizations will have replication configured at the disk or LUN level through the SAN. When the bandwidth is available between sites, synchronous replication can be used. Otherwise, for low-bandwidth or high-latency cluster scenarios, asynchronous replication would likely be more appropriate.

> **MORE INFO** **STORAGE REQUIREMENTS AND CSV**
>
> See *http://technet.microsoft.com/en-us/library/jj612869.aspx* for hardware and storage requirements and *http://technet.microsoft.com/en-us/library/jj612868.aspx* for information on the use of CSV in a cluster.

Cluster Aware Updating (CAU)

Cluster Aware Updating (CAU) is a new feature with Windows Server 2012 that enables clustered services to be updated while maintaining service availability with minimal disruption. Without CAU, the servers taking part in a cluster might be taken offline simultaneously to apply software updates. However, with CAU, the process is automated and follows these basic steps:

1. Place a node in maintenance mode.

2. Move clustered role service off of the node.

3. Install updates and restart if necessary.

4. Place the node back into service.

5. Restore clustered role service on the node.

6. Begin the update process on the next node.

> **NOTE** **FAILOVER CLUSTERING**
>
> **CAU is installed as a Windows feature called failover clustering.**

An important distinction between updating with CAU and updating with other methods is that using CAU for updating involves using the Cluster Aware Updating tool or using a Windows PowerShell CAU plug-in.

> **MORE INFO** **CAU PLUG-INS**
>
> See *http://technet.microsoft.com/en-us/library/jj134213.aspx* for more information on how CAU plug-ins work.

Using other methods for updates is not recommended and can lead to service downtime. CAU integrates with an existing update's infrastructure and can apply both Microsoft and non-Microsoft updates.

CAU operates in two modes, self-updating or remote-updating. In self-updating mode, the cluster updates itself according to the default Updating Run profile or by using a custom Updating Run profile. In remote-updating mode, the Update Coordinator computer (running Windows Server 2012 or Windows 8) starts the update process.

When planning CAU, the failover clustering feature is required on each node of the cluster. The CAU clustered role and failover clustering tools are required on all nodes for self-updating mode. For remote-updating mode, the failover clustering tools are required on the remote updating computer and on cluster nodes that run the Save-CauDebugTrace PowerShell cmdlet. The CAU clustered role is not required for remote-updating mode.

> **MORE INFO** **CAU**
>
> See *http://technet.microsoft.com/library/hh831694.aspx* for more information on CAU and *http://technet.microsoft.com/en-us/library/jj134234.aspx* for requirements and best practices for CAU.

> ## *Thought experiment*
> ### Configuring a Quorum for clusters
>
> In the following thought experiment, apply what you've learned about this objective to predict what steps you need to take. You can find answers to these questions in the "Answers" section at the end of this chapter.
>
> In this thought experiment, you'll be configuring a cluster with four servers to balance a DHCP configuration. Two of the servers are located in a remote data center. You need to configure a proper Quorum configuration for the cluster.
>
> Describe the options for Quorum configuration and where those options are configured.

Objective summary

- Multi-node and multi-site clustering is provided by failover clustering in Windows Server 2012.
- When configuring multi-site clustering, heartbeat settings can be important when there's network latency.
- Quorum should have an odd number of voting nodes when possible, and a witness can be added to make an odd number of votes.
- Replication for storage can be used in a synchronous or an asynchronous manner, with synchronous being recommended for low-latency, high-bandwidth clusters.

Objective review

Answer the following questions to test your knowledge of the information in this objective. You can find the answers to these questions and explanations of why each answer choice is correct or incorrect in the "Answers" section at the end of this chapter.

1. Which of the following commands shows IP and networking information specific to a cluster?

    A. Get-ClusterInfo

    B. Get-ClusterResouce | Get-ClusterParameter

    C. ifconfig /cluster

    D. Get-ClusterNetworkInfo

2. Which Quorum type prevents voting by all nodes except the witness?

   A. Node Majority (Witness Voting)

   B. Node Majority (Disk Witness)

   C. No Majority (Disk Witness Only)

   D. No Majority (Witness Vote Only)

3. Which of the following is not a valid reason for changing Quorum configuration?

   A. Long-term node or witness failure

   B. Adding or removing nodes

   C. Temporary failure of a network switch

   D. Multi-site cluster recovery

Objective 2.2: Plan and implement highly available network services

The second objective looks at creating a fault-tolerant environment at the network level. This is important to understand because networking is a key concept in an enterprise-level system administrator toolkit.

> **This objective covers how to:**
> - Plan for and configure Network Load Balancing (NLB)
> - Understand design considerations, including fault-tolerant networking, multicast versus unicast configuration, state management, and automated deployment of NLB using Virtual Machine Manager service templates

Planning for and configuring Network Load Balancing

Network Load Balancing (NLB) provides a means to distribute network traffic across two or more servers (up to 32 total), known as *hosts* in NLB terminology. NLB provides redundancy and scalability for basic stateless services, such as HTTP. NLB uses one or more cluster IP addresses to enable network traffic to the cluster.

NLB is added as a server feature in the Add Roles and Features Wizard. Doing so installs the Network Load Balancing Manager. Additionally, you can manage NLB using Windows PowerShell cmdlets.

Creating a new NLB cluster involves selecting New from the Cluster menu in the Network Load Balancing Manager. Doing so invokes the New Cluster Wizard. Within the New Cluster Wizard, enter the name of a host that will be part of the cluster and click Connect to reveal the available network adapters for the cluster, as shown in Figure 2-7.

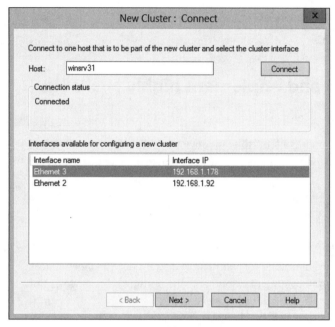

FIGURE 2-7 The New Cluster Wizard for creating an NLB cluster

The Host Parameters page will be shown next, within which you can add an IP address for the host by clicking Add. Doing so reveals the Add IP Address dialog box, shown in Figure 2-8.

The Host Parameters page is shown in Figure 2-9. On this page, you can configure the host priority, whether the host state will remain suspended when the computer restarts, and its default state from among three choices:

- Started
- Stopped
- Suspended

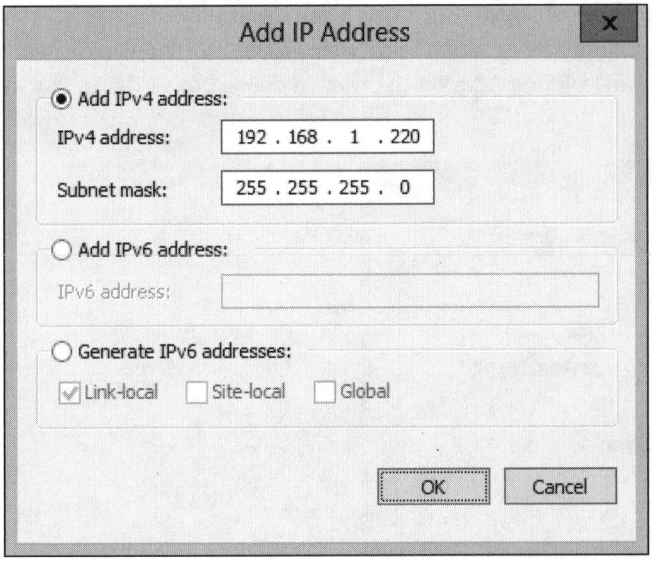

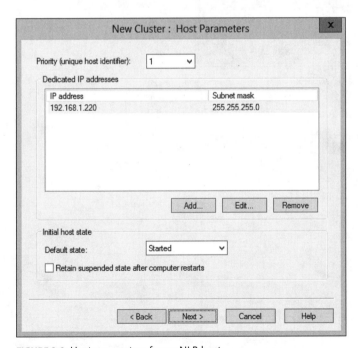

FIGURE 2-8 Adding an IP address to an NLB host

FIGURE 2-9 Host parameters for an NLB host

The Cluster IP Addresses page is shown next, within which you can configure the IP address(es) that will be used by clients connecting to the cluster. Figure 2-10 shows a cluster IP address that has been added by first clicking Add, which reveals a dialog box similar to that in Figure 2-8.

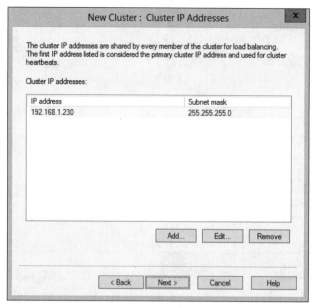

FIGURE 2-10 Configuring a cluster IP address

Cluster parameters are configured next, as shown in Figure 2-11.

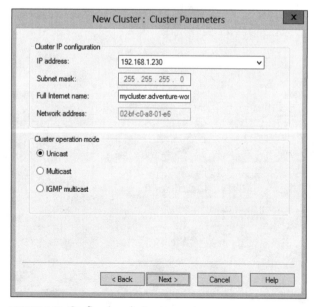

FIGURE 2-11 Configuring cluster parameters

On the Cluster Parameters page, you can configure the Full Internet Name for the cluster, along with its Cluster Operation Mode: Unicast, Multicast, or IGMP Multicast.

Port rules are configured on the Port Rules page, shown in Figure 2-12.

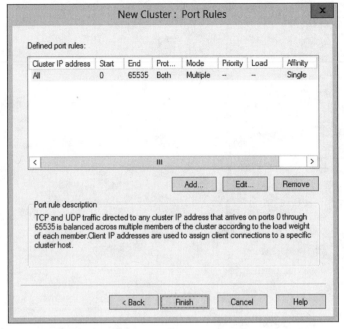

FIGURE 2-12 Configuring port rules for an NLB cluster

The default port rules direct all TCP and UDP traffic to the cluster (ports 0 through 65535). You can use this page to configure which ports will be allowed for the particular service being clustered. For example, if you're configuring web traffic, you can typically remove or edit the default rule and in its place add a rule to allow TCP ports 80 and 443 (if HTTPS is used) to the cluster IP address.

> **MORE INFO** **SERVICE PORTS AND PROTOCOLS**
>
> Technically, UDP ports 80 and 443 are reserved for HTTP traffic as well. See *http://www.iana.org/assignments/service-names-port-numbers/service-names-port-numbers.txt* for the authoritative list of service ports and protocols.

The Add/Edit Port Rule dialog box, shown in Figure 2-13, is where you can map the IP address to the port, along with protocols, filtering, and affinity.

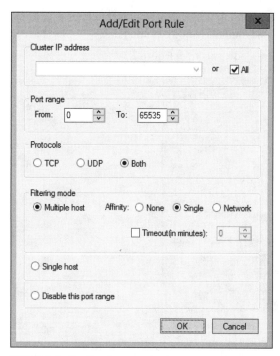

FIGURE 2-13 Configuring a port rule

> **NOTE   UNDERSTANDING DESIGN CONSIDERATIONS FOR NLB**
>
> When designing and planning an NLB implementation, you should consider the configuration of the hosts and the cluster as well.

Understanding design considerations

The next exam objective looks at some specific design-related aspects for creating a highly available network.

Fault-tolerant networking

NLB requires only a single network adapter, and each host participating in the cluster can have a different number of adapters. IP addresses on the adapters used for NLB need to be static, and NLB will disable DHCP on network adapters assigned to the cluster.

By itself, NLB provides for fault tolerance when more than one host is used. Hosts need to be on the same subnet. However, being on the same subnet many times implies that the hosts may connect to the same physical network hardware. Therefore, a single point of failure exists when hosts in an NLB cluster are connected in such a way. Adding fault tolerance at this level means adding redundant network hardware to reduce or remove the single point of failure and provide fault tolerance at the network level.

The filtering mode of a cluster, which is set at the port rule level, defines how network traffic is handled within the cluster. There are three options:

- Multiple Hosts
- Single Host
- Disable This Port Range

Multiple Hosts filtering mode indicates that cluster traffic will be distributed across multiple hosts in the cluster. Single Host filtering mode sends traffic for the given port rule to a single host based on its priority. If you choose Disable This Port Range, traffic will be blocked to the cluster IP address for the specified ports.

Multicast vs. unicast configuration

You can configure multicast and unicast settings at cluster creation or later by using the Cluster Parameters tab of the cluster Properties dialog box, shown in Figure 2-14.

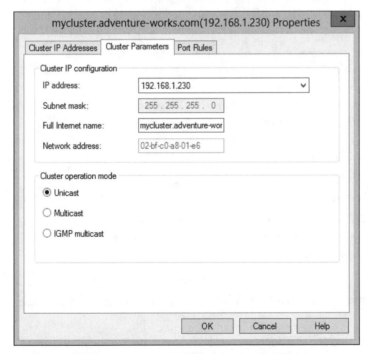

FIGURE 2-14 Cluster parameters related to unicast and multicast

In unicast mode, which is the preferred mode when there are two or more network adapters in a host, all traffic (for the configured ports) received on the cluster IP address is sent in a unicast manner to each of the hosts in the cluster. To do so, NLB will overwrite the MAC address of the adapter participating in the cluster with the cluster MAC address.

This means that the network adapter must allow its MAC address to be changed. Unicast is appropriate when there's more than one network adapter in the host.

When using unicast, the MAC address is made unique for outbound packets so as not to create problems when a switch sees the same MAC address through different ports. This modification is based on the host's priority. Even so, switch floods are still possible with unicast.

Multicast should be used when communication between the hosts is required and there's only one adapter in each host. The adapter MAC address is not overwritten with multicast mode, and each host receives cluster traffic using the multicast MAC address. However, a static Address Resolution Protocol (ARP) entry may be necessary for multicast to work correctly.

State management

State management refers to the maintaining of session state that's necessary for certain applications. For example, a web application where the user logs in will typically have a session associated with it. That session may be tied to the server.

NLB handles state through the affinity parameter, which is part of the port rules for a cluster. The affinity, configured as None, Single, or Network, defines how a session is handled. However, affinity is applicable only when the multiple-host filtering method is selected.

Selecting None for affinity indicates that connections, even from the same client IP address, can be handled by different hosts in the cluster. When Single affinity is chosen (the default), requests from the same client IP address are sent to the same NLB cluster host. Finally, the Network affinity option directs all traffic from a given Class C subnet to a specific cluster host. The Network affinity option is especially helpful if there are multiple exit points from a client location (such as multiple proxies) that would cause a single client's IP address to appear to be from a different source.

> **NOTE STATE MANAGEMENT**
>
> Selecting None for affinity improves performance of the cluster but doesn't provide any state management. Selecting Single or Network provides state management because each client request is sent to the same host.

Automated deployment of NLB using Virtual Machine Manager service templates

System Center 2012 Virtual Machine Manager (VMM) service templates can be used to deploy NLB. Doing so requires a Virtual IP (VIP) template for NLB.

The basic process for creating service templates in VMM involves using Service Template Designer to add the features necessary for the desired configuration. One such feature is a load balancer, which can be added to the service template using the Add Load Balancer button. Doing so adds a VIP connected to Client connection and Server connection objects. VMM will attempt to choose a VIP, but you can change the VIP by clicking on the object in Service Template Designer and selecting a different VIP.

With the correct VIP selected, you click on the Server connection object and, using the Connector, connect it to a NIC object for the appropriate host. Finally, the Client connection object is connected to a VM network. If the VM network hasn't already been added, it can be added by using the Add VM Network button. The final configuration looks like Figure 2-15.

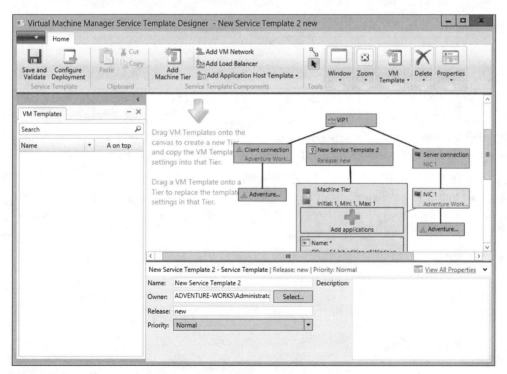

FIGURE 2-15 A service template with an NLB load balancer

Thought experiment

Using NLB for network redundancy

In the following thought experiment, apply what you've learned about this objective to predict what steps you need to take. You can find answers to these questions in the "Answers" section at the end of this chapter.

Your network is in need of redundancy for a web application, and you've chosen NLB for the solution. The servers involved in the web application each have one network adapter on the same subnet and are running Windows Server 2012. The web application needs to keep session state.

Describe the NLB configuration that you'll use, focusing specifically on multicast or unicast configuration and session management.

Objective summary

- Fault tolerance can be provided at the network level or by choosing a filter mode, such as multiple hosts.
- State management is achieved by sending all traffic from a client IP address to a single host (Single mode) or from a client network (Network mode) to a single host.
- NLB handles state through an affinity parameter within the cluster rules.
- NLB can be included as part of a VMM service template to make deployment easier. When using service templates, the operating system at the machine tier needs to have NLB installed.

Objective review

Answer the following questions to test your knowledge of the information in this objective. You can find the answers to these questions and explanations of why each answer choice is correct or incorrect in the "Answers" section at the end of this chapter.

1. Which of the following network affinity settings provides for state management?

   A. Single

   B. None

   C. Session

   D. Network

2. Which operation mode is appropriate when each host has more than one network adapter?

   A. Single

   B. Unicast

   C. Multicast

   D. Anycast

3. Which filter mode will send all traffic to a single host based on its priority?

   A. Single Host

   B. Multiple Hosts

   C. Failover

   D. Round-Robin

Objective 2.3: Plan and implement highly available storage solutions

High availability around storage is an area that has seen improvement in technology and support over the past decade. With standard tools and a small investment, you can create robust and scalable storage solutions for the enterprise. This section looks at a few ways you can make storage more redundant as it relates to the 70-414 exam objectives.

> **This objective covers how to:**
> - Plan for and configure storage spaces and storage pools
> - Design highly available, multi-replica DFS Namespaces
> - Plan for and configure multi-path I/O (MPIO)
> - Configure highly available iSCSI target and iSNS servers
> - Plan for and implement storage using RDMA and SMB multichannel

Planning for and configuring storage spaces and storage pools

Storage spaces and storage pools provide storage virtualization that brings another level of management and flexibility to Windows Server 2012. Storage pools, which are the underlying foundation of a storage space, use physical disks. Storage spaces provide a layer of abstraction to the physical infrastructure. Windows Server 2012 R2 adds several new features to storage spaces, including storage tiers, dual parity, and parity space for failover clusters, among others. Storage tiers improve performance by moving data to faster storage platforms, such as solid-state drives, based on the frequency of data access. Dual parity helps with resiliency in the event of a multi-disk failure by creating two copies of parity information. The parity space support for failover clusters enhances the use of storage spaces with failover clustering by enabling the creation of parity spaces.

> ***MORE INFO*** **NEW FEATURES OF STORAGE SPACES**
>
> See *http://technet.microsoft.com/library/dn387076.aspx* for more information on the new features of Storage Spaces in Windows Server 2012 R2.

Storagespaces require Serial Attached SCSI (SAS) or Serial Advanced Technology Attachment (SATA) disks with at least 4 gigabytes (GB) of available space that's unformatted and not part of a volume. The limitations are as important as the requirements. You can't use iSCSI or Fibre Channel controllers with storage spaces, and—while supported—USB disks are not recommended.

When planning storage spaces, you can choose from a simple, mirror, or parity resiliency. The resiliency type will determine the speed of the resulting data access as well as its resiliency to failure of a disk within the storage space. The resiliency is based on the disks available in the underlying storage pool. In other words, if the storage pool used as the basis for the storage space has only one disk, then the resiliency types will be limited.

Simple resiliency requires only one disk but doesn't provide any data protection in the event of disk failure. With simple resiliency, data is striped across the physical disks. Simple resiliency provides higher performance at the cost of protection; therefore, if you choose simple resiliency, you need to ensure that the data can be re-created easily in the event of disk failure.

Mirror resiliency provides a level of protection against disk failure by mirroring data across disks in the storage space. Mirror resiliency requires at least two disks and is slower than simple resiliency because data must be written across multiple disks. When used with five or more disks, mirror resiliency can protect against two disk failures. Mirror resiliency is appropriate for most cases.

Parity resiliency requires at least three disks and stores data and parity information across the disks. Parity resiliency is appropriate for sequential access scenarios where data is read or written in a certain order, such as with a backup system.

Both parity and mirror resiliency reduce the amount of available space on the storage space because each resiliency type needs to store additional information on each disk.

> **MORE INFO** **STORAGE SPACES**
>
> See *http://technet.microsoft.com/en-us/library/hh831739.aspx* for an overview of Storage Spaces.

Creating a storage pool

Because storage spaces are composed of storage pools, you need to have a storage pool available to create a storage space. You can configure a storage pool through the File and Storage Services section of the Server Manager. Selecting Storage Pools and then New Storage Pool invokes the New Storage Pool Wizard, within which you can enter the storage pool name and disk subsystem, as shown in Figure 2-16.

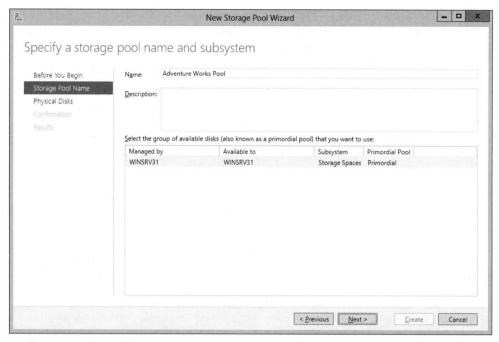

FIGURE 2-16 Configuring a storage pool

You can then select the physical disks to include as part of the storage pool, as shown in Figure 2-17.

The storage pool created in this section contains only one disk. Therefore, simple resiliency will be the only option available for the storage space. You can add another disk to the storage pool by selecting Add Physical Disk from the shortcut menu of the storage pool. Doing so reveals the Add Physical Disk dialog box, from which you can choose the disk to add to the storage pool.

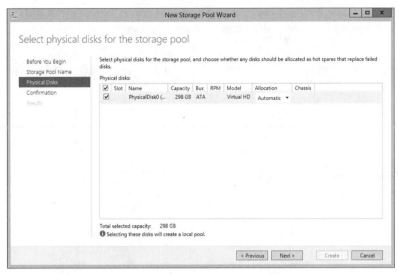

FIGURE 2-17 Selecting physical disks for a storage pool

Creating a storage space

Storage spaces are created by selecting New Virtual Disk from the shortcut menu of a storage pool. The New Virtual Disk Wizard walks through the process of creating a storage space. The first step in the wizard is to select a storage pool, as shown in Figure 2-18.

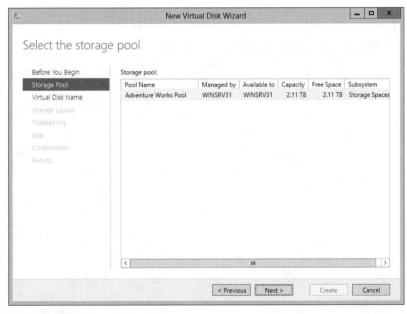

FIGURE 2-18 Creating a virtual disk

The name for the virtual disk is entered next, after which you choose the storage layout or resiliency type from among the choices discussed earlier in this section and depicted in Figure 2-19.

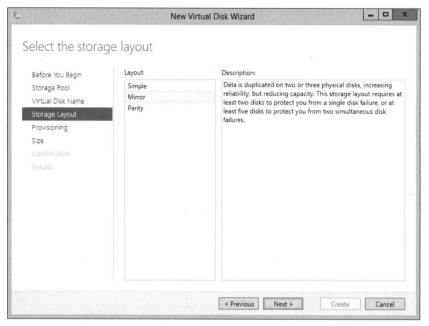

FIGURE 2-19 Choosing a resiliency type for a virtual disk

After choosing a resiliency type, the next step is to choose how the disk will be provisioned. You can choose Thin or Fixed, as shown in Figure 2-20. A thin provisioning type will use space only as needed, whereas fixed provisions the entire capacity right away.

With thin provisioning, you can create a virtual disk that's larger than the available capacity in the pool. You might do this if you know your storage needs will grow and you'll be adding physical disks at a later date to meet the needs. This scenario is shown in Figure 2-21, where the virtual disk size is specified as 10 terabytes but the available capacity is only 2.11 terabytes. It's worth noting that performance will be degraded with thin provisioning as opposed to fixed storage. Therefore, when provisioning a storage space where performance is a concern, you should use fixed storage.

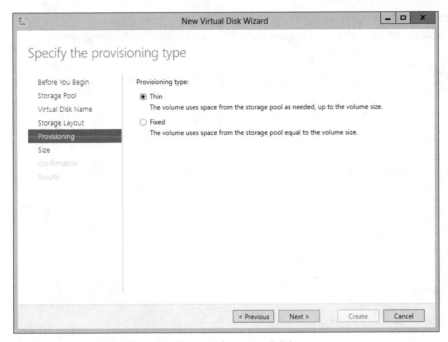

FIGURE 2-20 Choosing the provisioning type for a virtual disk

FIGURE 2-21 Setting the size of a virtual disk

Once the New Virtual Disk Wizard is complete, you'll be given the option to create a new volume. If you select the option, the New Volume Wizard will open, within which you can create a new volume, as shown in Figure 2-22.

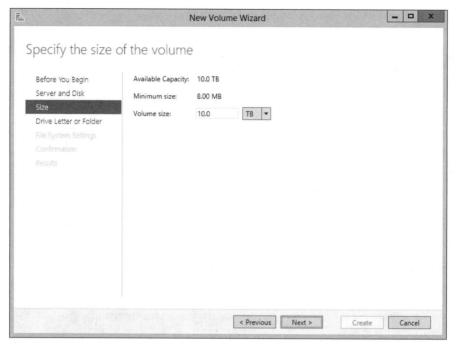

FIGURE 2-22 Creating a new volume

Other steps in the New Volume Wizard involve optionally choosing a drive letter for the volume and a format.

> **MORE INFO DEPLOYING STORAGE SPACES**
>
> See *http://technet.microsoft.com/en-us/library/jj822938.aspx* for deployment steps for Storage Spaces, including Windows PowerShell cmdlets.

Designing highly available, multi-replica DFS Namespaces

Distributed File System (DFS) provides a means for sharing files and folders within an organization. DFS is made up of two features: DFS Namespaces (DFSN or DFS-N) and DFS Replication (DFSR or DFS-R). DFSN creates a common name for shared folders so that users can access the share using that name, regardless of where or on what server the shared folder is hosted. DFSR provides replication of folders between servers using Remote Differential Compression (RDC), which makes the replication process more efficient.

The exam objective indicates that this is a design-related objective as opposed to a management-based objective. Therefore, this section looks at high-level concepts related to using DFS as a solution. Included in the section are several configuration touch points that you should consider when designing DFS. See *http://technet.microsoft.com/en-us/library/jj127250.aspx* for an overview of DFS that contains additional links to management-related topics.

DFS is a good solution for distributed file shares between a central location and one or more remote sites. The shared folders are replicated across the wide area network (WAN) to the remote sites, and users, regardless of their location, can access the shared folder through its DFS Namespace. However, the servers involved in DFS need to be in the same Active Directory forest. Other notable requirements include the use of NTFS volumes for shared folder storage and the need for the Active Directory Domain Services (AD DS) schema to be Windows Server 2003 R2 or newer for read-write folders and Windows Server 2008 or newer for read-only folders.

When designing a DFS-based solution, you should consider the available bandwidth and peak usage times. DFS Replication traffic can be optimized to occur only during certain hours.

> **MORE INFO** **DFS DESIGN**
>
> Though created for Windows Server 2003, the "Designing Distributed File Systems" document at *http://technet.microsoft.com/en-us/library/cc772778* contains helpful information. It's worth noting that configuration- and settings-related items may have changed since that document was written, and those settings are covered in this section.

DFS Namespace settings

When designing a namespace, you can create a standalone or domain namespace. Standalone namespaces can be clustered using a failover cluster and are also useful in environments where AD DS isn't available. A domain-based namespace uses the domain name as the path of the namespace. This makes it easier to migrate the namespace server in the future. For example, a domain-based namespace will have a name like this:

```
\\adventure-works.com\Public
```

Conversely, a standalone namespace will have the server's name in it:

```
\\WINSRV31\Public
```

When creating a domain-based namespace, you can optionally use Windows Server 2008 mode (enabled by default). When Windows Server 2008 mode is enabled, the Advanced tab of a domain-based namespace contains settings related to access-based enumeration, as shown in Figure 2-23. The polling settings shown in Figure 2-23 configure how the namespace servers will interact with the domain and are available for domain-based namespaces.

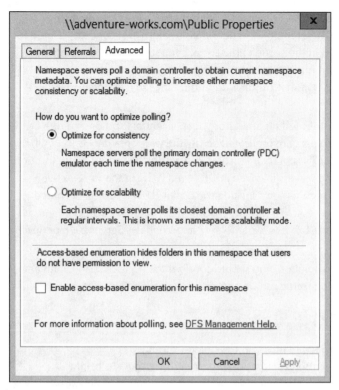

FIGURE 2-23 Configuring a domain-based namespace

If there are fewer than 16 namespace servers for the namespace, Optimize For Consistency should be used. The Optimize For Scalability option will cause an increase in the time it takes to replicate changes in a namespace, which may cause a temporary skew in the namespace view available to users.

Permissions can be configured when the namespace is created. By default, all users have read-only permissions. Other selections include:

- All Users Have Read And Write Permissions
- Administrators Have Full Access; Other Users Have Read-Only Permissions
- Administrators Have Full Access; Other Users Have Read and Write Permissions
- Use Custom Permissions

In addition to configuring permissions, the Edit Settings dialog box shown in Figure 2-24 can be used to set the path for the shared folder.

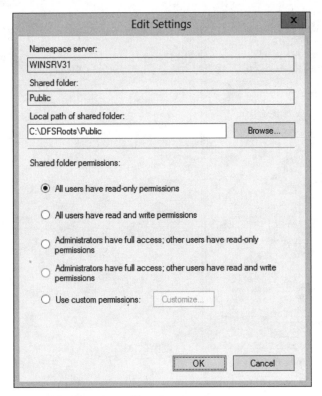

FIGURE 2-24 Changing settings for a namespace

When designing a namespace, you can also configure settings around referrals. When accessing a namespace, a user receives a list of namespace servers. If the first server in the list is unavailable, the client will attempt to reach the next server in the list. You can configure the length of time that the referral is cached, as well as the priority and ordering. Referral configuration is important for namespace design because the referral list can be set up to include only those servers at the client's physical site to prevent clients from accessing servers across a WAN link.

Referral settings are configured on the Referrals tab of a namespace's Properties dialog box, as shown in Figure 2-25. The default cache duration is 300 seconds. The ordering method options are:

- Random Order
- Lowest Cost (default)
- Exclude Targets Outside Of The Client's Site

Additionally, you can configure whether clients will fail back to their preferred target server.

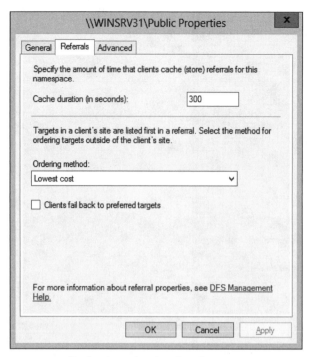

FIGURE 2-25 Configuring referral settings for a namespace

DFS Replication settings

DFS Replication is configured through replication groups. When creating a replication group, you can choose a multipurpose replication group or a replication group for data collection. The multipurpose replication group is a more generic approach and allows for two or more servers, whereas a data collection group is used for two servers and creates a two-way replication such that a branch (source) server sends its data to a central location (hub/destination server).

When creating a multipurpose replication group, there are three basic topologies, as described in Table 2-3.

TABLE 2-3 Multipurpose DFSR topologies

Topology	Description
Hub and spoke	A hub and spoke topology requires at least three servers and is typically used where there is a central hub location and data is replicated out to the destination spoke servers.
Full mesh	A full mesh topology, recommended for 10 or fewer servers, replicates data with all other members of the replication group.
No topology	This option doesn't specify a topology when the replication group is created, but a custom topology can be designed later.

When a topology is created, you can configure the hours within which replication will occur. The default is to replicate continuously using the full bandwidth (the default), as shown in Figure 2-26.

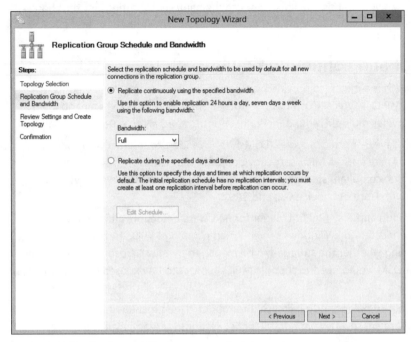

FIGURE 2-26 Configuring a replication group schedule

You can also configure a custom schedule for replication to occur, as shown in Figure 2-27.

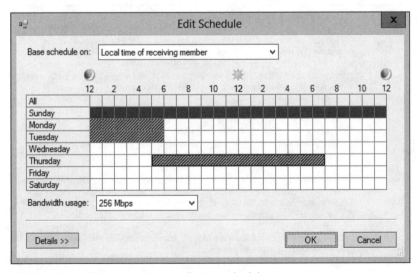

FIGURE 2-27 Configuring a custom replication schedule

When creating a replication group, you configure the folders to be replicated. When you do so, you can also publish the folder through DFS Namespace. This is accomplished within the Replicated Folders tab of a replication group's workspace by selecting Share And Publish In Namespace. When you do this, the folder will use the namespace settings for the chosen namespace.

Planning for and configuring multi-path I/O (MPIO)

Multipath I/O (MPIO) is a means to provide high availability for storage connected to Windows servers. MPIO is typically used with a storage area network (SAN) scenario in an enterprise and provides multiple redundant connections to the SAN to ensure reliability.

MPIO relies on device-specific modules (DSMs) from vendors to interact with various storage providers. There's also a Microsoft-provided DSM that works with SCSI Primary Commands-3 (SPC-3) compliant storage. MPIO is installed as a feature in Windows Server 2012 and is used with Fibre Channel, iSCSI, and SAS.

Windows uses Plug and Play (PnP) Manager for hardware detection, and MPIO also detects devices connected to a Windows server. When planning MPIO, the first step is typically determining whether the storage will be managed by the Microsoft DSM or a vendor DSM. The vendor DSM would need to support MPIO in order to be exposed through MPIO in Windows.

MPIO performs load balancing to increase throughput. When managed through the Microsoft DSM, there are several configurable policy settings for load balancing, as described in Table 2-4.

TABLE 2-4 Microsoft DSM settings

Setting	Description
Failover Only	No load balancing. Used for providing redundancy between an active path and one or more standby paths.
Least Blocks	Provides load balancing by sending the next I/O request to the path with the fewest outstanding data blocks being processed.
Least Queue Depth	Provides load balancing by sending the next I/O request to the path with the lowest current utilization.
Round Robin	The default policy for active/active storage that balances I/O among the available paths.
Round Robin with Subset	Enables a pool of active paths that will share load in a round-robin fashion, with other paths being standby. All active paths must be unavailable for the standby path to be used. In other words, if only one path becomes unavailable, the standby path doesn't automatically take its place.
Weighted Paths	Load balancing that uses a weight, or priority, for each path, with larger numbers being lower in priority.

When using the graphical interface, MPIO is configured through the MPIO Properties dialog box, shown in Figure 2-28.

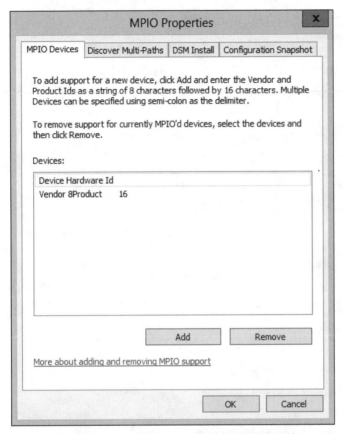

FIGURE 2-28 MPIO configuration through the graphical interface

The Discover Multi-Paths tab is where you can add multi-paths to the configuration.

When using the Server Core edition of Windows Server 2012, you configure MPIO through the command line. MPIO is added with the Windows PowerShell command as follows:

```
Enable-WindowsOptionalFeature -Online -FeatureName MultiPathIO
```

You can query the current state of the MPIO feature with this command:

```
Get-WindowsOptionalFeature -Online -FeatureName MultiPathIO
```

To enable the automatic claiming of iSCSI devices, use the following command:

```
Enable-MSDSMAutomaticClaim -BusType iSCSI
```

Changing the load balancing policy is achieved using the Set-MSDSMGlobalDefaultLoad-BalancePolicy -Policy <PolicyAbbreviation> command, where the <PolicyAbbreviation> is one of the following:

- **FOO** Failover Only
- **LB** Least Blocks
- **LQD** Least Queue Depth
- **None** Removes the default load balance policy
- **RR** Round robin

You can obtain the current load balance policy with the "get" version of the cmdlet:

`Get-MSDSMGlobalDefaultLoadBalancePolicy`

Various other settings for MPIO behavior are configured using the Set-MPIOSetting command. These include:

- CustomPathRecovery
- NewDiskTimeout
- NewPathRecoveryInterval
- NewPathVerificationPeriod
- NewPathVerificationState
- NewPDORemovePeriod
- NewRetryCount
- NewRetryInterval

The Get-MPIOSetting cmdlet shows current values.

> **MORE INFO** **WINDOWS POWERSHELL AND MPIO SETTINGS**
>
> See *http://technet.microsoft.com/en-us/library/hh826113.aspx* for a summary of the Windows PowerShell cmdlets available for MPIO and *http://www.microsoft.com/en-us/download/details.aspx?id=30450* for the MPIO Users Guide.

Configuring highly available iSCSI target and iSNS servers

Internet Small Computer System Interface (iSCSI) and Internet Storage Name Service (iSNS) are means to discover, manage, and provide storage over a standard network interface and connection. iSCSI provides block-level storage through targets. iSCSI targets are connected to clients, known as initiators. Windows Server 2012 R2 can act as an iSCSI target server by adding it as a role service through the graphical interface or with the Add-WindowsFeature fs-iscsitarget-server command. Windows Server 2012 R2 can also act as an iSCSI initiator.

iSNS also uses the concept of clients and servers. The iSNS Server feature in Windows Server 2012 R2 helps to connect and manage discovery and use of iSCSI devices. See *http://technet.microsoft.com/library/cc772568.aspx* for more information on iSNS Server.

You can configure highly available iSCSI and iSNS servers using failover clustering in Windows Server 2012 R2. The iSCSI target server is installed as part of the File and Storage Services role, and failover clustering is installed as a feature.

Both iSCSI Target Server and iSNS Server are predefined roles in Failover Cluster Manager. As such, you can add them easily using the High Availability Wizard, shown in Figure 2-29. However, prior to running the wizard, you should configure the iSCSI disk as storage in Failover Cluster Manager. It's worth noting that you'll need to manually bring the disks online using the standard Windows disk management tools, through either Server Manager or Computer Management. Once the disk has been brought online, it needs to be added to the available storage for the cluster.

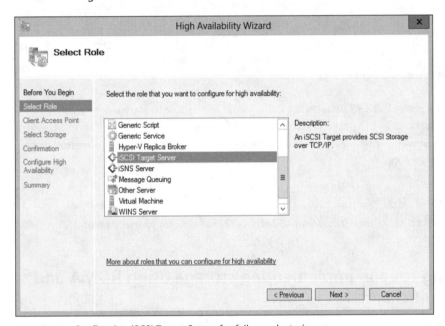

FIGURE 2-29 Configuring iSCSI Target Server for failover clustering

The client access point is configured next, as shown in Figure 2-30.

The storage previously added is selected next, after which you'll configure the high availability for the iSCSI cluster.

Like iSCSI, the High Availability Wizard can assist with creation of a clustered iSNS server. The steps are essentially the same as those for configuration of iSCSI in Failover Cluster Manager.

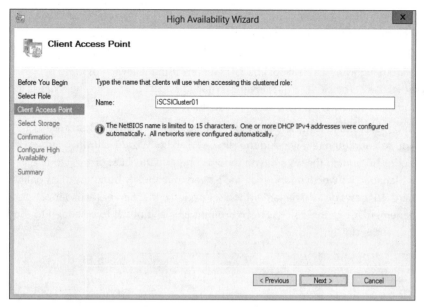

FIGURE 2-30 Setting the client access point

Windows Server 2012 R2 updates the iSCSI Target Server role to increase the maximum number of sessions and logical units to 544 and 256, respectively. With iSCSI Target Server in Windows Server 2012 R2, you can also utilize Virtual Hard Disk (VHD) 2.0 formatted disks (.vhdx file extension).

> **MORE INFO ISNS**
>
> See *http://technet.microsoft.com/en-us/library/cc772568.aspx* for an overview of iSNS.

Planning for and implementing storage using RDMA and SMB multichannel

A new feature introduced in Windows Server 2012 is the ability to utilize network adapters that have the *Remote Directory Memory Access (RDMA)* feature. The RDMA feature enables a remote file share to act like a local one due to the increased ability of RDMA-capable adapters. RDMA is useful for improving performance of SMB-based file servers because it offloads processing onto the RDMA-capable adapter, thereby reducing CPU utilization and latency for SMB-based access. SMB multichannel detects RDMA-capable network adapters and enables the use of SMB Direct.

Though SMB Direct is enabled with Windows Server 2012 or Windows Server 2012 R2, it will only be used when the appropriate hardware is available. You can disable the use of RDMA for a given network adapter using the command

```
Disable-NetAdapterRdma <AdapterName>
```

Alternatively, RDMA can be disabled for all adapters on a given server with the command

```
Set-NetOffloadGlobalSetting -NetworkDirect Disabled
```

EXAM TIP

Use Enable-NetAdapterRdma to enable RDMA for a given adapter or change the Network-Direct option to Enabled to enable RDMA for all adapters.

RDMA-capable network adapters shouldn't be placed in a teamed configuration. Doing so will disable the RDMA capabilities. SMB Multichannel creates two RDMA connections per interface and can be used in a failover cluster configuration.

> **MORE INFO   DEPLOYING SMB DIRECT**
>
> See *http://technet.microsoft.com/en-us/library/dn583825.aspx* for more information on SMB Direct deployment on iWARP adapters, see *http://technet.microsoft.com/en-us/library/dn583823.aspx* for more information on deployment with InfiniBand adapters, and see *http://technet.microsoft.com/en-us/library/dn583822.aspx* for more information on SMB Direct with RoCE adapters.

Thought experiment
Designing a DFS

In the following thought experiment, apply what you've learned about this objective to predict what steps you need to take. You can find answers to these questions in the "Answers" section at the end of this chapter.

You're designing a distributed file access method that will span three physical office locations. The network runs AD DS, and there's a domain controller located at each of the locations. There is a central data center and two remote offices in this organization. One of the concerns surrounds bandwidth usage for the replication and the subsequent usage of the shared file system.

Describe the configuration items that you can use with a distributed file system to limit or control bandwidth usage.

Objective summary

- Storage spaces provide a virtualized disk infrastructure built on storage pools of one or more disks.
- Storage spaces can be provisioned in a thin manner, giving them the ability to grow as needed.
- DFS Namespaces and replication are used to create a virtualized disk share that's accessible and replicated to multiple sites or locations if necessary.
- MPIO provides a method for accessing storage providers through multiple redundant and load-balanced paths.
- You can configure MPIO to use the Microsoft DSM or a vendor-supplied DSM, assuming that the DSM meets MPIO certification requirements.
- iSCSI Target Server and iSNS Server can be used as roles of failover clustering to provide redundancy and load balancing.

Objective review

Answer the following questions to test your knowledge of the information in this objective. You can find the answers to these questions and explanations of why each answer choice is correct or incorrect in the "Answers" section at the end of this chapter.

1. Which type of virtual disk resiliency requires three or more disks?

   A. Simple

   B. Parity

   C. Mirror

   D. Level 5

2. Which command would be used to change the load-balancing policy for MPIO to a policy that doesn't include any load balancing but still provides for fail over?

   A. Set-MPIOSetting -LoadBalancePolicy Failover

   B. Set-MSDSMGlobalDefaultLoadBalancePolicy -Policy All

   C. Set-MSDSMGlobalDefaultLoadBalancePolicy -Policy FOO

   D. Set-MPIOSetting -Policy None

3. Which DFSR topology can be used with two servers?

   A. Full mesh

   B. Hub and spoke

   C. Wheel

   D. Dual-mesh

Objective 2.4: Plan and implement highly available server roles

A network doesn't exist for itself alone; it exists for users to perform functions. That means providing services to support those functions. This section looks at methods in which server roles can be made highly available. This objective is largely a planning-related one, and the content reflects that requirement.

This objective covers how to:

- Plan for a highly available Dynamic Host Configuration Protocol (DHCP) server, Hyper-V clustering, Continuously Available File Shares, and a DFS Namespace server
- Plan for and implement highly available applications, services, and scripts using Generic Application, Generic Script, and Generic Service clustering roles

---

Planning for highly available services

This exam objective looks at planning around providing high availability for various applications, including DHCP, Hyper-V, file shares, and DFSN. (Availability for DFSN was discussed in the previous section.) All of these services can be made highly available using failover clustering in Windows Server 2012, but in the case of DHCP, there are different options available beginning with Windows Server 2012.

DHCP

DHCP can be made highly available through failover clustering or by implementing a split scope. You can also configure a failover relationship within the DHCP Manager tool, which is a preferred approach for most organizations running Windows Server 2012.

The failover relationship created with DHCP Manager can be configured in a load balance or hot standby mode with an authorized server and for specific scopes. When creating the new failover relationship with DHCP Manager, you can set these and other parameters, as shown in Figure 2-31.

When planning DHCP failover using this method, you should consider the amount of lead time that a server can provision an address before it needs to inform the other DHCP server (as defined by the Maximum Client Lead Time parameter). A longer amount of time means that the servers will be less likely to take over the entire scope in the event of a transient network issue or a quick reboot of one server. The State Switchover Interval is related insofar as it defines the amount of time that a server is marked as being down if it can't be contacted.

Note that Figure 2-31 depicts the Role Of Partner Server as Standby mode (sometimes called Active/Passive). The other option is Load Balance (sometimes called Active/Active), which reveals a load balance percentage (50/50 default) that will be used by each server.

When planning other types of failover, such as through failover clustering, you should consider the shared storage that will be used within the cluster. That storage should be redundant or clustered so that DHCP will still be available in the event of a failure of one part of the storage.

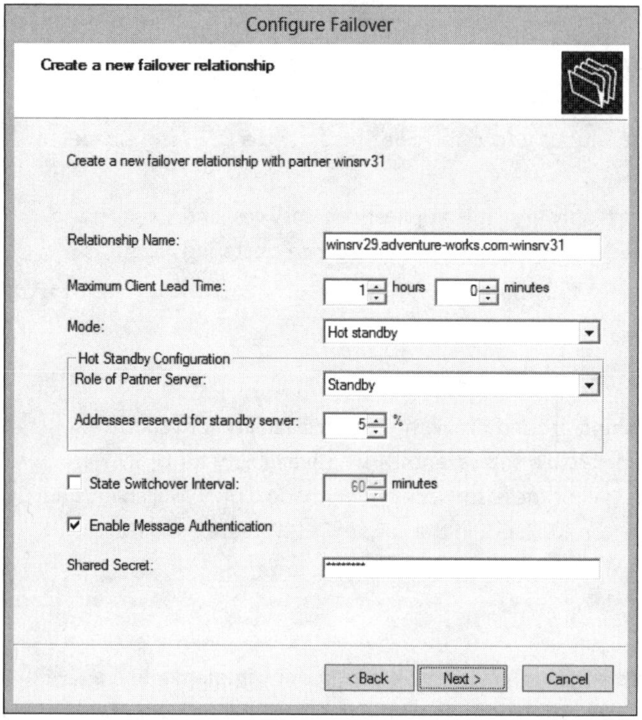

FIGURE 2-31 Configuring DHCP failover using DHCP Manager

Split-scope DHCP calls for the address scope for DHCP clients to be split among two or more servers. Those servers don't share information with each other, but rather simply respond to DHCP queries as received. The obvious limitation is that there will be fewer addresses available on a given server because the scope of available addresses is split. This can cause problems in networks where there are limited available addresses.

Hyper-V clustering

Hyper-V uses failover clustering to provide redundancy. Doing so requires some amount of planning to ensure that prerequisites and configuration requirements are met. Aside from the hardware requirements for Hyper-V and failover clustering (see the More Info sidebar later in this section), you also need to use a virtual switch, CSV, and configure virtual machines for high availability.

Creation of virtual machines that are to be highly available should be done through Failover Cluster Manager. Creating virtual machines through Failover Cluster Manager ensures that the machines are configured for high availability.

> **MORE INFO** **HYPER-V CLUSTERING**
>
> See *http://technet.microsoft.com/en-us/library/jj863389.aspx* for an overview of Hyper-V clustering, *http://technet.microsoft.com/library/hh831531* for an overview of Hyper-V, and *http://technet.microsoft.com/library/jj612869* for hardware requirements for failover clustering.

Continuously available file shares

File shares, available as the file server role in failover clustering, enable high availability of important files and data. When creating a highly available file server, you can choose between a clustered file server for general use (active/passive) or a scale-out file server (active/active). Choose a general file server for typical business-user patterns of opening and closing files regularly. Choose a scale-out file server for usage patterns that leave files open for long periods, such as for virtual machines.

General clustered file servers use one cluster node at a time, whereas scale-out file servers take advantage of the Distributed Network Name feature in Windows Server 2012 and distribute traffic across nodes. The use of CSVs will also determine the direction for the availability type. General file server clustering can't use CSVs, but CSVs are required for the scale-out file server option.

Related to CSVs are the types of file systems and file system–related features supported by each type of file server clustering option, as described in Table 2-5.

TABLE 2-5 Clustered file server support

Feature	General Clustered File Server	Scale-Out File Server
BranchCache	Available	Available in Windows Server 2012 R2 for Virtual Desktop Infrastructure (VDI) with remote storage separate from nodes.
Data Deduplication	Available	Not available
DFS Namespace server	Available	Not available
DFS Namespace folder target	Available	Available
DFS Replication	Available	Not available
File Classification Infrastructure	Available	Not available
File Server Resource Manager quotas, screening, reporting	Available	Not available

Feature	General Clustered File Server	Scale-Out File Server
Folder Redirection	Available	Available
Offline Files	Available	Available
SMB	Available	Available
Volume Shadow Copy Service Agent	Available	Available

> **MORE INFO** **SCALE-OUT FILE SERVERS**
>
> See *http://technet.microsoft.com/en-us/library/hh831349.aspx* for more information on scale-out file servers.

DFS Namespace Server

DFS enables an organization to use shared folders in a distributed manner. DFS Namespace Server enables the virtualization of those folders so that users can interact with the folders without knowing the underlying server location or folder structure. DFS Namespace Server is one of the applications that can be made highly available through the High Availability Wizard.

See the section titled "Designing highly available, multi-replica DFS Namespaces" earlier in this chapter for more information on highly available DFS.

> **MORE INFO**   **DFS NAMESPACE CMDLETS**
>
> Windows Server 2012 adds Windows PowerShell cmdlets for DFS Namespace Server management. See *http://technet.microsoft.com/en-us/library/jj884270.aspx* for more details on those cmdlets.

Planning and implementing highly available applications, services, and scripts

Failover clustering includes generic roles titled Generic Application, Generic Script, and Generic Service. These are used to create clusters for services and applications that wouldn't otherwise be aware of clustering or have options for high availability. To use a generic option, the underlying object being clustered should be IP-based, such as TCP, UDP, RPC over TCP/IP, DCOM, and so on.

The generic option chosen depends on the needs for clustering. For example, the Generic Application cluster simply looks to see whether a given process is running (and starts it if not). When configuring a Generic Application, you provide the application path and, optionally, registry keys to be replicated to other nodes. Like the Generic Application option, the Generic

Service option looks to see whether the configured service is running and is used for service-related clustering. Also like the Generic Application, Generic Service clustering can replicate registry entries.

The Generic Script option gives some amount of control over the process but is more complex to configure. With a Generic Script, an administrator creates a script that controls underlying applications, including monitoring their state. The script then interacts with failover clustering to determine whether an underlying application should be restarted or failed over.

Generic clustering is implemented through Failover Cluster Manager by creating a cluster and then choosing the appropriate role from the High Availability Wizard.

Thought experiment
Designing a DHCP failover solution

In the following thought experiment, apply what you've learned about this objective to predict what steps you need to take. You can find answers to these questions in the "Answers" section at the end of this chapter.

You're designing a DHCP failover solution for a client with a small network running Windows Server 2012 servers and a combination of Windows 7 and Windows 8 client computers. The client currently uses a split-scope DHCP solution. The client uses basic NAS and local storage and doesn't use virtual machines. The client has asked for an overview.

Describe the available solutions for DHCP failover and which one is recommended for this scenario.

Objective summary

- DHCP now has a native failover option that doesn't have the same limitations as other methods, such as failover clustering and split scope.
- File servers, Hyper-V, and generic services and applications can be clustered using failover clustering.
- Continuously available file shares use the Distributed Network Name feature and CSVs to ensure high availability of file shares.
- Generic services, applications, and scripts enable failover clustering to work with applications and technologies that aren't normally cluster-aware.

Objective review

Answer the following questions to test your knowledge of the information in this objective. You can find the answers to these questions and explanations of why each answer choice is correct or incorrect in the "Answers" section at the end of this chapter.

1. Which type of DHCP failover mode is considered active/passive?

   A. Standby

   B. Load Balance

   C. Passive Partner

   D. Split Address

2. Which of the following file system features is supported on scale-out file servers?

   A. SMB

   B. BranchCache

   C. Data Deduplication

   D. File Classification Infrastructure

3. Which type of generic clustering enables you to choose registry keys to be replicated during the cluster role configuration? (Choose all that apply.)

   A. Generic Application

   B. Generic Script

   C. Generic Service

   D. Generic Registry Application

Objective 2.5: Plan and implement a business continuity and disaster recovery solution

The final objective in this area looks at disaster recovery and the technologies and methods for providing the same. Newly added for Windows Server 2012 R2 is Microsoft Azure Hyper-V Recovery Manager and System Center Data Protection Manager (DPM). Both of those additions are addressed in this section.

Planning a backup and recovery strategy

Windows Server Backup can be installed as a feature in Windows Server 2012. You can back up locally or online to Microsoft Azure. When planning a backup and recovery strategy, you should consider several items, as described in this section.

When designing a backup solution, consider what you'll be backing up and where it will be sent.

- Do you need to back up the entire operating system? Doing so will include a significant amount of data that could possibly be re-created by reinstalling the operating system and then restoring data.

- How long will the backup take? You should ensure that the backup can complete before being kicked off again and that it doesn't run during times when the server is heavily loaded. Incremental backups can help with this issue.

- Where will backups be stored? If you're storing backups onsite, then the organization is susceptible to a disaster. Consider taking a backup set offsite or using an offsite backup destination.

Understanding planning considerations

There are some specific issues pertinent to Microsoft networks and some advanced features that you can take advantage of to provide backup and recovery of a Microsoft network. These include the use of Microsoft Azure Hyper-V Recovery Manager, Hyper-V Replica, and issues related to recovery of Active Directory.

Using Hyper-V Replica and Microsoft Azure Hyper-V Recovery Manager

Hyper-V Replica enables replication for select virtual machines. This replication can be enabled within a data center or across data centers to ensure recovery in the event of a disaster. When using Hyper-V Replica in a failover cluster scenario, the Hyper-V Replica Broker cluster service should be used to manage the replica.

In Windows Server 2012, the replication frequency was set at 5 minutes. This meant a gap of 5 minutes in replication between Hyper-V hosts, which could result in a large amount of data loss in the event of an unplanned outage that caused failover to the replicated virtual machine. In Windows Server 2012 R2, you can configure the frequency on which replication will occur from three choices: 30 seconds, 5 minutes, and 15 minutes. This enables greater control over important virtual machines and less frequent updates for those virtual machines that don't change much.

The introduction of Microsoft Azure Hyper-V Recovery Manager enables replication control from an external entity. This means that in disaster-recovery scenarios, you're no longer dependent on having access to the Hyper-V host at either site. It's important to note that Microsoft Azure Hyper-V Recovery Manager does not replicate a virtual machine to a third-party data center, but rather provides management capabilities only; replication is still done between the Hyper-V hosts.

> **MORE INFO** **MICROSOFT AZURE HYPER-V RECOVERY MANAGER**
>
> See *http://msdn.microsoft.com/en-us/library/windowsazure/dn469074.aspx?fwLinkID=321294*
> for more information on Microsoft Azure Hyper-V Recovery Manager.

Recovering an Active Directory domain and forest and restoring and cloning a domain controller

Active Directory is vital to an organization's continuity. Therefore, it's important that you plan for backup and recovery of Active Directory. It's a good idea to keep the operating system files and Active Directory database as well as SYSVOL on separate volumes. You should back up the system state, which is an option found when configuring a custom backup in Windows Server Backup, as shown in Figure 2-32.

System state plays an important role in domain controller operation. You can restore system state with the command wbadmin start systemstaterecovery.

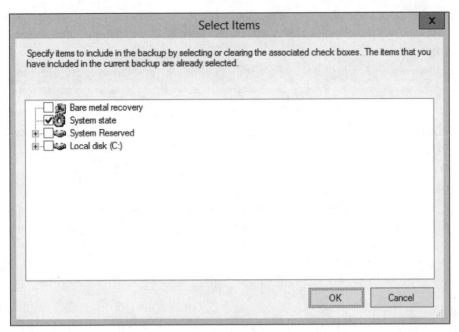

FIGURE 2-32 Backing up system state as part of a backup strategy

MORE INFO **DOMAIN CONTROLLER RECOVERY**

See *http://technet.microsoft.com/library/cc732238* for scenario overviews for backing up and recovering Active Directory Domain Services.

Restoring an Active Directory object and container using authoritative restore and the Recycle Bin

The Active Directory Recycle Bin keeps track of objects that have been removed from Active Directory. With the Active Directory Recycle Bin, objects are logically deleted and moved to the Deleted Objects container. Objects in the Deleted Objects container are eventually migrated to being recycled objects. Recycled objects eventually expire, after which the object is subject to garbage collection and removed entirely from the Active Directory database.

Performing an authoritative restore of an Active Directory container or object brings that container or object back to the state it was in prior to being deleted. Objects within domain directory partitions, application directory partitions, and configuration directory partitions can be restored. Active Directory objects are typically restored using the Active Directory Administrative Center (ADAC) but can also be restored using Windows PowerShell. The msDS-deletedObjectLifetime and tombstoneLifetime attributes determine the lifetime for the deleted object and the recycled object, respectively. By default, the value for these attributes are set to null, which in effect gives msDS-deletedObjectLifetime the same lifetime as tombstoneLifetime, or 180 days. Note that Active Directory objects can also be restored using the ldp.exe command, specifically by removing the isDeleted attribute from the CN=Deleted Objects container.

You can also restore Active Directory objects using Windows Server Backup, but doing so has several drawbacks over the Recycle Bin–based method discussed here. See *http://technet. microsoft.com/en-us/library/dd379542* for more information.

Planning for and implementing backup and recovery using System Center Data Protection Manager (DPM)

System Center Data Protection Manager (DPM) provides a robust backup and recovery solution for SQL Server, Exchange Server, Hyper-V, and other products. DPM can also provide backup and recovery for standard file servers and Windows client computers. DPM is installed on its own servers and also uses a SQL Server instance, which can be installed locally or on a remote SQL server. DPM uses an agent on each protected computer. The agent can be installed using the Protection Agent Installation Wizard in the DPM console, as shown in Figure 2-33.

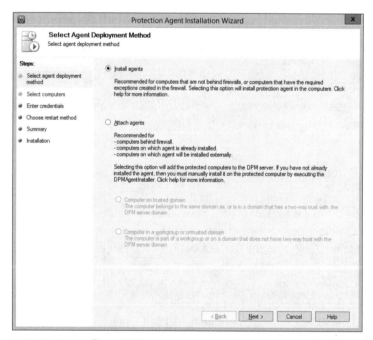

FIGURE 2-33 Installing a DPM agent

DPM uses a storage pool to manage the available space to which data sources are backed up. Both agent installation and storage pools are managed from within the Management workspace in the DPM administrator console. The storage pool must exist at the operating-system level, after which it can be added in the DPM console, as shown in Figure 2-34.

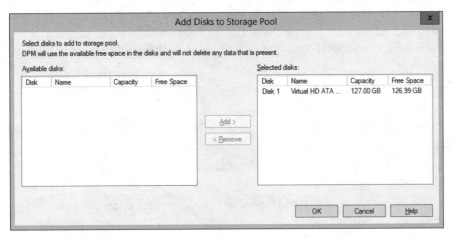

FIGURE 2-34 Adding disks to a DPM storage pool

Planning for a DPM deployment

Part of the planning for a DPM deployment is determining how many servers are necessary based on the existing infrastructure. You should consider network bandwidth between the DPM server and the servers or clients to be backed up. A minimum of 512 kilobytes (KB) is required for the connection. A DPM server can provide backup for up to 2,000 SQL Server databases or 3,000 client computers. The recommended disk space is 80 terabytes per DPM server for SQL Server and Exchange Server and 25 terabytes for SharePoint Server.

EXAM TIP

When planning snapshots, the limit is 9,000 snapshots per DPM server for express full backups and file recovery points. The limit does not apply to incremental synchronizations.

DPM needs to be used in an Active Directory environment but can provide backups across domains in the same forest and across forests as long as two-way trust exists between the domains or forests.

DPM uses the concept of protection groups to help organize data sources. Protection groups are nothing more than those data sources that share the same DPM configuration for backup. DPM provides a varying level of recovery for certain products. For example, different versions of Exchange Server can be protected at different levels by DPM. The article at *http://technet.microsoft.com/en-us/library/jj627977.aspx* provides an overview of protection groups and a table noting the protectable data for various sources.

In addition to the protectable data, Microsoft has created a deployment checklist, available at *http://technet.microsoft.com/en-us/library/hh758205.aspx*, which includes these overall steps:

- Identify each data source to be protected, including the type, size, fully qualified domain name, cluster name (if part of a cluster), and anything to be excluded from the backup.
- Identify the protection method, such as short-term disk-based, long-term tape-based, and so on.
- Determine the requirements around recovery in the event that a client being protected fails.
- Organize protection groups, decide whether to encrypt tapes, and determine the replica creation method.

Based on the requirements and information already determined, you can then calculate the amount of space needed to meet those requirements with DPM. This, along with the placement of servers, will lead you to determine the number of DPM servers necessary for your deployment.

Various firewall settings may need to be changed to support DPM on computers in untrusted domains. Specifically, support for DCOM on port 135 and WINSOCK on port 5718 for the agent coordinator and 5719 for the protection agent needs to be allowed on the computer to be protected. Additional considerations for non-domain joined computers can be found at *http://technet.microsoft.com/library/hh757954.aspx*.

Certificate-based authentication can also be used with DPM in both trusted and untrusted domains for the file server and Hyper-V data sources. See *http://technet.microsoft.com/library/hh916530.aspx* for more information.

Deploying DPM

Once the implementation has been planned, deploying DPM includes tasks such as installing the DPM server and any SQL Server instances to be used by DPM, installing protection agents, creating DPM storage pools, and creating protection groups.

Protection groups are created from within the Protection workspace in the DPM administrator console using the Create New Protection Group Wizard. Within the wizard, you first select whether to protect servers or clients, as shown in Figure 2-35.

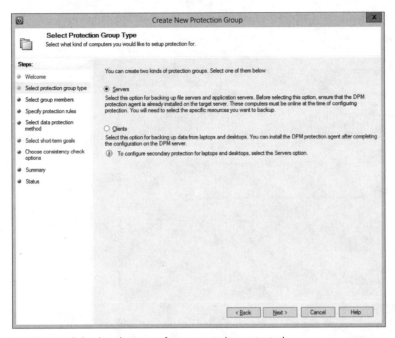

FIGURE 2-35 Selecting the type of resource to be protected

Next, the servers to be protected are selected, along with the data to be protected on each server, as shown in Figure 2-36.

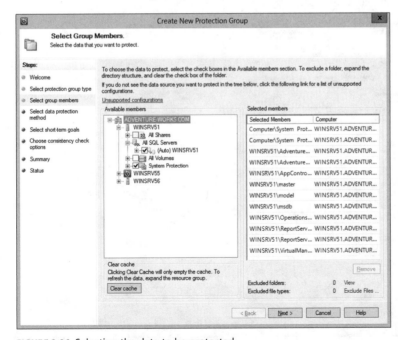

FIGURE 2-36 Selecting the data to be protected

The protection group name and mode are selected next, as shown in Figure 2-37.

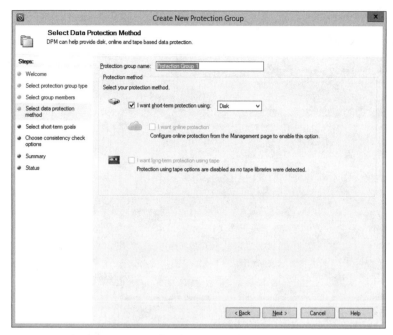

FIGURE 2-37 Setting parameters for the protection group

The protection schedule is set next, as shown in Figure 2-38.

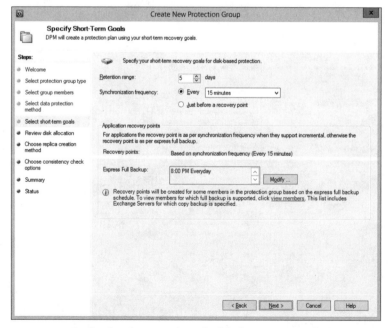

FIGURE 2-38 Configuring the protection schedule for a protection group

The disk allocation based on the initial calculation of data size is shown next, enabling you to make changes to the location and settings related to protection. This is illustrated in Figure 2-39.

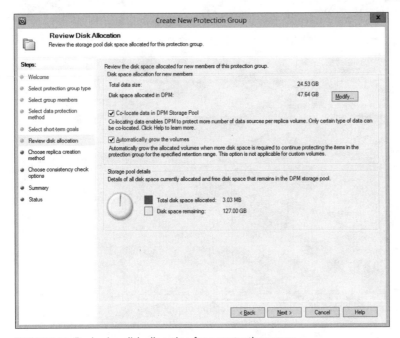

FIGURE 2-39 Reviewing disk allocation for a protection group

The replica creation method is set next in the wizard, as shown in Figure 2-40.

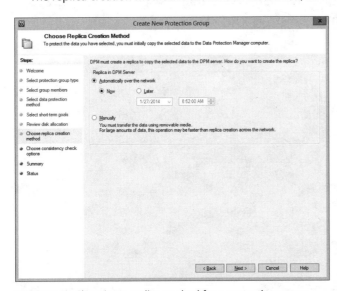

FIGURE 2-40 Choosing a replica method for a protection group

Finally, the consistency check options are set for the protection group, as shown in Figure 2-41.

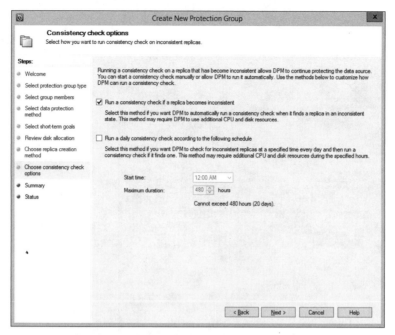

FIGURE 2-41 Choosing consistency check options for a protection group

---

MORE INFO DEPLOYING DPM

See *http://technet.microsoft.com/en-us/library/hh757840.aspx* for specific information on protecting various types of servers and clients with DPM.

Thought experiment

Planning a backup strategy

In the following thought experiment, apply what you've learned about this objective to predict what steps you need to take. You can find answers to these questions in the "Answers" section at the end of this chapter.

You're planning a backup strategy for an organization. The organization consists of eight Windows Server 2012 servers along with shared storage on an NAS device. The network runs Active Directory Domain Services along with standard file shares, DHCP, DNS, and so on. The NAS device is automatically backed up to the cloud and is outside of the scope of your engagement. Your task is to plan for backup of the Windows Server 2012 servers.

Discuss the overall considerations for backup of the servers and any other items that you can recommend to help ensure availability in the event of a server outage or a site-wide disaster.

Objective summary

- Backup and recovery strategies center around ensuring business continuity in the event of disaster.
- Windows Server Backup can be used to create a backup of Windows servers and can back up system state, which is important for Active Directory.
- The Active Directory Recycle Bin provides an easy way to recover objects that have been deleted from Active Directory.
- DPM can be used to provide backup and recovery for various services and server types.
- DPM can protect computers joined to the domain and those outside of the domain.

Objective review

Answer the following questions to test your knowledge of the information in this objective. You can find the answers to these questions and explanations of why each answer choice is correct or incorrect in the "Answers" section at the end of this chapter.

1. Which item should be included in a backup for Active Directory?

   A. System state

   B. AD DS

   C. Service Master

   D. FSMO

2. Which property defines the lifetime of a deleted object in the Active Directory Recycle Bin?

   A. tombstoneState

   B. tombstoneLife

   C. msDS-deletedObjectLifetime

   D. msDS-recycleBinLifeTime

3. Which portions of an Active Directory implementation should be kept on a separate volume?

   A. SYSVOL

   B. Active Directory database

   C. ENTVOL

   D. Recycle Bin

Answers

This section contains the solutions to the thought experiments and answers to the lesson review questions in this chapter.

Objective 2.1: Thought experiment

Ideally, you would have an odd number of votes in the Quorum configuration. Therefore, you can configure a witness so that it also has a vote. Because the servers are located in different data centers, it's likely that you'll use a file-share witness. The Configure Cluster Quorum Wizard is used to reconfigure Quorum settings and is found in the More Actions area of a cluster's shortcut menu.

Objective 2.1: Review

1. **Correct answer:** B

   A. **Incorrect:** Get-ClusterInfo is not a real cmdlet.

   B. **Correct:** Get-ClusterResouce | Get-ClusterParameter shows current IP and networking information.

   C. **Incorrect:** ifconfig /cluster is not a valid command.

   D. **Incorrect:** Get-ClusterNetworkInfo is not a valid command.

2. **Correct answer:** C

   A. **Incorrect:** Node Majority (Witness Voting) is not a valid Quorum type.

   B. **Incorrect:** Node Majority (Disk Witness) is not a valid Quorum type.

   C. **Correct:** No Majority (Disk Witness Only) allows only the witness to have a vote.

   D. **Incorrect:** No Majority (Witness Vote Only) is not a valid Quorum type.

3. **Correct answer:** C

   A. **Incorrect:** Long-term node or witness failure is a valid reason for changing Quorum configuration.

   B. **Incorrect:** Adding or removing node failure is a valid reason for changing Quorum configuration.

   C. **Correct:** Temporary failure of a network switch is not a valid reason for changing Quorum settings.

   D. **Incorrect:** Multi-site cluster recovery failure is a valid reason for changing Quorum configuration.

Objective 2.2: Thought experiment

For this experiment, you'll most likely need to use multicast because each of the servers has only one adapter. Multicast enables the servers to still communicate with each other if necessary. It's likely that the default setting, Single affinity, will be appropriate for the port rule for the web application, because this will keep the client served by the same server as long as the client IP address remains the same for a given session.

Objective 2.2: Review

1. **Correct answers:** A, D

    A. **Correct:** Single affinity provides state management.

    B. **Incorrect:** None is not a valid option.

    C. **Incorrect:** Session is not a valid option.

    D. **Correct:** Network affinity provides state management.

2. **Correct answer:** B

    A. **Incorrect:** Single is not a valid operating mode.

    B. **Correct:** Unicast is used when there's more than one adapter and the hosts need to communicate with each other.

    C. **Correct:** Multicast can be used when there's more than one adapter but is typically used when there's only one adapter.

    D. **Incorrect:** Anycast is not a valid operating mode.

3. **Correct answer:** A

    A. **Correct:** Single Host distributes traffic to a single host based on priority.

    B. **Incorrect:** Multiple Hosts distributes traffic across hosts.

    C. **Incorrect:** Failover is not a valid filter mode.

    D. **Incorrect:** Round-Robin is not a valid filter mode.

Objective 2.3: Thought experiment

You can create a domain-based namespace for this solution because the organization uses AD DS. The Optimize For Scalability option should be used because there are domain controllers at each location that the clients can use to get namespace information.

For replication, hub and spoke can be used if the main place for information is the central location; otherwise, full mesh can be used. You should also configure referrals so that there's a priority for local site. Optionally, you can configure referral traffic to only use servers at the local site.

You can configure replication traffic and its accompanying bandwidth usage according to a schedule that makes sense for the client. For example, if it's acceptable for there to be a delay in changes being replicated, you can disable replication during business hours or limit the bandwidth usage during that time.

Objective 2.3: Review

1. **Correct answer:** B

    A. **Incorrect:** Simple resiliency requires only one disk.

    B. **Correct:** Parity resiliency requires at least three disks.

    C. **Incorrect:** Mirror resiliency requires at least two disks.

    D. **Incorrect:** Level 5 is not a virtual disk resiliency type.

2. **Correct answer:** C

    A. **Incorrect:** Set-MPIOSetting -LoadBalancePolicy Failover is not an available command.

    B. **Incorrect:** There is not an All option to the Set-MSDSMGlobalDefaultLoadBalance-Policy command.

    C. **Correct:** Set-MSDSMGlobalDefaultLoadBalancePolicy -Policy FOO sets the policy to failover only.

    D. **Incorrect:** Set-MPIOSetting -Policy None is not a valid command.

3. **Correct answer:** A

    A. **Correct:** Full mesh can be used with two servers.

    B. **Incorrect:** Hub and spoke requires at least three servers.

    C. **Incorrect:** Wheel is not an available option.

    D. **Incorrect:** Dual-mesh is not an available option.

Objective 2.4: Thought experiment

There are three basic options for DHCP failover: native DHCP failover in the DHCP service, failover clustering, and split scope. Split scope is limited because it doesn't provide a true failover, but only a temporary solution in the event that the primary server fails, requiring manual intervention to remediate failure. A failover cluster won't work for this client because they use NAS and local storage. The native DHCP failover is recommended for this scenario because it provides redundancy while requiring little management or intervention.

Objective 2.4: Review

1. **Correct answer:** A

    A. **Correct:** Standby is active/passive with a secondary server taking over if needed.

    B. **Incorrect:** Load Balance is active/active.

    C. **Incorrect:** Passive Partner is not a valid type.

    D. **Incorrect:** Split Address is not a valid type.

2. **Correct answer:** A

    A. **Correct:** SMB is supported by both scale-out and generic file server clustering.

    B. **Incorrect:** BranchCache is not supported by scale-out file server.

    C. **Incorrect:** Data Deduplication is not supported by scale-out file server.

    D. **Incorrect:** File Classification Infrastructure is not supported by scale-out file server.

3. **Correct answers:** A, C

    A. **Correct:** Generic Application can replicate registry settings.

    B. **Incorrect:** Generic Script doesn't include registry replication.

    C. **Correct:** Generic Service can replicate registry settings.

    D. **Incorrect:** Generic Registry replication doesn't exist.

Objective 2.5: Thought experiment

Overall considerations include the amount of traffic available and what to back up. Because the organization already backs up to the cloud, you may be able to use a cloud-based remote solution for Windows backup. You should ensure that system state is backed up. You should ensure that the day-to-day issues, such as adequate domain controllers, exist as well. Adding the Active Directory Recycle Bin can also help alleviate issues surrounding inadvertent deletion of AD DS objects.

Objective 2.5: Review

1. **Correct answer:** A

    A. **Correct:** System state should be included in a backup strategy for Active Directory.

    B. **Incorrect:** AD DS is not an available option.

    C. **Incorrect:** Service Master is not a valid role.

    D. **Incorrect:** FSMO is not related to backup.

2. **Correct answer:** C

    A. **Incorrect:** tombstoneState is not a valid property for this question.

    B. **Incorrect:** tombstoneLife is not a valid property (though tombstoneLifetime is, and it defines the lifetime for recycled objects).

    C. **Correct:** msDS-deletedObjectLifetime defines the lifetime for a deleted object.

    D. **Incorrect:** msDS-recycleBinLifeTime is not a real property.

3. **Correct answers:** A, B

    A. **Correct:** SYSVOL should be kept on a separate volume.

    B. **Correct:** Active Directory database should be kept on a separate volume.

    C. **Incorrect:** ENTVOL is not part of an Active Directory implementation.

    D. **Incorrect:** Recycle Bin is not kept on a separate volume

CHAPTER 3

Plan and implement a server virtualization infrastructure

Virtualization has grown over the years to become the primary method for server deployment in many enterprise data centers. The increased use of virtualization makes this skillset highly valuable for an administrator. This chapter looks at the exam objectives surrounding planning and implementation of server virtualization.

Objectives in this chapter:

- Objective 3.1: Plan and implement virtualization hosts
- Objective 3.2: Plan and implement virtual machines
- Objective 3.3: Plan and implement virtualization networking
- Objective 3.4: Plan and implement virtualization storage
- Objective 3.5: Plan and implement virtual machine movement
- Objective 3.6: Manage and maintain a server virtualization infrastructure

Objective 3.1: Plan and implement virtualization hosts

The first objective for the 70-414 exam relates to basic planning and implementation for virtualization hosts, or the computers on which virtual machines will be deployed. As virtual machines provide the infrastructure necessary for many enterprises, planning and implementation of the hosts is a key aspect for success of the deployment.

> **This objective covers how to:**
> - Plan for and implement delegation of virtual environment (hosts, services, and VMs), including self-service capabilities
> - Plan and implement multi-host libraries, including equivalent objects
> - Plan for and implement host resource optimization
> - Integrate third-party virtualization platforms
> - Deploy Hyper-V hosts to bare metal

Planning for and implementing virtual environment delegation

System Center Virtual Machine Manager (VMM) enables role-based delegation of management. In addition, VMM also has self-service capabilities that enable users to deploy virtual machines and services to private clouds, as well as create templates and change other settings. This section examines both delegation and self-service.

Delegation with VMM

VMM contains several user roles that contain the various capabilities necessary to perform certain tasks. This section examines the roles available and how to assign users to those roles.

DEFINING USER ROLES IN VMM

User roles delegate administration of certain tasks within VMM. For example, you might have several host groups defined, such as a host group for developers. You can delegate administration of that host group to a development team lead so that he or she can create virtual machines when needed. User roles can be assigned with a limited scope so that actions performed by an administrator apply only to the host group or cloud for which they have permissions.

VMM defines four built-in user roles profiles. User role profiles contain various capabilities that define what a given user role can do. Table 3-1 describes the user role profiles and their capabilities in VMM.

TABLE 3-1 User role profiles in VMM

Role Profile	Description
Fabric Administrator (Delegated Administrator)	The Fabric Administrator role can perform all administrative tasks in VMM for the resources under its control. This typically means a host group but can also include a cloud or library server. Members of this group also cannot modify membership in the Administrator group and can't add XenServer hosts and clusters or WSUS servers.
Read-Only Administrator	Members of the Read-Only Administrator group can view information related to their assigned host groups, clouds, and library servers, as well as specified Run-As account information.
Tenant Administrator	Members of the Tenant Administrator group manage self-service users and networks. Tenant Administrators can also create and manage their own virtual machines and specify the tasks that self-service users can perform. Additionally, Tenant Administrators can create quotas on resources and virtual machines.
Application Administrator (Self-Service User)	A self-service user can create and manage his or her own virtual machines and services.

DELEGATING ADMINISTRATION IN VMM

Delegating administration in VMM involves either adding users to the built-in Administrator user role or creating user roles with the user role profiles covered in the previous section. As with most other user role management tasks in Windows, you can nest groups inside of the user roles in VMM. For example, you might add the Domain Admins group to the Administrator user role in VMM, thereby enabling anyone in the Domain Admins group to administer the VMM deployment.

Adding users to the Administrator user role is accomplished in the Settings workspace in VMM, by selecting the Properties of the Administrator user role. When you do so, clicking the Members tab shows the current members of the user role, from which you can add or remove as necessary. This is illustrated in Figure 3-1.

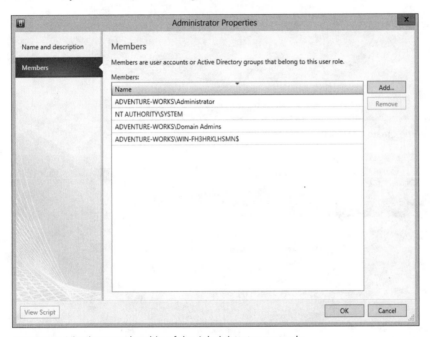

FIGURE 3-1 Viewing membership of the Administrator user role

Creating a user role is also accomplished from the Settings workspace in the VMM console. Selecting Create User Role invokes the Create User Role Wizard, which first gathers name and description information about the user role to be created, as shown in Figure 3-2.

On the next page of the wizard, you select the user role profile to apply to the user role being created. You can choose from the profiles described in Table 3-1. This page is shown in Figure 3-3.

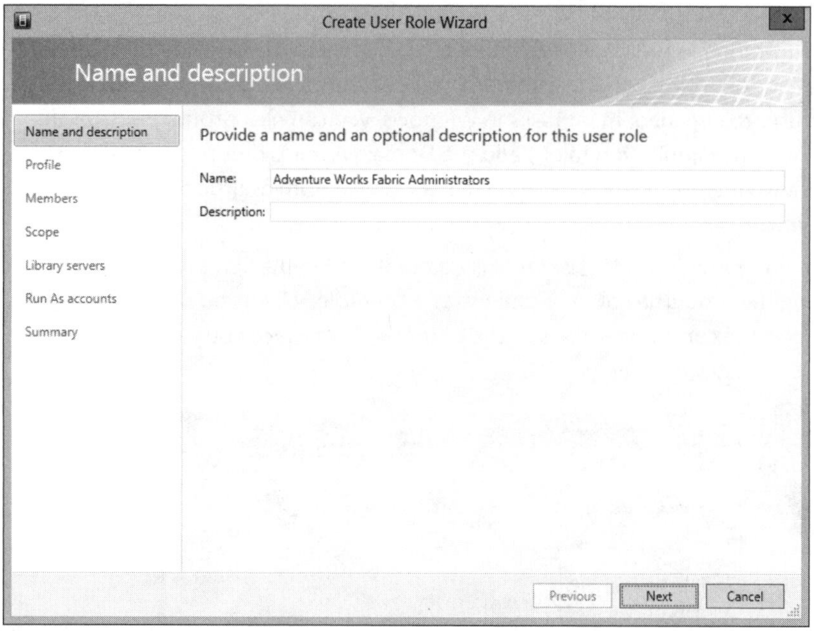

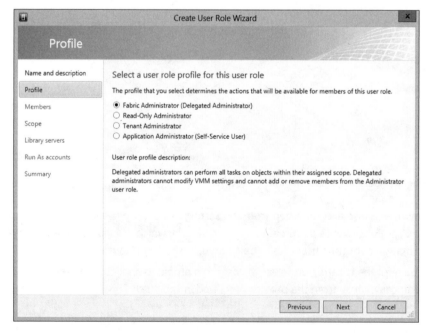

FIGURE 3-2 Using the Create User Role Wizard to create a new user role

FIGURE 3-3 Selecting a user role profile

Next, membership for the user role is chosen, as shown in Figure 3-4.

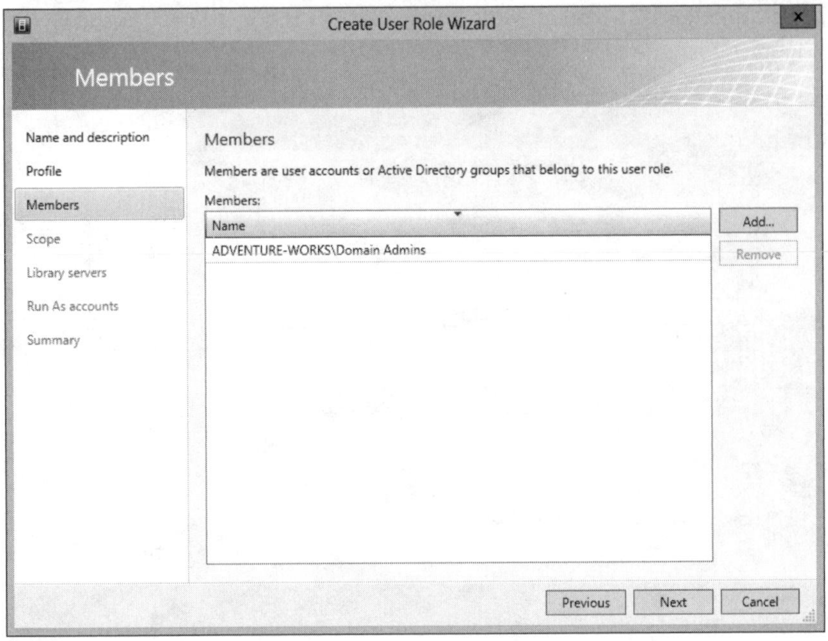

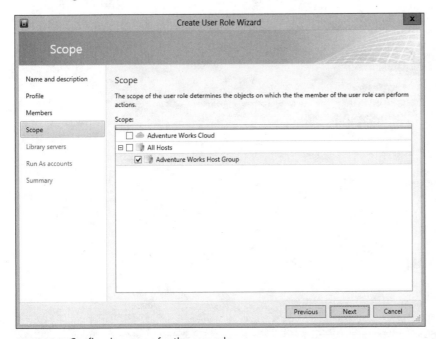

FIGURE 3-4 Configuring membership for the user role

The scope to which the user role will apply is configured in the next page of the wizard, shown in Figure 3-5.

FIGURE 3-5 Configuring scope for the user role

The library servers and Run As accounts for the user role are configured next, as shown in Figure 3-6 and Figure 3-7.

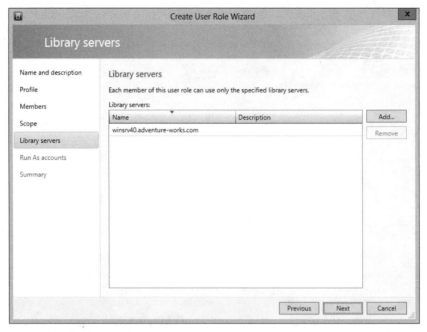

FIGURE 3-6 Configuring library servers

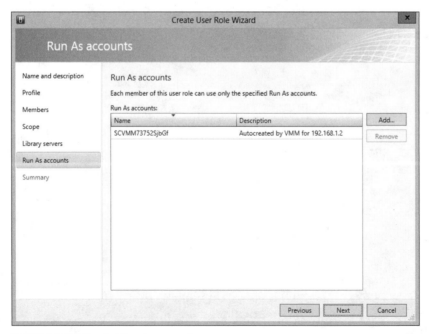

FIGURE 3-7 Configuring Run As accounts

Similar steps are used to create other user roles, with the exception of the Tenant Administrator role. The Tenant Administrator role has additional settings that can be configured, including quotas, networking, resources, and actions. Quotas can be set at the role level or at the member level, as shown in Figure 3-8.

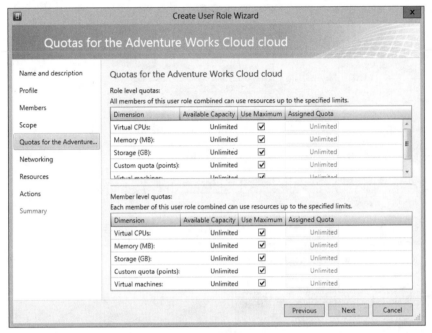

FIGURE 3-8 Setting Quotas for a Tenant Administrator user role

Permitted actions need to be specified for the Tenant Administrator and Application Administrator user roles. This is also accomplished in the Create User Role Wizard, as shown in Figure 3-9.

You can test the permissions and view of a given user role right within the VMM console by selecting Open New Connection from the down arrow in the top-left corner of the VMM console ribbon. The Connect To Server dialog box will display and, once connected, the Select User Role dialog box will display (see Figure 3-10), within which you can select a user role for the session.

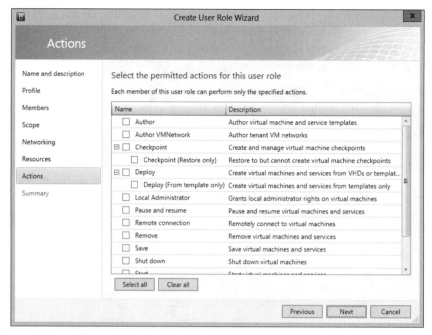

FIGURE 3-9 Configuring permitted actions for a user role

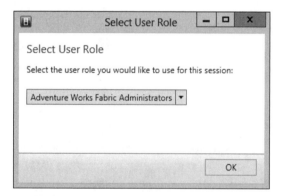

FIGURE 3-10 Selecting a user role for a new session

There are also Windows PowerShell cmdlets for working with user roles, several of which are described in Table 3-2. Virtual Machine Manager in System Center 2012 R2 adds new cmdlets. You can see a full list of cmdlets, including those for System Center 2012 R2, at *http://technet.microsoft.com/en-us/library/jj654428.*

TABLE 3-2 Windows PowerShell cmdlets for working with user roles

Cmdlet	Description
Get-SCUserRole	Displays information on a user role
Get-SCUserRoleMembership	Displays membership information on a user role
New-SCUserRole	Creates a new user role
Remove-SCUserRole	Deletes a user role
Grant-SCResource	Grants access to a resource to a user or user role
Revoke-SCResource	Removes access to a resource from a user or user role
Set-SCUserRole	Changes settings for a user role

> *MORE INFO* **USER ROLES IN VMM**
>
> See *http://technet.microsoft.com/en-us/library/gg696971.aspx* for more information on user roles in VMM.

Self-service in VMM

Self-service in VMM enables users to deploy virtual machines and services as well as create templates and profiles. Enabling self-service means creating one or more roles with the Application Administrator (Self-Service User) role capabilities using the Create User Role Wizard already discussed. When configured, users in the role can log in using the VMM console.

> *MORE INFO* **VMM SELF-SERVICE**
>
> See *http://technet.microsoft.com/en-us/library/gg610573.aspx* and *http://technet.microsoft.com/en-us/library/jj860419.aspx* for more information on self-service in VMM.

Planning and implementing multi-host libraries

Multi-host libraries entail library objects that are shared or distributed across multiple library servers in VMM. When an object, such as a template, is shared among multiple library servers, you can mark the object as being the same by making it an equivalent object.

Planning libraries means choosing the location or locations where library servers will be placed. You might place a library server at a remote site to enable local virtual machines to take advantage of that library server's objects.

Library servers need to be in the same domain or a two-way trusted domain with the VMM management server. Additionally, the firewall rules need to allow File and Print Sharing traffic from the VMM management server. Adding library servers requires the Administrator or Delegated Administrator user role.

Creating a multi-host library involves copying the same files or objects to each server taking part in the multi-host library. File-based library resources can be marked as equivalent objects, as discussed later in this section. The following steps are used to create a multi-host library:

1. Create a file share on each server and copy files there or copy the files to an already-created library share in VMM. Alternatively, you can also import a physical resource in VMM.

2. Mark files as equivalent objects as appropriate.

Creating equivalent objects

Equivalent objects enable a file-based object in a library share to be used by VMM without needing to retrieve it from a specific site. Equivalent objects are created by associating them through the VMM console in the Library workspace. Specifically, you click an object and then select its equivalent object while holding Ctrl and select Mark Equivalent from the ribbon or the shortcut menu. Doing so reveals the Equivalent Library Objects dialog box, shown in Figure 3-11.

The family and release should be entered for the library objects being marked as equivalent. For example, in Figure 3-11, the family being created is Large VHD Templates and its release is 1. These values should be changed to the necessary values based on your equivalent objects.

Equivalent objects are helpful when you have large files, such as an ISO in multiple VMM libraries, and you need to ensure that the local copy is used. For example, you might provision a virtual machine and want to ensure that the ISO in the local library is used. You could mark the ISOs as equivalent so that the local ISO is used.

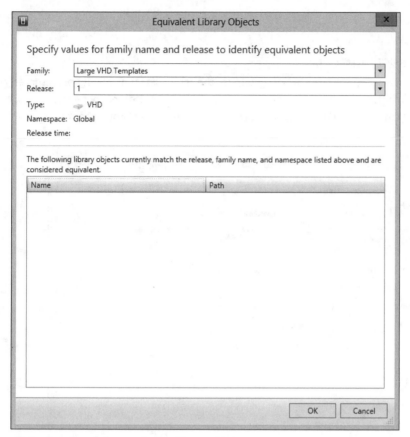

FIGURE 3-11 Creating an equivalent library object

MORE INFO **EQUIVALENT OBJECTS**

See *http://technet.microsoft.com/en-us/library/gg610650.aspx* for more information on creating or modifying equivalent objects.

Planning for and implementing host resource optimization

Optimizing host resources involves ensuring that the virtual machine host servers have enough resources to service their virtual machines and enough resources for normal operation of the server itself. VMM contains settings related to host reserves. Host reserves are used to keep a certain level of resources available to the host server. You can set the following parameters related to host reserves:

- CPU percentage
- Memory

- Disk space
- Maximum disk I/O per second
- Network capacity percentage

When using host reserves, the parent host group for the server sets the default host reserves for the servers within its group. However, host reserves can be changed on a per-server basis by selecting the Override Host Reserve Settings From The Parent Host Group check box, as shown in Figure 3-12.

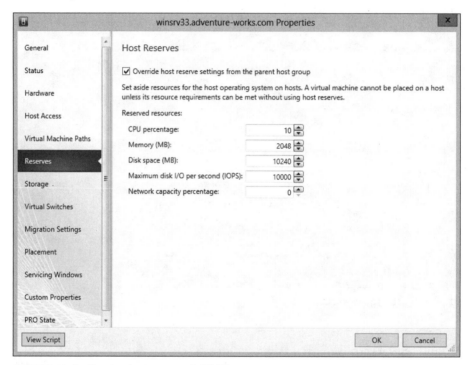

FIGURE 3-12 Configuring host reserves in VMM

Beyond manual configuration of host reserves, you can also configure reserves dynamically using dynamic optimization and power optimization. Dynamic optimization is discussed later in this chapter. Power optimization is used to conserve power by turning off hosts when additional resources are required. Power optimization requires that the host group be configured for migration using dynamic optimization.

> **MORE INFO POWER OPTIMIZATION**
>
> See *http://technet.microsoft.com/en-us/library/gg675109.aspx* for more information on power optimization.

Integrating third-party virtualization platforms

VMM integrates with third-party virtualization platforms, such as VMware vCenter Server and Citrix XenServer. VMM can then manage virtual machines on those platforms.

Adding a VMware vCenter Server is accomplished within the Fabric workspace by selecting VMware vCenter Server from the Add Resources menu. When adding a server, you enter the computer name, the port to use for communication, a Run As account, and whether to communicate in secure mode, as illustrated in Figure 3-13.

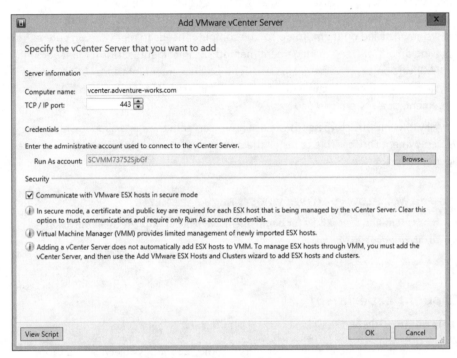

FIGURE 3-13 Adding a VMware vCenter Server to the Fabric workspace

MORE INFO **VMWARE VCENTER SERVER AND ESX HOSTS**

Once the VMware vCenter Server has been added, you can then proceed to adding the ESX hosts. See *http://technet.microsoft.com/en-us/library/gg610652.aspx* for more information on adding ESX hosts to VMM and *http://technet.microsoft.com/en-us/library/gg610683.aspx* for an overview of management tasks for ESX hosts.

Unlike the VMware vCenter Server integration, adding Citrix XenServer hosts and clusters doesn't require adding the XenServer first. XenServer hosts and clusters can be added by simply selecting Citrix XenServer Hosts and Clusters from the Add Resources menu of the Fabric workspace.

MORE INFO CITRIX XENSERVER

See *http://technet.microsoft.com/en-us/library/gg610628.aspx* for an overview of Citrix XenServer in VMM.

Deploying Hyper-V hosts to bare metal

As of System Center 2012 SP1, Virtual Machine Manager can find computers that are candidates for deployment as Hyper-V hosts from bare metal—in other words, with no operating system installed on them. To do so, the computer needs to meet certain criteria, such has having an out-of-band management method like Intelligent Platform Management Interface (IPMI) version 1.5 or version 2.0, Data Center Management Interface (DCMI) version 1.0, System Management Architecture for Server Hardware (SMASH) version 1.0 on WS-Management, or a custom protocol.

Additionally, the infrastructure needs to have a PXE server in the same subnet with the Windows Deployment Services role to install the operating system along with an appropriate operating system image.

MORE INFO WORKFLOW FOR HYPER-V HOSTS FROM BARE METAL

Microsoft has identified a workflow for deployment available at *http://technet.microsoft. com/en-us/library/gg610634.aspx.*

Thought experiment
Delegating VMM

In this thought experiment, apply what you've learned about this objective. You can find an answer in the "Answers" section at the end of this chapter.

You're tasked with designing and implementing the delegation for the VMM implementation in your organization. The VMM implementation includes three Hyper-V servers. Your organization consists of an infrastructure team along with two development teams. The development teams have enough expertise to be able to create their own virtual machines.

Describe the user roles that you might use for the delegated administration.

Objective summary

- Several built-in user profiles in VMM can be used to build user roles.
- You can use multi-host libraries as a means to keep equivalent objects, such as templates, located on servers close to the client.
- VMM enables you to provide reserved host resources to ensure that the host has enough memory, CPU, and other resources to continue normal operations.
- VMM integrates with VMware vCenter Server and Citrix XenServer and can manage virtual machines hosted on those platforms.

Objective review

Answer the following questions to test your knowledge of the information in this objective. You can find the answers to these questions and explanations of why each answer choice is correct or incorrect in the "Answers" section at the end of this chapter.

1. Which of the following is *not* a valid host reserve setting?

   A. Memory

   B. Disk Status

   C. CPU Percentage

   D. Disk Space

2. Which role or roles can add XenServer hosts and clusters to VMM?

   A. Fabric Administrator

   B. Administrator

   C. Self-Service Role

   D. Tenant Administrator

3. What is the default port used for communication between VMM and a VMware vCenter Server?

   A. 443

   B. 5150

   C. 5297

   D. 3389

Objective 3.2: Plan and implement virtual machines

Once the underlying infrastructure has been planned and implemented, you can begin planning the virtual machines (VMs) that will act as guests atop the Hyper-V hosts. This section looks at highly available virtual machines and other aspects related to the virtual machines themselves.

> **This objective covers how to:**
> - Plan for and implement highly available VMs
> - Plan for and implement guest resource optimization, including shared VHDx
> - Configure placement rules
> - Create Virtual Machine Manager templates

Planning and implementing highly available VMs

Making a virtual machine highly available is easier than ever with System Center 2012. When planning highly available VMs, you should consider the hosts on which the virtual machines will reside. For example, making a highly available VM hosted on two servers located physically next to each other in the data center isn't really helpful if there's a power loss or other catastrophic event at that data center. An option for configuration in VMM is the possible nodes to which a VM can migrate. This option can be used to configure both the preferred owner of a VM and the hosts to which the VM can fail.

> **MORE INFO** **PREFERRED HOSTS**
>
> See *http://technet.microsoft.com/en-us/library/jj628161.aspx* for more information on preferred and possible owner configuration in VMM.

You should consider each point of failure in the VM's availability chain. The host servers should have different power sources, physical locations, network connectivity, and so on. Reducing or removing the single points of failure will help to make the VM highly available.

Another option for high availability for VMs is an availability set. An availability set is used to ensure that VMs providing the same service are located on separate nodes of a cluster. This helps to alleviate service downtime if a given VM host goes offline.

> **MORE INFO** **AVAILABILITY SETS**
>
> See *http://technet.microsoft.com/en-us/library/jj628165.aspx* for more information on configuring availability sets in VMM.

When configuring high availability, you have four options for the priority of the VM:

- High
- Medium
- Low
- Do not restart automatically

When a node in a cluster fails, higher priority VMs are allocated resources before those with lower priority. If the node to which the VM is moved doesn't have enough available resources, those VMs with lower priority may not be started. This is important for planning in that you should ensure that important VMs are given high priority over those that serve a less valuable role in the organization.

Implementing highly available VMs is accomplished when creating a virtual machine or after creation through the virtual machine's Properties dialog box.

Adding the high availability option is accomplished by selecting Make This Virtual Machine Highly Available at the Configure Hardware phase of virtual machine creation, within the Availability section, as shown in Figure 3-14.

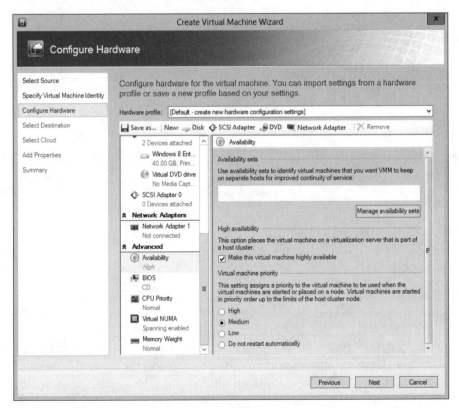

FIGURE 3-14 Adding high availability to a virtual machine

Planning for and implementing guest resource optimization

Several items can be configured to help optimize VM resource usage. Among these are dynamic memory, smart page file, and RemoteFX.

Dynamic memory enables the host to allocate a range of RAM (Random Access Memory) to a virtual machine and to recover that RAM when it's not needed by the VM. Four dynamic memory settings are found within the Hardware Configuration section of a VM's properties (shown in Figure 3-15) or at configuration time:

- Startup Memory
- Minimum Memory
- Maximum Memory
- Memory Buffer Percentage

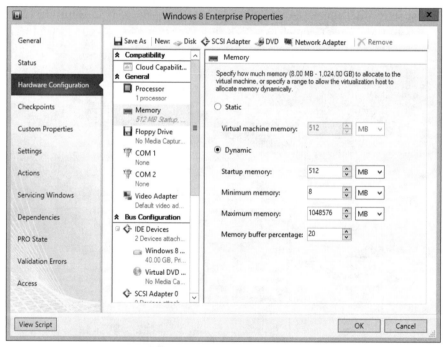

FIGURE 3-15 Dynamic memory settings

Startup Memory defines the amount of RAM that will be allocated to the VM on boot, while Minimum and Maximum Memory define the lowest and highest amounts of RAM that will be available to the virtual machine at any given time.

The Memory Buffer Percentage defines the amount of additional memory that will be allocated to the virtual machine to account for incremental changes to the amount of RAM needed at a given point in time. While Hyper-V can allocate memory very quickly, there are times when the virtual machine would benefit from having slightly more RAM available. The Memory Buffer Percentage is calculated as a percentage of the currently allocated RAM. For example, if the virtual machine has 1,000 megabytes (MB) of memory currently in use and a 10 percent buffer, then Hyper-V will actually allocate 1,100 MB.

Another setting not directly related to dynamic memory is Memory Weight. Memory Weight defines how the host allocates memory to a given virtual machine. There are four settings related to Memory Weight:

- High
- Normal
- Low
- Custom

When a host is low on memory, the virtual machines with higher priority will have memory allocated before those with a lower priority. While these settings aren't directly related to dynamic memory, they can affect performance of a virtual machine.

Smart Paging, which creates paging files for virtual machine startup, is used when the Hyper-V host doesn't have enough startup memory available. Assume a virtual machine has 2,048 MB startup memory allocated to it, but the last time it was running, it was using 500 MB. Now when the virtual machine is restarted, it will need all 2,048 MB of startup memory. In this way, Smart Paging helps to alleviate virtual machine restart failures. Hyper-V uses the following rules, all of which need to be met, for determining when Smart Paging will be used:

- The virtual machine is being restarted (but not started from an Off state).
- The Hyper-V host has no physical memory available.
- The Hyper-V host cannot recover memory from its other virtual machines.

Smart Paging files exist only during virtual machine startup and are only used for this purpose.

RemoteFX requires the Remote Desktop Virtualization Host role service on the Hyper-V hosts that will provide RemoteFX to virtual machines. RemoteFX can be added to a virtual machine through the Display section of its Properties dialog box.

EXAM TIP

RemoteFX is no longer within the objective domain for the 70-414 exam.

Shared VHDx

Storage for a virtual machine cluster can be made using a shared virtual hard disk (.vhdx file). Shared VHDx can be used with cluster-shared volumes (CSV) or on Scale-Out File Servers on an SMB-based share. In either case, both servers need to be capable of failover clustering, running Windows Server 2012 R2, and within the same Active Directory domain.

> **NOTE SHARED VHDX**
>
> Shared VHDx is not appropriate for the operating system itself.

A prerequisite for using a shared VHDx is to have clustered virtual machines already created through a Hyper-V cluster. Once the virtual machines are created, adding a shared VHDx is accomplished through the Failover Cluster Manager. Specifically, add a SCSI Controller and new virtual hard disk to one of the virtual machines and then select Enable Virtual Hard Disk Sharing within the SCSI Controller Advanced Features.

> **EXAM TIP**
>
> The Add-VMHardDiskDrive Windows PowerShell cmdlet can be used with the -ShareVirtualDisk parameter to share the virtual hard disk.

Once the disk has been added and shared, the final step is to create a guest cluster on the virtual machines.

Configuring placement rules

When a virtual machine is created, VMM evaluates the possible hosts for the virtual machine using several performance criteria for the host and also the expected utilization of the VM. The result is a scale of 1 to 5 stars based on how well VMM believes a given host can service the virtual machine being created (see Figure 3-16).

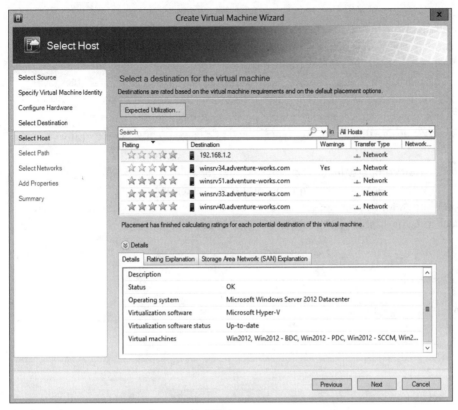

FIGURE 3-16 Virtual machine placement in VMM

Clicking Expected Utilization enables you to change how the hosts are rated according to the expected usage pattern for the virtual machine. You can change four criteria:

- Expected CPU Utilization (default 20%)
- Required Physical Disk Space (GB) (default 0)
- Expected Disk I/O Per Second (default 0)
- Expected Network Utilization In Megabits Per Second (default 0)

MORE INFO **PLACEMENT AND HOST RATINGS**

See *http://technet.microsoft.com/en-us/library/jj860428.aspx* for more information on placement and host ratings.

Placement rules are created at the host group level, and by default host groups inherit placement rules from their parent host group. Placement rules are created by first creating custom properties. Several custom properties are already available, and you can create your own as well. For example, you might create a custom property that defines the application layer on which virtual machines operate (such as data layer, web layer, business rules layer, and so on). In such a scenario, you may have certain hosts designated for servicing virtual machines in the web layer. Creating a custom property and assigning that as a placement rule would then ensure that virtual machines would be placed on hosts that met the custom property.

Create a custom property in the Manage Custom Properties dialog box (shown in Figure 3-17), which is accessed through host group, virtual machine, and other Properties dialog boxes in VMM. The custom property can then be associated with various objects in VMM, such as hosts, host groups, virtual machines, and so on.

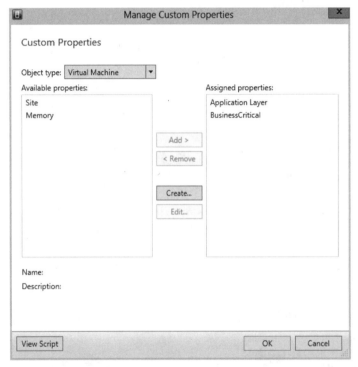

FIGURE 3-17 Managing a custom property and assigning it to a virtual machine object type

Once the custom property is created, you then assign values for it through each of the appropriate hosts, host groups, or virtual machines. Placement rules are then configured within the host group to which the custom property should apply. For example, Figure 3-18 shows placement rules for the All Hosts host group, with one placement rule defined for the Application Layer custom property previously defined.

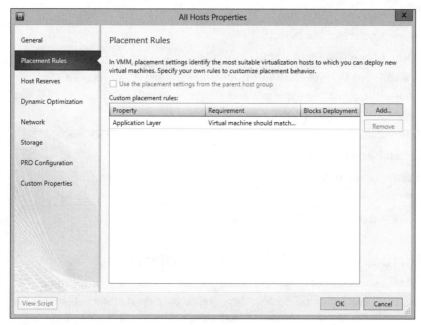

FIGURE 3-18 Viewing placement rules for the All Hosts group

Adding a placement rule is accomplished by clicking Add, which reveals the Create Custom Requirement dialog box shown in Figure 3-19.

FIGURE 3-19 Creating a placement rule

There are four criteria for matching the rule, contained in the Requirement drop-down list:

- Virtual Machine Must Match Host

- Virtual Machine Should Match Host
- Virtual Machine Must Not Match Host
- Virtual Machine Should Not Match Host

These criteria enable you to configure how the placement rules will be evaluated. For example, when one of the "must" criteria is selected, the deployment of a virtual machine will be blocked if it doesn't meet the placement rule.

There are also Windows PowerShell cmdlets related to placement rules, including:

- Add-SCCustomPlacementRule
- Get-SCCustomPlacementRule
- Remove-SCCustomPlacementRule
- Set-SCCustomPlacementRule

Creating Virtual Machine Manager templates

Virtual Machine Manager templates are library resources that contain information about the configuration for a virtual machine. Being a library resource, Virtual Machine Manager templates are created in the Library workspace by selecting Create VM Template from the Home ribbon. Doing so invokes the Create VM Template Wizard, shown in Figure 3-20.

As displayed in Figure 3-20, you can create a VM template by using a virtual hard disk, by using another VM template, or by using an existing virtual machine. The VM Template Identity page enables you to set the name for the template and its description. The Configure Hardware page is used to configure hardware settings for the template and is shown in Figure 3-21.

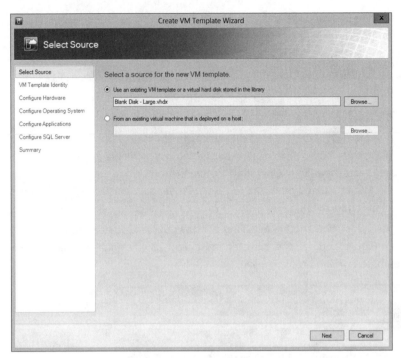

FIGURE 3-20 Beginning the Create VM Template Wizard

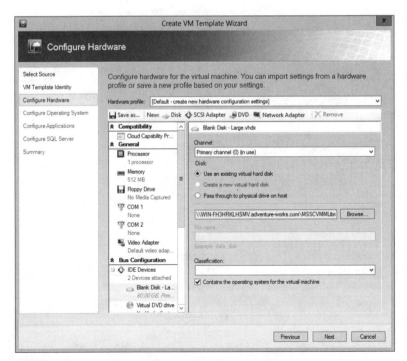

FIGURE 3-21 Configuring hardware settings for the template

The Configure Operating System page, shown in Figure 3-22, is used to configure operating system parameters for the template. It's important to note that you can choose a Guest OS Profile from among these options:

- Default - Create New Windows Operating System Customization Settings (as depicted in Figure 3-22)

- None - Customization Is Not Required

- Create New Linux Operating System Customization Settings

The Guest OS Profile option chosen determines what settings are available for configuration. For example, when the Create New Linux Operating System Customization Settings option is chosen, only Operating System, Identify Information, Root Credentials, and Time Zone can be set and a RunOnce set of scripts defined.

If you choose the default option and are installing Windows Server 2003 or above, the next page shown is Configure Applications, depicted in Figure 3-23. Clicking Add enables you to add an application based on the profile chosen.

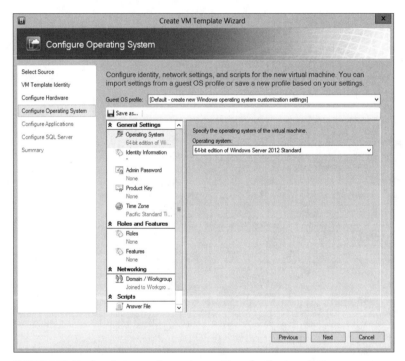

FIGURE 3-22 Configuring operating system settings for the template

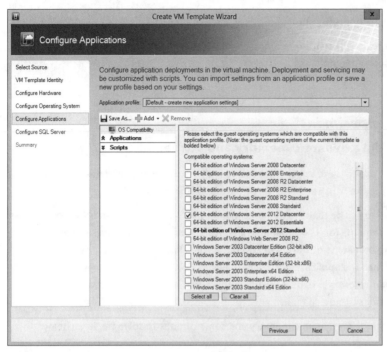

FIGURE 3-23 Configuring applications in the template

Finally, you can also deploy SQL Server, as shown in Figure 3-24.

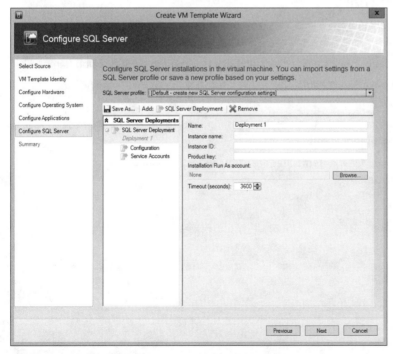

FIGURE 3-24 Configuring SQL Server as part of a VM template

MORE INFO CREATING TEMPLATES

See *http://technet.microsoft.com/en-us/library/bb963734.aspx* for more information on creating virtual machine templates.

Thought experiment

Understanding dynamic memory and virtual machines

In this thought experiment, apply what you've learned about this objective. You can find an answer in the "Answers" section at the end of this chapter.

Your organization has been using dynamic memory as a means to maintain memory requirements for its v irtual machine hosts. However, recently users have been reporting that some of the client computers are slow when starting new applications. Once the application is open, the users don't report any issues and the application performs as expected. You suspect that it might be related to the dynamic memory settings.

Discuss the settings for dynamic memory and some options to solve the issue being reported.

Objective summary

- When planning highly available VMs, you can set priority for the VM, availability sets, and preferred hosts.
- Guest resources can be optimized by using dynamic memory and by using RemoteFX.
- Hyper-V can use a Smart Paging file to help restart a virtual machine when there isn't enough available memory.
- Placement rules are used as part of the measurements to determine the host on which a virtual machine should reside.
- Virtual Machine Manager templates are used to rapidly configure virtual machines with the same configurations.

Objective review

Answer the following questions to test your knowledge of the information in this objective. You can find the answers to these questions and explanations of why each answer choice is correct or incorrect in the "Answers" section at the end of this chapter.

1. When planning high availability, the priority of a virtual machine can be set. Which of the following is *not* an option for that priority?

    A. High

    B. Do Not Restart Automatically

    C. Medium

    D. Automatic

2. Which of the following criteria must be met for Smart Paging to be used?

    A. The host is out of physical memory.

    B. The virtual machine is off and is being started.

    C. The virtual machine is running and needs a larger paging file.

    D. The Dynamic Memory Smart Paging option is enabled.

3. Which of the following cannot be used as the basis for a virtual machine template?

    A. A virtual machine that has already been deployed

    B. An existing template in the library

    C. A virtual hard disk in the library

    D. A predefined operating system image

Objective 3.3: Plan and implement virtualization networking

Creating specialized networks for virtual machines can help with security and provide advanced configurations where virtual machines can communicate only with each other. This section looks at the objectives surrounding virtual networks. Several of the objectives, such as Virtual Local Area Networks (VLANs) and converged networks, relate closely to each other and are addressed throughout this section.

> **This objective covers how to:**
>
> - Plan for and configure Virtual Machine Manager logical networks
> - Plan for and configure IP address and MAC address settings across multiple Hyper-V hosts, including IP virtualization
> - Plan for and implement Windows Server Gateway
> - Plan for and configure virtual network optimization
> - Plan and implement VLANs and pVLANS
> - Plan and implement VM networks
> - Plan and implement converged networks

Planning for and configuring Virtual Machine Manager logical networks

Logical networks are collections of networking objects, such as IP addresses and subnets, VLANs, and related information used to help organize the structure of virtual machines. Logical networks are conceptual, which means they aren't tied directly to (though they are still dependent on) the physical network infrastructure. This means you can set up a logical network to support virtual machines based on business need, even though those virtual machines may be physically connected to different switches in different geographical locations.

Planning logical networks

When planning for logical networks, you might use various strategies. For example, you might create a logical network based on an application layer (such as the database layer, web or frontend layer, and so on) or based on a purpose, such as quality assurance.

VMM requires that a logical network exist in order to deploy virtual machine services. However, VMM creates a logical network automatically when a Hyper-V host is added. The automatically created logical network matches the first DNS suffix label on each of the host's network adapters. These logical networks essentially match the physical topology.

Three important concepts surround logical networks:

- Network sites
- Static IP address pools
- Media Access Control (MAC) address pools

MORE INFO LOGICAL NETWORKS

See *http://technet.microsoft.com/en-us/library/jj721568.aspx* for more information on logical networks and *http://technet.microsoft.com/en-us/library/jj870823.aspx* for common scenarios for logical networks. You can also view common scenarios for networking at *http://technet.microsoft.com/en-us/library/jj870823.aspx*.

NETWORK SITES

A network site provides the link between a subnet or subnets, VLANs, and subnet/VLAN pairs and a logical network. Network sites enable you to further refine a logical network. For example, assume that you have two physical data centers in different locations. For redundancy, you want to service web traffic from each of these data centers. You could create a logical network to represent the web traffic and then create a network site for each data center. Doing so would enable you to maintain host groups for each data center while still using the same logical network for ease of management.

STATIC IP ADDRESS POOLS

Static IP address pools provides a means by which VMM can assign IP addresses to Windows-based virtual machines. Static IP address pools can optionally contain information such as DNS servers, default gateway, and Windows Internet Name Service (WINS) servers.

Static IP address pools aren't necessary where Dynamic Host Configuration Protocol (DHCP) has already been deployed. However, if your configuration uses network virtualization, then an IP address pool must be created so that VMM can provide IP information to the virtual machines deployed on the virtual network.

EXAM TIP

When you use static IP addresses assigned by VMM, you need to configure a static MAC address for the virtual machine as well.

Static IP address pools can also be created to support multicasting on the virtual machine network, with a few prerequisites:

- Network virtualization must be enabled on the logical network.
- Multicast must be selected for the IP address pool.
- The IP version (IPv4 or IPv6) needs to be the same for both the VM network and the logical network.

EXAM TIP

Prior to the Windows Server 2012 R2 release, the GET-SCVMNetwork cmdlet was the only way to view the IP address version information.

IP address pools are covered in the section titled "Planning for and configuring IP address and MAC address settings across multiple Hyper-V hosts" later in this chapter.

MAC ADDRESS POOLS

VMM can also be used to assign MAC addresses to network devices on Windows-based virtual machines. There are two default MAC address pools, one for Hyper-V and Citrix XenServer hosts and another for VMware ESX hosts. You can add MAC address pools as needed for your topology. Doing so is discussed in the section titled "Planning for and configuring IP address and MAC address settings across multiple Hyper-V hosts" later in this chapter.

Creating a logical network

Logical networks are created in the Fabric workspace by selecting Logical Network from the Create drop-down list. Doing so invokes the Create Logical Network Wizard, shown in Figure 3-25 and Figure 3-26.

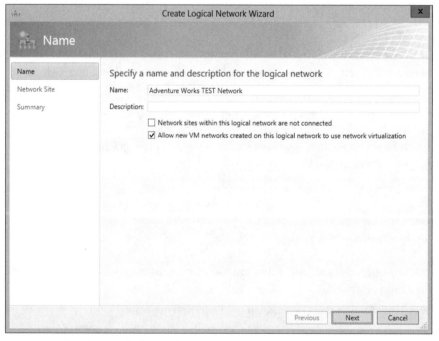

FIGURE 3-25 Creating a logical network

The two options shown on the Name page of the wizard are:

- Network Sites Within This Logical Network Are Not Connected
- Allow New VM Networks Created On This Logical Network To Use Network Virtualization

If you select the first option, indicating that the network sites aren't connected, another option is revealed:

- Network Sites Within This Logical Network Contain Private VLANs (pVLANs)

This option, along with its parent option indicating that the networks are not connected, is used for topologies that contain VLANs. If the virtual machines will use Hyper-V hosts, then the Allow New VM Networks Created On This Logical Network To Use Network Virtualization option can be chosen.

Another possibility when creating networks is that virtual machines will be connected to an external network. In this case, you shouldn't create a logical network using VMM; rather, you should add a virtual switch. See *http://technet.microsoft.com/en-us/library/jj614619.aspx* for more information on this scenario.

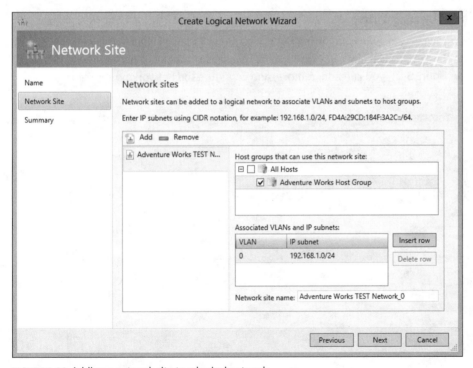

FIGURE 3-26 Adding a network site to a logical network

Once the network is configured, you can change settings related to the logical network in its Properties dialog box.

Virtual switch extensions are add-ons that enhance virtual switches to enable features that you might find on a traditional network switch, such as traffic shaping. Virtual switch extensions also enable third-party vendors to write add-ons that hook into the virtual switch. Virtual switch extensions can be managed through the Hyper-V console and also using Virtual Machine Manager. See *http://technet.microsoft.com/en-us/library/dn249411.aspx* for more information on virtual switch extension management with System Center 2012 R2.

Converged networks are networks that handle both normal network traffic and traffic for storage. Windows Server 2012 and Windows Server 2012 R2 both support converged networks.

Planning for and configuring IP address and MAC address settings across multiple Hyper-V hosts

You can use VMM to manage IP address and MAC address settings across Hyper-V hosts. This can be accomplished by managing each host through the Fabric workspace in VMM and by using logical network items and IP address and MAC address pools.

Hyper-V networking

Managing Hyper-V networking through VMM is accomplished by selecting the host and then opening the Virtual Switches page of the Properties dialog box. On the Virtual Switches page, shown in Figure 3-27, you can add, remove, and configure the networking for the Hyper-V host.

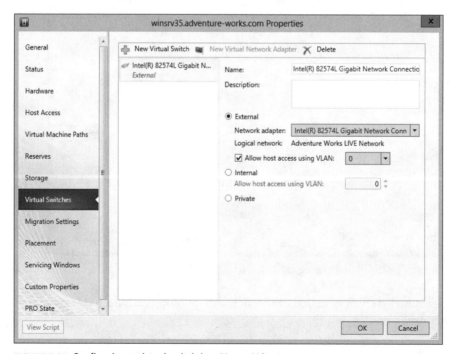

FIGURE 3-27 Configuring a virtual switch in a Hyper-V host

As Figure 3-27 shows, three types of network bindings can be created:

- **External**   Use the External option when the virtual machines need to communicate with servers outside of the virtual machine fabric, such as external servers and the Hyper-V host operating system itself.

- **Internal**   An internal switch is used for communication to other virtual machines on the same host and to the Hyper-V host itself.

- **Private**   A private switch is used to enable communication only with other virtual machines on the host and not on the Hyper-V host or any other external network.

> **MORE INFO** **HYPER-V NETWORKING**
>
> See *http://technet.microsoft.com/en-us/library/gg610603.aspx* for additional network settings for Hyper-V. Logical switches enable you to apply virtual switch settings across multiple Hyper-V hosts. See *http://technet.microsoft.com/en-us/library/jj628154.aspx* for more information on logical switches.

IP address pools

IP address pools are configured within the Fabric workspace by selecting Create IP Pool from the Home ribbon. Doing so invokes the Create Static IP Address Pool Wizard, shown in Figure 3-28.

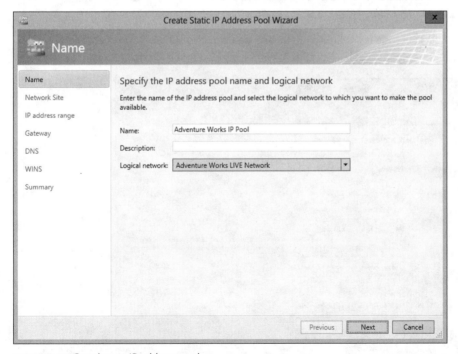

FIGURE 3-28 Creating an IP address pool

The network site is configured next. You can choose an existing network site or create a new one, as shown in Figure 3-29.

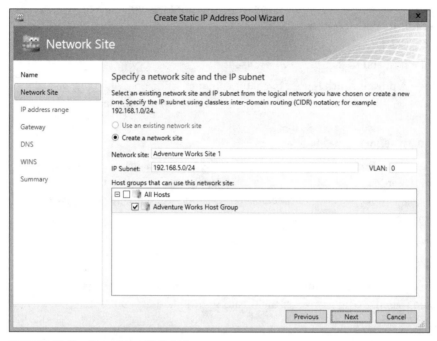

FIGURE 3-29 Creating a new network site

The IP address range is configured next, and you can also set aside reserved addresses within the subnet for virtual IPs (VIPs) or for other purposes. See Figure 3-30 for an example.

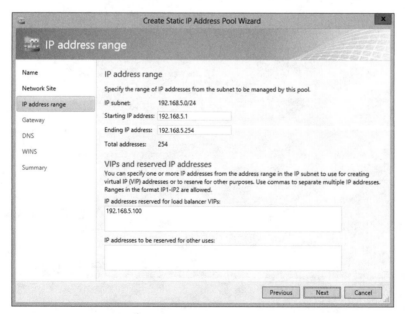

FIGURE 3-30 Configuring the IP address range

The next several screens in the Create Static IP Address Pool Wizard enable you to specify optional settings, such as the default gateway (or multiple default gateways), DNS servers, and WINS servers. Providing these settings is a good idea when VMM will manage the IP addresses for virtual machines, because the virtual machines will receive all of this basic networking information without any additional configuration necessary.

IP address pools are helpful for a delegation scenario, where normal IP address management would be accomplished by a separate team, such as a network team. In these instances, the network team can designate a range of IP addresses, which can then be added to Virtual Machine Manager for actual assignment to virtual machines.

> **MORE INFO IP ADDRESS POOLS**
>
> See *http://technet.microsoft.com/en-us/library/gg610590.aspx* for more information on creating IP address pools.

MAC address pools

MAC address pools are created in the Fabric workspace by selecting Create MAC Pool from the Home ribbon. Doing so invokes the Create MAC Address Pool Wizard, shown in Figure 3-31.

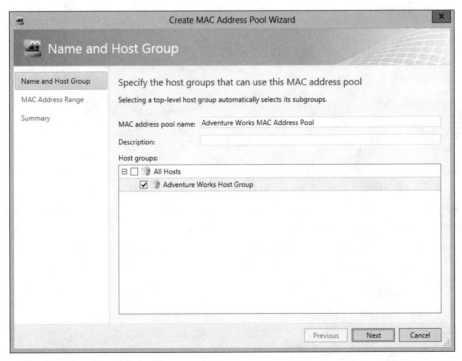

FIGURE 3-31 Creating a MAC address pool

As in IP address pool creation, you select the host group(s) to which the pool will apply. On the next page you enter the range of MAC addresses to use.

Creating a VM network

When network virtualization is enabled, you can create a virtual machine network. This is accomplished through the VMs and Services workspace by selecting Create VM Network from the Home tab. Doing so begins the Create VM Network Wizard, shown in Figure 3-32.

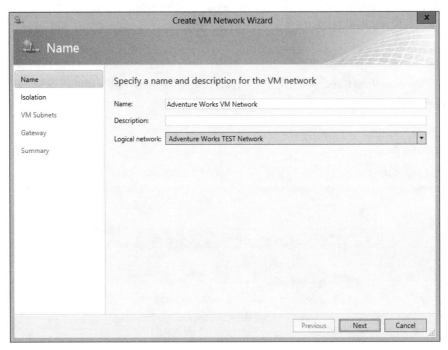

FIGURE 3-32 Beginning the Create VM Network Wizard

Once the name and logical network (and optionally a description) are chosen, you choose the isolation for the VM network, as shown in Figure 3-33.

It's worth noting that if the only option available is No Isolation, that typically means the logical network doesn't have network virtualization enabled.

The subnet(s) to use for the VM network are specified next, as shown in Figure 3-34.

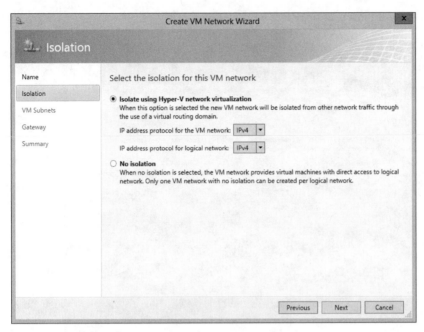

FIGURE 3-33 Choosing an isolation type for a VM network

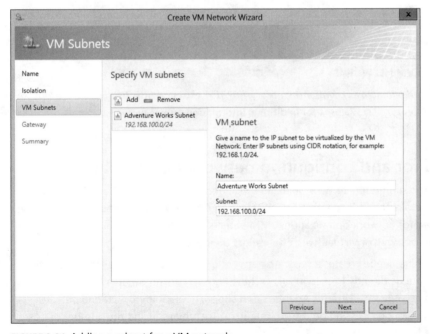

FIGURE 3-34 Adding a subnet for a VM network

Finally, a gateway is chosen, as depicted in Figure 3-35.

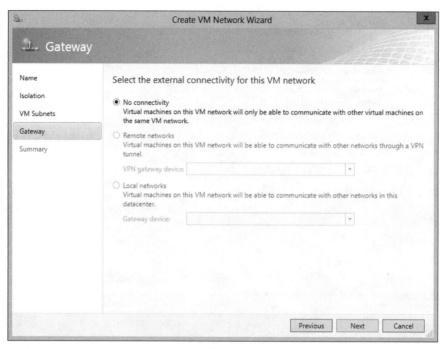

FIGURE 3-35 Choosing a gateway for the VM network

> **MORE INFO VM NETWORKS**
>
> See *http://technet.microsoft.com/en-us/library/jj628157.aspx* and *http://technet.microsoft.com/en-us/library/jj721575.aspx* for additional information on VM networks.

Planning for and configuring network optimization

Network optimization refers to two capabilities included with Windows Server 2012 and available on certain network adapters. Specifically, TCP Chimney Offload and virtual machine queue are used for network optimization. VMM detects when these capabilities are available, and the virtual network or virtual switch will reflect their availability.

Virtual machine queue creates a separate network queue for each virtual machine and connects that queue directly to the virtual machine, thus bypassing other layers involved in the processing of network traffic. Adapters that support TCP Chimney Offload perform much of the network processing on the adapter itself, thereby reducing the number of host resources needed for this purpose.

Network optimization is configured at the virtual machine level by adding a network adapter to the virtual machine and selecting the Enable Virtual Network Optimizations check box.

Planning for and implementing Windows Server Gateway

Windows Server Gateway provides routing between virtual and physical networks to facilitate advanced scenarios, such as tenant isolation and virtual private network (VPN) connections between virtual machines in the cloud and those on site. See *http://technet.microsoft.com/en-us/library/dn313101.aspx* for more information on scenarios for Windows Server Gateway.

Implementing Windows Server Gateway has several requirements, depending on the configuration and need. You'll need more hardware to run a clustered Windows Server Gateway configuration, for example. See *http://technet.microsoft.com/en-us/library/dn423897.aspx* for more information on the specific hardware requirements.

Thought experiment

Configuring virtual switches

In this thought experiment, apply what you've learned about this objective. You can find an answer in the "Answers" section at the end of this chapter.

You're configuring network settings for your virtual network. Specifically, you're configuring virtual switches. You need to configure a switch that enables WSUS virtual machines to connect to Microsoft to obtain updates. You also need to configure a network with a credit card application, and those virtual machines should only be able to communicate with each other.

Discuss the options available for the virtual switch that will facilitate this scenario.

Objective summary

- Logical networks are used to abstract the physical network from that used for virtual machines.
- VMM enables complex network configurations based on the need for the virtual machine network.
- VMM can configure IP address and MAC address pools and create virtual IP addressing and virtual networks for isolated communication.
- Network optimization is a function of the network adapter hardware and, when available, can be configured through VMM.
- Windows Server Gateway is used to facilitate advanced networking, such as VPN and tenant isolation for virtual machines.

Objective review

Answer the following questions to test your knowledge of the information in this objective. You can find the answers to these questions and explanations of why each answer choice is correct or incorrect in the "Answers" section at the end of this chapter.

1. When creating a logical network, which option needs to be chosen to enable network virtualization?

    A. Allow New VM Networks Created In This Logical Network To Use Network Virtualization

    B. This Logical Network Can Use Network Virtualization

    C. Allow This Logical Network To Be Virtualized

    D. This VM Network Can Use Network Virtualization

2. Which of the following are features of network optimization? (Choose all that apply.)

    A. TCP Chimney Offload

    B. Virtual Network Queue

    C. Virtual machine queue

    D. TCP Chimney Stack Offload

3. Which of the following is a prerequisite for configuring network virtualization?

    A. At least one virtual machine

    B. Hyper-V hosts

    C. TCP Offload enabled

    D. Network adapter support

Objective 3.4: Plan and implement virtualization storage

Virtualization storage is a key element to a successful virtual machine deployment. Understanding the options and choosing the correct solution will help you prepare for this task when you encounter it.

> **This objective covers how to:**
>
> - Plan for and configure Hyper-V host clustered storage, including standalone and clustered setup using SMB and CSV
> - Plan for and configure Hyper-V guest storage, including virtual Fibre Channel, iSCSI, and shared VHDx
> - Plan for storage optimization
> - Plan for and implement storage using SMB 3.0 file shares

Planning for and configuring Hyper-V host clustered storage

Hyper-V can use local storage, such as that directly connected to the server, or remote storage, such as a file share. At a different level, storage support in VMM consists of block storage, such as that provided through logical unit numbers (LUNs) by iSCSI, Fibre Channel, and SAS, and file storage, such as that provided through SMB or NAS. This section examines the basic configuration of Hyper-V storage as well as the objective surrounding SMB 3.0 file shares for Hyper-V storage.

The type of storage available in the organization will determine the planning involved in its configuration. VMM helps to abstract the storage layer for virtual machines and Hyper-V hosts. For example, VMM can create logical units rather than relying on the underlying storage configuration.

Storage can be assigned at the host group level. Therefore, when planning storage you should consider allocating storage according to the needs of the host group. For example, a host group for development servers likely doesn't need the fastest (and probably most expensive) storage in the organization. Storage classifications, discussed later in this section, can help with the assignment of storage.

Microsoft has identified a workflow for configuration storage in VMM. The workflow consists of the following steps. These steps are prerequisites for adding storage to Hyper-V hosts and clusters.

1. Use the Add Storage Devices Wizard to configure the storage discovery. See the section titled "Configuring SMB and CSV storage" later in this chapter for more details.

2. Assign a classification to the discovered storage based on organizational criteria. See *http://technet.microsoft.com/en-us/library/gg610685.aspx* for more information.

3. Select a method for creating logical units for use with rapid provisioning. This step is especially important when using rapid provisioning with SAN-based cloning and snapshots. See *http://technet.microsoft.com/en-us/library/gg610624.aspx* for more information on this step.

4. Provision the logical units using VMM or using a native method for logical unit creation provided by the storage vendor. See *http://technet.microsoft.com/en-us/library/gg696973.aspx* for more information.

5. Allocate storage to a host group within VMM. See *http://technet.microsoft.com/en-us/library/gg610686.aspx* for additional details on this step.

One of the more important areas in which you can plan storage for virtual machines is around the classifications. You can create classifications based on your organization's storage capacity, speed, and availability. For example, your organization may have a large storage area network (SAN) that's highly available and mirrored across sites. However, space on the SAN is expensive and therefore limited to production servers. You might create a classification that indicates this storage is to be used for production-level purposes.

> *NOTE* **AWINDOWS POWERSHELL CMDLET FOR ADDING STORAGE PROVIDERS**
>
> The Add-SCStorageProvider Windows PowerShell cmdlet can be used to add storage providers.

Configuring SMB and CSV storage

Selecting Storage Devices from the Add menu of the Fabric workspace reveals the Add Storage Devices Wizard, shown in Figure 3-36. From here, you can add a Windows-based file server or other storage devices to the VMM fabric.

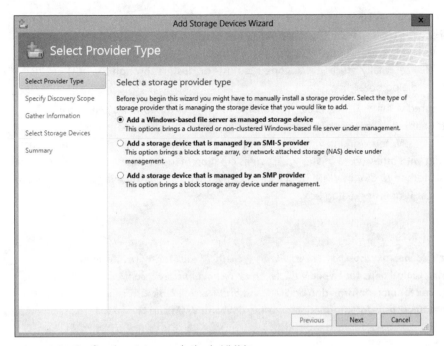

FIGURE 3-36 Configuring a storage device in VMM

The next step is to enter the details of the server on which the storage resides (not depicted here) and then select the SMB share, shown in Figure 3-37.

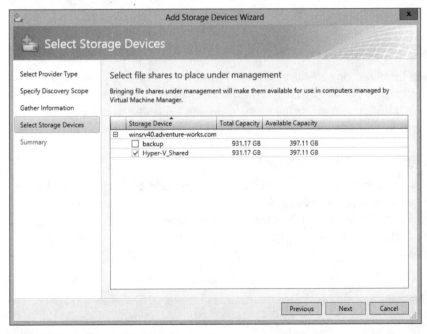

FIGURE 3-37 Choosing a file share

After the storage has been discovered, you create a file share. This step may be confusing for storage devices created from existing SMB shares because there's already an SMB share exposed by the underlying Windows server. You essentially create another share on top of that storage device. Finally, storage is assigned to hosts or clusters through the host or cluster's Properties dialog box.

Cluster-shared volumes (CSVs) are also available for use in VMM and enable cluster members to share the same disk. This helps to provide faster failover capabilities, among other advantages. When working with CSVs, there are several tasks similar to those needed when working with other types of storage, such as creation of logical units and so on. You can also convert storage to CSV in VMM by selecting Convert To CSV on the Available Storage tab of a host cluster Properties dialog box.

> **MORE INFO** SMB AND CSV
>
> See *http://technet.microsoft.com/en-us/library/gg610696.aspx* for more information on configuring logical units for Hyper-V hosts, *http://technet.microsoft.com/en-us/library/ jj134187.aspx* for more information on SMB, and *http://technet.microsoft.com/en-us/ library/gg610692.aspx* for information on using CSV with VMM and Hyper-V.

Planning for and configuring Hyper-V guest storage

Guest storage refers to the storage used by virtual machines. There are several methods for providing this storage, three of which will be covered in this section:

- Virtual Fibre Channel
- iSCSI
- Pass-through disk

Like planning for storage in general, planning for guest storage is largely dependent on the available infrastructure. For instance, you need Fibre Channel capabilities to deploy virtual Fibre Channel, so if that's not available then there's no need to plan for its use. However, for the exam you should still understand how to add Fibre Channel devices.

Working with virtual Fibre Channel

Fibre Channel is added in the Storage area of the Fabric workspace. Selecting Storage Devices from the Add Resources menu reveals the Add Storage Devices Wizard (seen previously in Figure 3-36). On the Select Provider Type page, shown in Figure 3-36, selecting the Add A Storage Device That Is Managed By An SMI-S Provider option enables the Fibre Channel storage to be added.

MORE INFO **FIBRE CHANNEL**

The "How to Add and Classify Virtual Fibre Channel Devices in VMM" article on TechNet contains additional information on this process. See *http://technet.microsoft.com/en-us/library/dn303340.aspx* for the article.

Working with iSCSI

As of System Center 2012 SP1, VMM can manage the iSCSI Target Server functionality in Windows Server 2012. The iSCSI Target Server can be configured using the Add-SCStorageProvider Windows PowerShell cmdlet.

MORE INFO **ISCSI AND WINDOWS POWERSHELL**

See *http://technet.microsoft.com/en-us/library/jj860422.aspx* for limitations and Windows PowerShell cmdlets for iSCSI and VMM.

Working with pass-through disks

Pass-through disks enable Hyper-V to work directly with an underlying physical disk, such as a disk connected directly to the server or through a SAN LUN. Pass-through disks typically offer better performance than a traditional VHD stored on another disk. Pass-through disks are managed at the virtual machine level.

Planning for storage optimization

When considering optimization of storage in VMM, one way guest performance can be improved is by using fixed disks rather than dynamically expanding disks. The underlying disk architecture is vital for performance with SAN-based technologies, typically offering higher performance than file share–based disks for virtual machine storage.

Operations Manager offers Performance and Resource Optimization (PRO) tip integration with VMM, and this integration offers an opportunity for performance improvement as well. Integration with Operations Manager is discussed in the "Manage and maintain a server virtualization infrastructure" section of this chapter.

Thought experiment

Configuring host and guest storage

In this thought experiment, apply what you've learned about this objective. You can find answers to these questions in the "Answers" section at the end of this chapter.

You'll be configuring both the overall host storage solution and guest storage for your organization. The organization consists of a single data center with three sites, all with high-speed connections. Your organization utilizes a SAN for all disk storage, including physical servers.

1. Discuss the process of configuring host storage from a high level.

2. Discuss the options for guest storage and how those might be configured for optimal performance.

Objective summary

- VMM can manage storage for Hyper-V hosts, both standalone and clustered.
- Storage devices are added (discovered), classified, and provisioned, all from within the Fabric workspace of VMM.
- VMM can use storage on SMB-based file shares and through SMI-S and SMP.
- Guest storage for virtual machines is accomplished using virtual Fibre Channel, iSCSI, and pass-through disks.
- Storage optimization is achieved through multiple methods, including use of pass-through disks where appropriate and by utilizing Performance and Resource Optimization (PRO) tips through integration with Operations Manager.

Objective review

Answer the following questions to test your knowledge of the information in this objective. You can find the answers to these questions and explanations of why each answer choice is correct or incorrect in the "Answers" section at the end of this chapter.

1. Which cmdlet is used to add a storage provider to VMM?

   A. Add-SCStorageHost

   B. Add-SCStorageProvider

   C. Add-VMMStorageHost

   D. Add-SCStorageUnit

2. During which phase of host storage provisioning do you apply ratings to discovered storage?

    A. Classify

    B. Discover

    C. Provision

    D. Allocate

3. Which of the following is a prerequisite for using virtual Fibre Channel for guest storage?

    A. An environment with NAS storage

    B. A supported Fibre Channel adapter

    C. Appropriate IP addressing

    D. iSCSI Target Server role

Objective 3.5: Plan and implement virtual machine movement

Being able to move virtual machines between hosts is a powerful and highly useful feature in an enterprise. The scenario is useful to provide load balancing and disaster recovery, and to migrate a virtual machine to a new host when needed for an upgrade or other feature. This section looks at virtual machine movement and its related exam objectives.

> **This objective covers how to:**
> - Plan for and configure live and storage migration between Hyper-V hosts
> - Plan for and manage P2V and V2V
> - Plan for and implement virtual machine migration between clouds

Planning for and configuring live and storage migration between Hyper-V hosts and clouds

There are several types of migrations for virtual machines, including live and storage migration, as identified in the exam objectives. There are also quick migrations and quick storage migrations. A quick migration, sometimes called a *cluster transfer*, is used to migrate virtual machines between cluster nodes using Windows Failover Cluster. Quick migrations involve some downtime because the virtual machine state is saved (hibernated) while the disk is brought online by the other cluster node. Quick storage migrations move the storage for a virtual machine from one storage provider to another. Quick storage migrations also involve downtime.

When planning migrations, the underlying storage and network infrastructure will dictate the available options. If SAN-based infrastructure is not in place, none of the SAN options are available. Obviously, live migrations are preferred for environments where downtime is not acceptable, but live migrations can also consume resources, so setting a concurrency limit (discussed in the section titled "Live migrations" in this chapter) is important.

Also consider the use of snapshots. Migrating a virtual machine that has snapshots can take longer over networks, and the migration may fail if the snapshots are removed but not yet deleted by Hyper-V. Use the Status column in Hyper-V Manager to ensure that the status is not Merge In Progress, or wait until the merge is complete.

> **MORE INFO** **MIGRATIONS**
>
> See *http://technet.microsoft.com/en-us/library/jj628158.aspx* for additional information on migrations, including limitations for live migrations.

Network-based storage migrations

When migrating a virtual machine, using network-based storage migrations are the slowest solution. Network migrations use Background Intelligent Transfer Service (BITS) to copy the virtual machine between locations.

You can also perform a manual migration using the Migrate VM Wizard, shown in Figure 3-38.

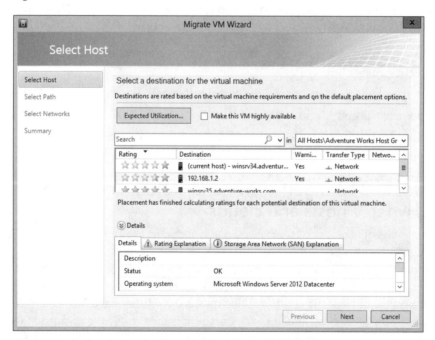

FIGURE 3-38 Performing a migration using the Migrate VM Wizard

SAN-based migrations

Though no longer mentioned directly on the newly revised objectives for the Windows Server 2012 R2 exam, SAN migrations are still a viable option for migration. When Hyper-V hosts have access to the LUN on a SAN, a SAN migration can be performed. SAN migrations can transfer virtual machines into and out of a cluster. However, a dedicated LUN (not using CSV) needs to be available when transferring out of a cluster. SAN migrations are supported with the following infrastructure:

- Fibre Channel
- iSCSI SAN
- N_Port ID (NPID) Virtualization

Using SANs with VMM involves certain configuration steps depending on the needs of the environment and the type of SAN deployed. For example, older SAN technology may require Virtual Disk Service (VDS) be installed. See *http://technet.microsoft.com/en-us/library/ gg610594.aspx* for details on rapid provisioning, which contains insight into creating templates that can be used for SAN migrations.

SAN migrations are used by default when migrating virtual machines using the Migrate VM Wizard. This can be changed on the Select Path page of the Migrate VM Wizard by selecting Transfer Over The Network Even If A SAN Transfer Is Available.

Live migrations

As its name implies, a live migration takes place without downtime. As of System Center 2012 SP1, live migrations can be performed both within and outside of a failover cluster, including between standalone hosts and between nodes in different clusters, though the hosts must be domain joined. System Center 2012 SP1 also enables live storage migration and live virtual system migration, which migrates both the machine and underlying storage at the same time. Finally, live migrations can also take place simultaneously, and there's a configurable limit on the number of migrations that can take place at once.

Migration settings are configured at the host level within the Migration Settings page of the host's Properties dialog box, shown in Figure 3-39.

When manually performing a migration, if the hosts can see the same SMB 3.0 file share, the Live transfer type is available for the migration. There are three settings related to live migrations available with System Center 2012 R2. These include compression and using SMB as a transport, both of which are configured within the Advanced Features section of Hyper-V Live Migration settings on the Hyper-V host.

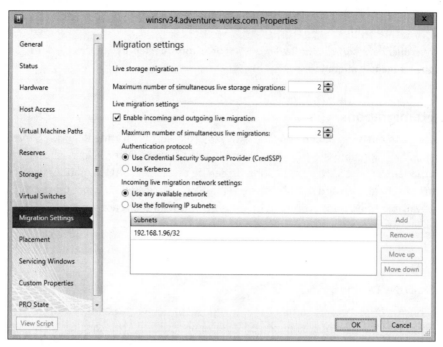

FIGURE 3-39 Live migration settings in VMM

> ***MORE INFO*** **LIVE MIGRATIONS**
>
> See *http://technet.microsoft.com/en-us/library/jj860434.aspx* for more information on live migrations.

Planning for and managing P2V and V2V

Physical to virtual (P2V) and virtual to virtual (V2V) migrations help facilitate management of virtual machines by VMM. P2V typically occurs when organizations move from physical to virtualized infrastructure. When planning P2V, there are certain limitations and other considerations. First among those limitations is that P2V has been removed from Virtual Machine Manager 2012 R2. Therefore, if you have a scenario that involves Virtual Machine Manager 2012 R2, you can automatically know that P2V is not an option. However, other scenarios may appear, in which case it's helpful to also know other limitations and considerations for P2V. The physical computer being migrated needs to have at least 512 MB of RAM and an ACPI BIOS while also residing in a nonperimeter network. The physical computer also cannot have encrypted volumes or volumes larger than 2,048 GB, and cannot be on Itanium architecture.

P2V migrations can be performed in online or offline mode. In online mode (the default for most situations), the physical computer being migrated remains online while Volume

Shadow Copy Service (VSS) is used to create a copy of NTFS volumes and data from VSS-aware applications. Offline mode, which is recommended for domain controller migrations and is required for FAT volumes, takes the physical computer offline, boots it into the Windows Preinstallation Environment (Windows PE), and then creates a clone of the physical volumes into a virtual hard disk (VHD).

P2V migrations to VMM are compatible with numerous Windows-based operating systems, as denoted in Table 3-3.

TABLE 3-3 P2V operating system support

Operating System	P2V Migration Possible
Windows Web Server 2012	Yes
Windows Server 2012 (Standard, Enterprise, Datacenter)	Yes
Windows 8	Yes
Windows Web Server 2008 and 2008 R2	Yes
Windows Server 2008 R2 (Standard, Enterprise, Datacenter)	Yes
Windows 7	Yes
Windows Vista with SP1	Yes
Windows Server 2003 Web Edition	Yes
Windows Server 2003 (Standard, Enterprise, Datacenter)	Yes with SP2 or later
Windows XP Professional with SP3	No (System Center 2012 SP1); Yes (System Center 2012)
Windows NT 4.0	No

Migrating a virtual machine for P2V is accomplished from within the VMs and Services workspace in VMM by selecting Convert Physical Machine from the Create Virtual Machine drop-down list. Doing so invokes the Convert Physical Server (P2V) Wizard, shown in Figure 3-40.

> **MORE INFO** **PERFORMING A P2V MIGRATION**
>
> See *http://technet.microsoft.com/en-us/library/hh427286.aspx* for a walkthrough of a P2V migration.

A virtual to virtual (V2V) migration is done for conversions of existing virtual machines hosted in Citrix XenServer and VMware vCenter. Like P2V migrations, there are certain limitations to V2V scenarios. Specifically, virtual machines hosted on XenServer can't be migrated in a V2V manner, but rather need to be converted using P2V methods. Like P2V methods, XenServer migrations can only be performed on Windows-based virtual machines.

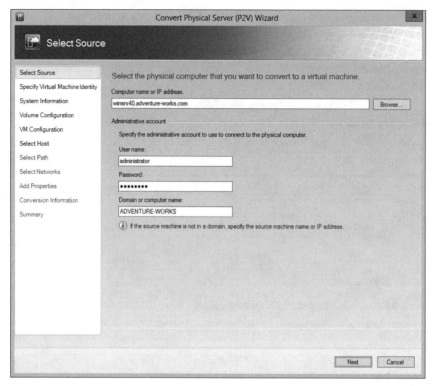

FIGURE 3-40 Beginning the conversion process

When using System Center 2012, V2V conversions from VMware can be accomplished if the VMware server is running ESX/ESXi 3.5 Update 5 or ESX/ESXi 4.0, 4.1, or 5.1. System Center 2012 SP1 only supports migrations from ESX/ESXi 4.1 and 5.1. Additionally, VMware tools must be uninstalled from the virtual machine before beginning the migration.

Like P2V conversions, beginning a V2V conversion is accomplished in the VMs and Services workspace by selecting Convert Virtual Machine from the Create Virtual Machine drop-down list.

> **MORE INFO VMWARE V2V**
>
> See *http://technet.microsoft.com/en-us/library/gg610672.aspx* for a step-by-step migration process for V2V from VMware.

Thought experiment

Migrating computers to virtual machines

In this thought experiment, apply what you've learned about this objective. You can find an answer in the "Answers" section at the end of this chapter.

You'll be migrating a set of physical computers for a legacy Windows NT 4.0 domain. The domain has two domain controllers running Windows NT 4.0 and three Windows XP Professional computers.

Describe the options for migrating these computers to virtual machines, along with limitations therein.

Objective summary

- Several types of migrations are available for virtual machines, including SAN-based, live, network, quick, and quick storage.
- SAN migrations can be performed with the appropriate underlying architecture, including Fibre Channel, iSCSI SAN, and NPID.
- P2V migrations help facilitate a virtualized infrastructure.
- V2V migrations can be accomplished from VMware ESX hosts, but XenServer hosts follow a P2V path.

Objective review

Answer the following questions to test your knowledge of the information in this objective. You can find the answers to these questions and explanations of why each answer choice is correct or incorrect in the "Answers" section at the end of this chapter.

1. Which mode of migration is recommended for domain controllers in a P2V scenario?

    A. Online

    B. Offline

    C. SAN

    D. Cluster

2. Which migration type results in minimal or no downtime?

    A. Network

    B. Quick

    C. Offline

    D. Live

3. Simultaneous live migrations are configured in which area of VMM?

    A. Per host

    B. Per virtual machine

    C. Per SAN

    D. For each virtual machine template

Objective 3.6: Manage and maintain a server virtualization infrastructure

This entire chapter is dedicated to planning and implementing the infrastructure necessary for virtualization. However, a few areas of the infrastructure can be further enhanced. These areas include integration with System Center Operations Manager, resource optimization, and the creation of service templates, among others. This section looks at some of those additional features that can help with an enterprise virtualization infrastructure.

> **This objective covers how to:**
> - Manage dynamic optimization and resource optimization
> - Integrate Operations Manager with System Center Virtual Machine Manager and System Center Service Manager
> - Update virtual machines in libraries
> - Plan for and implement backup and recovery of virtualization infrastructure by using System Center Data Protection Manager (DPM)

Managing dynamic optimization and resource optimization

Dynamic optimization performs live migrations of virtual machines within host clusters that are configured for such migrations. Additionally, there's a power optimization setting that can turn off hosts when they're not needed. This section focuses on optimization through VMM.

> **NOTE DYNAMIC OPTIMIZATION**
>
> As discussed later in this chapter, many of the same functions previously performed using Performance and Resource Optimization (PRO) are also performed with dynamic optimization.

Dynamic optimization and power optimization are configured on a host group basis. The Administrator or Delegated Administrator role is necessary to configure these optimizations, though delegated administrators are limited to configurations for their predefined host groups. From the Fabric workspace, selecting Dynamic Optimization from a host group's Properties dialog box reveals the screen shown in Figure 3-41.

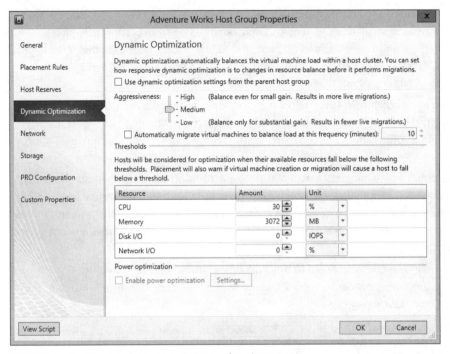

FIGURE 3-41 Configuring dynamic optimization for a host group

You can configure the aggressiveness with which VMM will attempt to optimize the virtual machine load within a group. The three basic settings for aggressiveness are High, Medium (the default setting), and Low. There are intermediary settings as well, between Medium and High and between Medium and Low.

A High aggressiveness setting means that optimization will occur more frequently when VMM deems that a small gain might be had by doing so. On the other hand, Low aggressiveness means that VMM will perform fewer migrations and only do so when there's a large performance gain or a large resource utilization imbalance between hosts within the host group.

> **NOTE** **DEFAULT FREQUENCY**
>
> The default frequency is 10 minutes.

There are four configurable resource thresholds after which dynamic optimization may occur. These include:

- CPU
- Memory

- Disk I/O
- Network I/O

These thresholds can be thought of as available resources, or the resources that the host must keep available at all times to keep dynamic optimization from occurring. Figure 3-41 shows a Medium aggressiveness and 30 percent CPU utilization. This means that if the available CPU on a host falls below 30 percent, it becomes a candidate for dynamic optimization of its virtual machines.

You can also configure VMM to perform dynamic optimization automatically, and you can set the interval in which the dynamic optimization will occur. If you don't configure automatic dynamic optimization, you can manually trigger the optimization through the Fabric workspace.

Power optimization migrates virtual machines and turns off the host when not needed. It's important to recognize that power optimization applies to *hosts* and not virtual machines. Power optimization requires a quorum be maintained for host clusters. If the host cluster was created outside of VMM, then at least four hosts will remain active at all times and not subject to power optimization.

Power optimization is scheduled to run at all times but can be configured through the Settings dialog box, shown in Figure 3-24, found within the Power Optimization area of the Dynamic Optimization page.

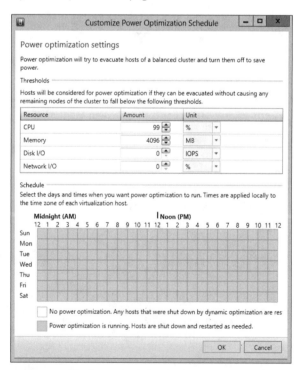

FIGURE 3-42 The Power Optimization Settings page in VMM

MORE INFO DYNAMIC OPTIMIZATION AND POWER OPTIMIZATION

See *http://technet.microsoft.com/en-us/library/gg675109.aspx* and *http://technet. microsoft.com/en-us/library/gg675118.aspx* for more information on dynamic and power optimization.

Integrating Operations Manager with VMM and Service Manager

Integrating Operations Manager with VMM involves installing the Operations Manager console on the VMM management server, installing Operations Manager agents on the VMM management server, virtual machines, and hosts (as appropriate), and importing management packs. Integration of Operations Manager and VMM was covered in Chapter 1. This objective focuses on taking advantage of that integration through the use of PRO tips.

Dynamic optimization replaces some of the PRO functionality previously achieved with integration with Operations Manager. Specifically, the PRO CPU Utilization and PRO Memory Utilization monitors for hosts that are no longer used. However, Operations Manager and PRO tips are still quite useful for VMM. This section looks at integration of Operations Manager and enabling PRO tips.

Working with PRO tips

Once integration is complete, you can manage the connection between Operations Manager and VMM from within the Settings workspace of VMM. In the Operations Manager Settings dialog box, you can enable the connection, as well as enable PRO, enable Maintenance Mode, and test PRO. See Figure 3-43 for the Operations Manager Settings dialog box.

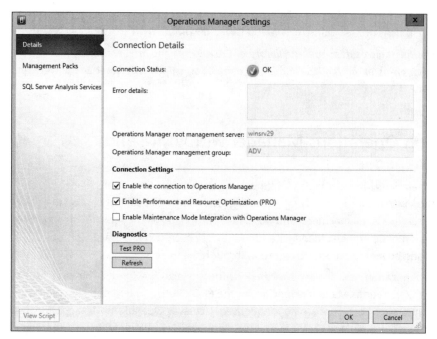

FIGURE 3-43 The Connection Details page in VMM

Clicking Test PRO reveals a PRO tip alert like the one shown in Figure 3-44.

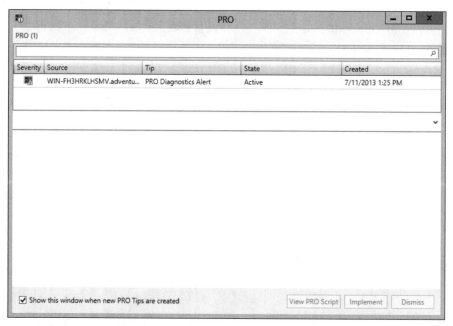

FIGURE 3-44 A test PRO alert in VMM

If the test PRO alert isn't generated, you may find some useful debug information in the Jobs workspace in VMM. You can also use the Windows PowerShell cmdlet Test-SCPROTip to generate the test PRO tip.

PRO can be configured for host groups, host clusters, clouds, services, hosts, and virtual machines. With System Center 2012, you can change the configuration of PRO for each type of monitor being used. For instance, you may want to remediate certain PRO monitors but just view others.

Configuring PRO is accomplished in the Properties dialog box of a given host or host group. Figure 3-45 shows an example of two host monitors, one configured for Monitor and one for Remediate.

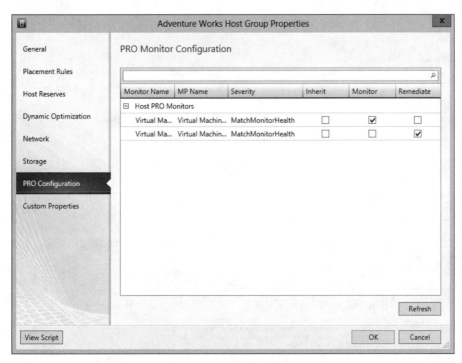

FIGURE 3-45 The PRO Monitor Configuration page for a host group

Integration of System Center Service Manager and Operations Manager is accomplished through the use of connectors. Connectors for Operations Manager can be used for alerts and configuration items. Connectors are created in Service Manager through the Connectors pane in the Administration workspace. When Create Connector is selected, the choice of whether to create an Operations Manager alert connector or an Operations Manager configuration item (CI) connector will be among the available connectors.

A wizard is used to create both types of connectors. When creating an alert connector, you'll define the routing rule containing the criteria for the alert, shown in Figure 3-46.

FIGURE 3-46 Creating an alert routing rule for Operations Manager

Alternatively, when creating a CI connector, the configuration items are chosen as part of the wizard, as shown in Figure 3-47.

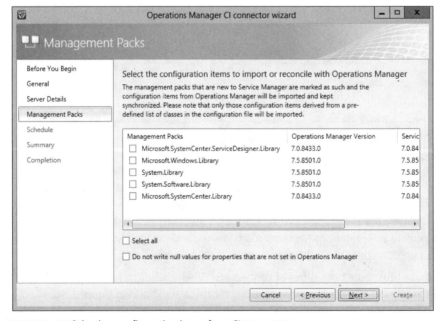

FIGURE 3-47 Selecting configuration items for a CI connector

MORE INFO OPERATIONS MANAGER CONNECTORS

See *http://technet.microsoft.com/en-us/library/hh524325.aspx* for more details on creating connectors.

Update virtual machine images in libraries

As discussed in the first objective in this chapter, libraries are used to store common objects that can be used across a virtual environment, including images for virtual machines. Library objects can be versioned, which assists in managing updates.

Figure 3-48 shows a library resource called test.iso that's currently in release 3.

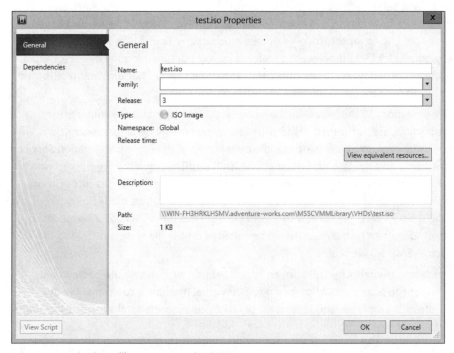

FIGURE 3-48 Viewing a library resource in VMM

You can view the dependencies of the resource on the Dependencies tab. Doing so enables you to see any other objects that are currently using the resource.

Updating the library resource is typically accomplished outside of VMM. For instance, updating a template or a new ISO image would be done independent of VMM. You can then use VMM to update the release and other details.

Planning for and implementing backup and recovery of virtualization infrastructure using DPM

Data Protection Manager (DPM), part of System Center 2012, can be used to protect virtual machines, whether the virtual machine is hosted on a standalone Hyper-V server or a cluster. To do so, DPM installs a protection agent on the host servers (and on the file server in the case of SMB 3.0 storage). DPM provides real-time, live backups of virtual machines and doesn't require downtime. DPM can send backups to disk, Windows Azure backup, or tape. When backed up to tape, recovery will take much longer than a disk-based backup. Therefore, planning for DPM usage in this scenario involves determining the needs for rapid recovery. One option would be to use disk-based storage for recent backups and tape-based storage for long-term storage for archival purposes.

There are limitations to the live online backups, however. If any of these limitations apply, then offline backups are performed. If the virtual machine has any dynamic disks or disks that are not NTFS, then an offline backup is the only option. If the Backup Integration Service (Volume Snapshot) isn't running or if the machine itself is offline, then the live backup won't be able to run. When running DPM in a cluster environment, if the Cluster Resource Group is not available, then DPM will also need to perform a backup in offline mode. In many instances, DPM works in conjunction with VSS to perform its online backups. This means that the File Server VSS Agent role service should be installed on the file servers providing shared storage, such as SMB 3.0 file shares.

The storage requirements for DPM are an important part of planning the deployment. Each DPM server can provide backups for up to 800 virtual machines. You can arrive at a rough estimate of the storage requirement simply by calculating the total allocated storage for each virtual machine.

Regardless of the storage and other factors in use, the DPM protection agent needs to be installed. This can be installed using the DPM console or manually. The manual option needs to be used for nondomain computers or those where a firewall or other limitation prevents the DPM console method from working.

One additional concept for DPM concerns protection groups. You can create logical groupings in DPM to gather similar resources or group together resources that should be treated the same from a data-protection standpoint.

> **MORE INFO** **CONFIGURING DPM**
>
> See *http://technet.microsoft.com/en-us/library/hh757970.aspx* for more information on configuring DPM for various storage scenarios and for live migrations.

Thought experiment
Dynamic optimization

In this thought experiment, apply what you've learned about this objective. You can find an answer in the "Answers" section at the end of this chapter.

Your virtual infrastructure consists of 56 virtual machines running Windows Server 2012, running across eight Hyper-V hosts. You've configured dynamic optimization along with live migrations between Hyper-V hosts. You've found that there has been an unacceptable increase in network traffic, and you believe it's being caused by dynamic optimization.

Discuss some things you can do to adjust dynamic optimization.

Objective summary

- Operations Manager can be integrated with VMM to provide PRO tips.
- Service templates can be versioned, and new versions can be applied to running services, thereby applying the updates to the services.
- The library stores objects that are used within a VMM environment. Library objects can be versioned and updated.

Objective review

Answer the following questions to test your knowledge of the information in this objective. You can find the answers to these questions and explanations of why each answer choice is correct or incorrect in the "Answers" section at the end of this chapter.

1. Which of the following are valid resource thresholds for dynamic optimization?

   A. CPU

   B. Memory

   C. Disk I/O

   D. Available Disk

2. Which command generates a test PRO tip when configuring VMM and Operations Manager integration?

   A. Set-SCPROTip

   B. Test-SCPROTip

   C. Gen-SCPROTip

   D. Set-OpsPROTip

3. To which of the following does power optimization apply?

   A. Virtual machines

   B. Hosts

   C. Grids

   D. Library objects

Answers

This section contains the solutions to the thought experiments and answers to the lesson review questions in this chapter.

Objective 3.1: Thought experiment

Solving this thought experiment can involve two user roles—the main Administrator role and the Application Administrator (Self-Service) user role. Because there's only one infrastructure team, you shouldn't need a Tenant or Fabric Administrator role.

Objective 3.1: Review

1. **Correct answer:** B

   A. **Incorrect:** Memory is a valid host reserve setting.

   B. **Correct:** Disk status is not a valid host reserve setting.

   C. **Incorrect:** CPU percentage is a valid host reserve setting.

   D. **Incorrect:** Disk space is a valid host reserve setting.

2. **Correct answer:** B

   A. **Incorrect:** Fabric Administrator cannot perform this operation.

   B. **Correct:** Administrator is the only role that can add XenServer hosts and clusters.

   C. **Incorrect:** Self-Service users cannot perform this operation.

   D. **Incorrect:** Tenant Administrators cannot perform this operation.

3. **Correct answer:** A

   A. **Correct:** Port 443 is the default port for this communication.

   B. **Incorrect:** 5150 is not the default port.

   C. **Incorrect:** 5297 is not the default port.

   D. **Incorrect:** 3389 is not the default port and is typically used for Remote Desktop.

Objective 3.2: Thought experiment

There are four settings related to dynamic memory: Startup Memory, Minimum Memory, Maximum Memory, and Memory Buffer Percentage. There's also an ancillary setting, Memory Weight, that defines how the host allocates memory resources.

Because users are reporting slow application start times, it's not likely that the Startup Memory is to blame, since that relates to the virtual machine itself. You might be tempted to increase the Minimum Memory, and if the host has enough memory, this is a reasonable step. However, another option would be to increase the Memory Buffer Percentage, because that will keep additional memory in reserve based on the amount of RAM currently in use on the VM.

Objective 3.2: Review

1. **Correct answer:** D

   A. **Incorrect:** High is an option for priority.

   B. **Incorrect:** Do not restart automatically is an option for priority.

   C. **Incorrect:** Medium is an option for priority.

   D. **Correct:** Automatic is not an option for priority.

2. **Correct answer:** A

   A. **Correct:** The host is out of physical memory is one of the criteria for use of Smart Paging.

   B. **Incorrect:** The virtual machine needs to be in a restart state, not coming from an Off state.

   C. **Incorrect:** Smart Paging is not used for virtual machines that are running.

   D. **Incorrect:** The Dynamic Memory Smart Paging option does not exist.

3. **Correct answer:** D

   A. **Incorrect:** A virtual machine that has already been deployed can be used.

   B. **Incorrect:** An existing template in the library can be used.

   C. **Incorrect:** A virtual hard disk in the library can be used.

   D. **Correct:** A predefined operating system image cannot be used for this purpose.

Objective 3.3: Thought experiment

There are three options for communicating with virtual switches: external, internal, and private. The WSUS server will need to use a virtual switch with external access. The virtual machines involved in the credit card application will need to use a private virtual switch. The internal virtual switch enables communication between the virtual machine and any other virtual machine on the host or the host itself.

Objective 3.3: Review

1. **Correct answer:** A

   A. **Correct:** Allow New VM Networks Created In This Logical Network To Use Network Virtualization is the correct option for this question.

   B. **Incorrect:** This Logical Network Can Use Network Virtualization is not an available option.

   C. **Incorrect:** Allow This Logical Network To Be Virtualized is not an available option.

   D. **Incorrect:** This VM Network Can Use Network Virtualization is not an available option.

2. **Correct answers:** A, C

   A. **Correct:** TCP Chimney Offload is one of the ways in which VMM can optimize network traffic.

   B. **Incorrect:** Virtual Network Queue is not an option.

   C. **Correct:** Virtual machine queue is one of the ways in which VMM can optimize network traffic.

   D. **Incorrect:** TCP Chimney Stack Offload is not an option.

3. **Correct answer:** B

   A. **Incorrect:** Virtual machines are not a prerequisite for network virtualization configuration.

   B. **Correct:** Hyper-V hosts are required to use network virtualization.

   C. **Incorrect:** TCP Offload is not related to this question.

   D. **Incorrect:** Network adapter support is not related to this question.

Objective 3.4: Thought experiment

1. The high-level process for configuring storage is identified by Microsoft as:

   A. Discover storage.

   B. Classify storage.

   C. Select logical unit method.

   D. Provision storage.

   E. Allocate storage.

2. Guest storage can use virtual Fibre Channel or pass-through disks, depending on how the hosts are configured. Both options offer good performance, since they would both be using the underlying SAN.

Objective 3.4: Review

1. **Correct answer:** B

   A. **Incorrect:** Add-SCStorageHost is not used to add a storage provider to VMM.

   B. **Correct:** Add-SCStorageProvider

   C. **Incorrect:** Add-VMMStorageHost is not used to add a storage provider to VMM.

   D. **Incorrect:** Add-SCStorageUnit is not used to add a storage provider to VMM.

2. **Correct answer:** A

   A. **Correct:** Classify is the phase of host storage provisioning where you apply ratings to discovered storage

   B. **Incorrect:** Discover is not the phase of host storage provisioning where you apply ratings to discovered storage.

   C. **Incorrect:** Provision is not the phase of host storage provisioning where you apply ratings to discovered storage.

   D. **Incorrect:** Allocate is not the phase of host storage provisioning where you apply ratings to discovered storage.

3. **Correct answer:** B

   A. **Incorrect:** An environment with NAS storage s not a prerequisite for using virtual Fibre Channel for guest storage.

   B. **Correct:** A supported Fibre Channel adapter

   C. **Incorrect:** Appropriate IP addressing s not a prerequisite for using virtual Fibre Channel for guest storage.

   D. **Incorrect:** iSCSI Target Server role s not a prerequisite for using virtual Fibre Channel for guest storage.

Objective 3.5: Thought experiment

Because the domain controllers run Windows NT 4.0, you can't perform a P2V migration. You must upgrade the servers to a later, supported operating system before performing the migration. Assuming that the Windows XP Professional computers are running at least SP3, they can be migrated.

Objective 3.5: Review

1. **Correct answer:** B

   A. **Incorrect:** Online is not the recommended mode of migration for domain controllers in a P2V scenario.

   B. **Correct:** Offline migration is the recommended mode of migration for domain controllers in a P2V scenario.

   C. **Incorrect:** SAN is not the recommended mode of migration for domain controllers in a P2V scenario.

   D. **Incorrect:** Cluster is not the recommended mode of migration for domain controllers in a P2V scenario.

2. **Correct answer:** D

   A. **Incorrect:** Network migrations are the slowest solution.

   B. **Incorrect:** Quick migrations involve some downtime.

   C. **Incorrect:** In offline migration, the physical computer is taken offline, resulting in some downtime.

   D. **Correct:** Live migration results in minimal or no downtime.

3. **Correct answer:** A

   A. **Correct:** Simultaneous live migrations are configured at the host level.

   B. **Incorrect:** Simultaneous live migrations are not configured per virtual machine.

   C. **Incorrect:** Simultaneous live migrations are not configured per SAN.

   D. **Incorrect.** Simultaneous live migrations are not configured for each virtual machine template.

Objective 3.6: Thought experiment

First, you can disable dynamic optimization automatic live migrations to see whether that has any effect on the network traffic. If the network traffic goes down with dynamic optimization automatic live migrations disabled, then it's time to look for additional configuration settings to help.

Dynamic optimization has several settings that can be configured to define its behavior. Notably, you can configure how aggressive dynamic optimization is. The aggressiveness setting will determine the amount of benefit needed for VMM to undertake a dynamic optimization operation. Additionally, you can configure the interval on which dynamic optimization is run. Finally, you can configure the available resources on each host or as a group.

Objective 3.6: Review

1. **Correct answers:** A, B, C

   A. **Correct:** CPU is a valid threshold.

   B. **Correct:** Memory is a valid threshold.

   C. **Correct:** Disk I/O is a valid threshold.

   D. **Incorrect:** Available Disk is not a valid threshold.

2. **Correct answer:** B

   A. **Incorrect:** Set-SCPROTip is not a valid command.

   B. **Correct:** Test-SCPROTip generates a test PRO diagnostic.

   C. **Incorrect:** Gen-SCPROTip is not a valid command.

   D. **Incorrect:** Set-OpsPROTip is not a valid command.

3. **Correct answer:** B

   A. **Incorrect:** Power optimization does not apply to virtual machines.

   B. **Correct:** Power optimization applies to hosts.

   C. **Incorrect:** Grids are not valid objects in VMM.

   D. **Incorrect:** Power optimization does not apply to library objects.

Design and implement identity and access solutions

The previous chapters looked at various aspects of maintaining an advanced server infrastructure for today's enterprise environment. Chapter 4 addresses enterprise needs related to security certificates, rights management, and other related aspects. Though the objectives are heavily weighted toward certificate infrastructure and Active Directory, you should also be familiar with basic concepts of least privilege and the three basic tenets of security: confidentiality, integrity, and availability.

Objectives in this chapter:

- Objective 4.1: Design a Certificate Services infrastructure
- Objective 4.2: Implement and manage a Certificate Services infrastructure
- Objective 4.3: Implement and manage certificates
- Objective 4.4: Design and implement a federated identity solution
- Objective 4.5: Design and implement Active Directory Rights Management Services (AD RMS)

Objective 4.1: Design a Certificate Services infrastructure

The first set of objectives looks at design of certificate services. The next section, Objective 4.2, looks at implementation related to the design discussion in this section.

This objective covers how to:

- Design a multi-tier certification authority (CA) hierarchy with offline root CA
- Plan for multi-forest CA deployment
- Plan for Certificate Enrollment Web Services and Certificate Enrollment Policy Web Services
- Plan for Network Device Enrollment Services (NDES)
- Plan for certificate validation and revocation
- Plan for disaster recovery
- Plan for trust between organizations, including Certificate Trust Lists (CTL), cross-certifications, and bridge CAs

Designing a multi-tier certification authority hierarchy

The first objective in this chapter examines planning and design issues while the second looks at many of the same topics from a management standpoint. When designing a Certificate Services infrastructure, the first task is to determine the requirements. This includes where the certificates will be used, specifically the CA hierarchy involved in deployment and certificate validation. For example, in a typical web scenario, validation occurs first at the client browser, even though the certificate itself is deployed on the web server and the root CA is on another server as well. Including and planning for failover is also important with Certificate Services, so examining single points of failure in the hierarchy is essential to a design.

At the top of a multi-tier CA hierarchy is the root certification authority. A single root CA can be used, but multiple root CAs might be needed for regulatory or other reasons, such as a need for the root CA to be physically hosted in a certain geographical location. There are three types of root CAs, as described in Table 4-1.

TABLE 4-1 Root CA types

Type	Description
Standalone root CA	Not integrated with Active Directory Domain Services (AD DS) and can be taken offline. Supports subordinate CAs of either enterprise or standalone types.
Enterprise root CA	Integrated with AD DS and does not support offline CA or subordinate standalone CAs.
External root CA	A CA that exists outside of the organization and is operated by a third party. An external root CA is typically used to generate certificates for externally facing websites.

There are two tiers involved in a typical CA hierarchy, the root tier and the issuing tier, as shown in Figure 4-1.

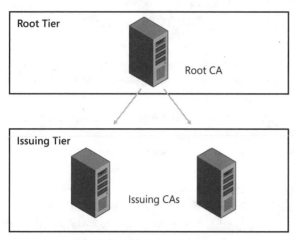

FIGURE 4-1 Multi-tier CA hierarchy

The first or highest tier of the CA hierarchy is the root tier. A standalone root CA can be operated in offline mode and should exist at the top of the hierarchy. With an offline CA, you need to include a subordinate CA that is online. A subordinate CA is any CA that's not the root CA, which includes CAs that issue certificates or ones that exist to enforce policy.

The next tier in a CA hierarchy, called the issuing tier, is where CAs that can issue certificates exist. The issuing CAs handle enrollment, validation, and revocation of certificates. When using a root CA in offline mode, there should be at least two issuing CAs in the intermediate tier. You can add more issuing CAs to the design if necessary to account for remote sites and fault tolerance.

An intermediate tier is sometimes included between the root and issuing tiers for management purposes, but its use is typically not recommended. A scenario where this tier might be used is for legal or political reasons, such as when companies merge. This tier is sometimes known as a policy tier because it's where those business policies are enforced. While the tier isn't required for technical reasons, the policy might dictate that such a tier is created. See the More Info link for additional details.

Planning for multi-forest CA deployment and trust between organizations

Using a multi-forest CA deployment can reduce management and administration overhead that would otherwise occur if each forest managed its own CA independently. When planning a multi-forest CA deployment, one forest will be the resource forest and other forests will be account forests. The resource forest hosts the enterprise CAs and is used for certificate enrollment for the entire organization. The resource forest becomes the master copy for all certificate-related objects. Account forests include domain members that perform certificate enrollment from the resource forest.

Thinking back to the tiers in Figure 4-1, the root tier exists logically outside of the multi-forest deployment, and the issuing tier logically includes the resource forest, which is then responsible for certificate-related management to other forests through a two-way trust. Another option is to include an enterprise CA in each forest, which requires no forest trust between forests. In this scenario, the enterprise CA in each forest works directly with the root CA. Finally, Certificate Enrollment Web Services can also be used to provide certificates between forests without a trust relationship. The next section includes a discussion of the planning steps around Certificate Enrollment Web Services.

An organization might have one or more self-signed certificates issued by internal CAs. Certificate Trust Lists (CTLs) are lists of certificates for these internal CAs. Using a CTL enables trust to be established, especially in multi-forest scenarios, because the internal CA certificate can be trusted. CTLs can also have different lifetimes than the underlying certificate, thereby enabling you to have greater control over the trust. See *http://technet.microsoft.com/en-us/library/dn265983.aspx* for more information on trusted root certificates as it relates to CTLs.

Cross-certification and bridge CAs are useful for migration scenarios where you need to establish a new CA, for example on Windows Server 2012, but your existing CA runs Windows Server 2003. In such a case, you can cross-certify the new CA by using a Cross-Certification Authority Certificate.

Planning for Certificate Enrollment Web Services

Certificate Enrollment Web Services enable certificate enrollment between forests and certificate issuance to external entities, such as contractors. Certificate Enrollment Web Services can be used regardless of domain trusts and in scenarios where certificate enrollment is needed by nondomain devices.

The Certificate Enrollment Web Services server needs to be a member of the domain and should be running at least Windows Server 2008 R2, though Windows Server 2012 is required if automatic renewal of certificates will be used across forests or for nondomain members.

> *NOTE* **ENTERPRISE CA REQUIRED**
>
> Certificate Enrollment Web Services requires an enterprise CA and cannot be used with a standalone CA.

The section titled "Implement and manage a Certificate Services infrastructure" discusses Certificate Enrollment Web Services in more depth, with a specific focus on configuration and management.

> **MORE INFO CERTIFICATE ENROLLMENT WEB SERVICES**
>
> See *http://social.technet.microsoft.com/wiki/contents/articles/7734.certificate-enrollment-web-services-in-active-directory-certificate-services.aspx* for more information on Certificate Enrollment Web Services.

Planning for Network Device Enrollment Services (NDES)

Network Device Enrollment Services (NDES) provides a means by which network devices such as routers can obtain certificates even if those devices aren't part of the domain. NDES uses the Simple Certificate Enrollment Protocol (SCEP). NDES acts as an intermediary by sending enrollment requests to the CA and then retrieving the certificate and sending it back to the requesting network device.

NDES is an Internet Server API (ISAPI) extension and therefore requires a server with IIS. The server works with a CA through DCOM, so that communication will need to be allowed through any firewalls that sit between the NDES server and the server hosting the CA.

You can configure NDES with an enterprise or standalone CA. When configured in an enterprise scenario, the permissions and certificate requests are based on certificate templates. NDES can also be used with a standalone CA. When deploying with an enterprise CA, the server hosting NDES and the server hosting the CA should be separate, whereas when using a standalone CA, the NDES should be on the same server.

> **MORE INFO NDES**
>
> See *http://social.technet.microsoft.com/wiki/contents/articles/9063.network-device-enrollment-service-ndes-in-active-directory-certificate-services-ad-cs.aspx* for more information about NDES in AD CS.

Planning for certificate validation and revocation

Clients need to validate a certificate both for its expiration and its overall chain of trust. You might need to revoke a certificate for various reasons, including compromise of the chain of trust for certificates or a change that affects the certificate, such as a name change or an organizational change.

Certificate revocation uses Certificate Revocation Lists (CRLs). CRLs contain a list of certificates that are no longer valid, and the CRL can become large. To solve this, you can use a delta CRL that contains changes or new revocations.

CRLs are sent through CRL distribution points, which are part of a CA role in Windows Server 2012. When designing a CRL distribution point, you can optionally use HTTP, FTP, LDAP, or file-based addresses as URLs. You should take care in doing so, however, because any change in the CRL URL will be seen only by newly issued certificates; old certificates will use the old URL for revocation list operations.

Another planning point is around the validity period and publishing intervals for CRLs. You can configure the interval between publication of a revocation list or delta list as well as the period in which the CRL is valid. As discussed in the next section, the interval and validity periods have implications for disaster recovery.

Planning for disaster recovery

Planning for disaster recovery of a CA involves many of the same steps and thought processes that go into planning redundancy and fault tolerance in other areas. For example, eliminating single points that cannot be restored is a goal in any disaster recovery scenario, as is mitigating risks of failure as much as feasible.

Mitigating with CAs in mind means installing clustered issuing CAs. Beyond that, the publication interval for the CRL can also be increased, though doing so also increases the time it takes for clients to become aware of a new revocation.

Planning for backups, including backup of the CA database, is important for disaster recovery. System state should be included in a backup for a CA.

Thought experiment
Certificate infrastructure design

You need to design a certificate infrastructure that spans three entities within the same organization. There is one major data center and a small infrastructure at each location. The entities would like to manage their own CAs.

Describe the infrastructure considerations that go into this design.

You can find the solution in the "Answers" section at the end of this chapter.

Objective summary

- Certificate infrastructure in a multi-tier environment involves a root CA tier along with an issuing tier that contains issuing CAs, and optionally an intermediate tier between the root and issuing tiers.
- Multi-forest CA deployment involves establishing a method so that clients in different forests can trust a CA from a different forest.
- Certificate Enrollment Web Services provide a means for external multi-forest CA deployment.
- Certificate validation and revocation is handled through CRLs.
- NDES can be configured with an enterprise or standalone CA.
- Disaster recovery of certificate infrastructure involves configuring the validity period, performing backups, and performing many of the other steps that are taken for disaster recovery planning of other services.

Objective review

Answer the following questions to test your knowledge of the information in this objective. You can find the answers to these questions and explanations of why each answer choice is correct or incorrect in the "Answers" section at the end of this chapter.

1. Which type of CA can be operated in offline mode?

   A. Enterprise

   B. Standalone

   C. Offline

   D. On/off

2. Which period defines the amount of time that a CRL can be used?

   A. Publishing interval

   B. Validation

   C. Validity

   D. Revocation interval

3. When using NDES, which type of CA should be installed on the same server?

   A. Standalone

   B. Enterprise

   C. Multi-forest

   D. CA trust

Objective 4.2: Implement and manage a Certificate Services infrastructure

The certificate infrastructure design accomplished in Objective 4.1 will now be implemented through the tasks related to Objective 4.2. This section looks at configuring several of the items previously discussed and a few new areas as well.

> **This objective covers how to:**
> - Configure and manage offline root CA
> - Configure and manage Certificate Enrollment Web Services and Certificate Enrollment Policy Web Services
> - Configure and manage NDES
> - Configure Online Certificate Status Protocol (OCSP) responders
> - Migrate CA
> - Implement administrator role separation
> - Implement and manage trust between organizations, including CTLs, cross-certifications, and bridge CAs
> - Monitor CA health

Configuring and managing offline root CA

Active Directory Certificate Services is installed as a role on Windows Server 2012. Within the role are several role services, one of which is a certification authority, as shown in Figure 4-2.

Once the CA role has been installed, configuration is required. The configuration steps include specifying the role services, the setup type (standalone or enterprise), the private key, and other details. The Standalone CA option should be chosen for an offline root CA, as shown in Figure 4-3.

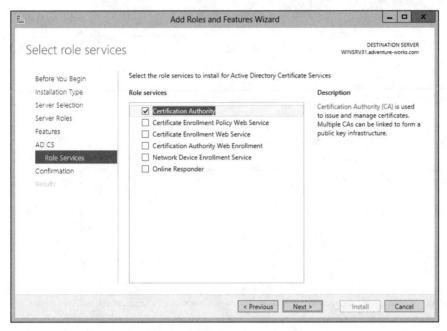

FIGURE 4-2 Installing the Certification Authority role service

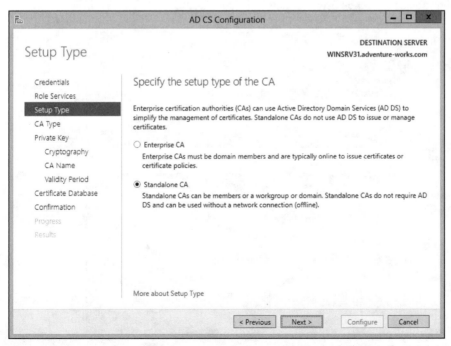

FIGURE 4-3 Choosing the Standalone CA option

The CA type is next, within which the Root CA option should be chosen, as shown in Figure 4-4.

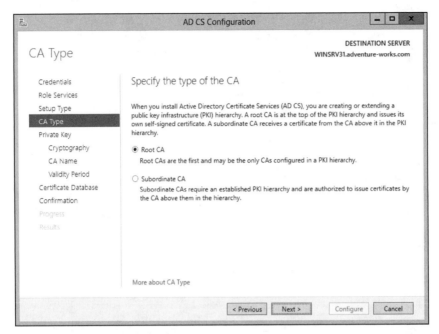

FIGURE 4-4 Selecting a Root CA type

The next page enables you to choose whether a new private key should be created or an existing private key should be used, as shown in Figure 4-5.

FIGURE 4-5 Choosing the key type for a CA installation

When creating a new private key, you can choose the cryptography type, the CA name, and the validity period. Once the details of the private key are specified, you next choose the location for the certificate database, as shown in Figure 4-6.

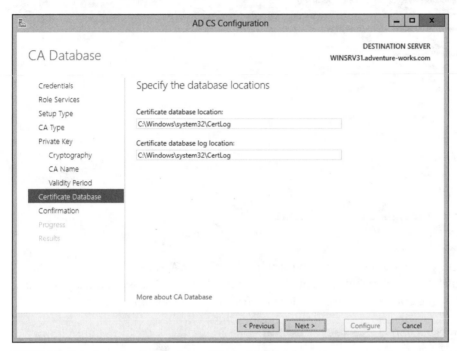

FIGURE 4-6 Choosing a location for the certificate database

> **MORE INFO CA CONFIGURATION**
>
> See *http://technet.microsoft.com/en-us/library/cc731183.aspx* for more details on CA configuration, including an overview of CA naming.

Once configured, the Certification Authority tool is used to manage a CA. One of the configuration items to verify with a root CA is the policy regarding request handling, to ensure that certificate requests are set to pending by the root CA. This is accomplished on the Policy Module tab of the Properties dialog for the CA. On the Policy Module tab, clicking Edit reveals the properties for Request Handling, as shown in Figure 4-7.

FIGURE 4-7 Ensuring that the request-handling mode is set to pending

The CRL distribution point should be configured for your CA as well. This is accomplished by selecting the CRL Distribution Point (CDP) extension from the Extensions tab, as shown in Figure 4-8. The CDP should be set to a location from which clients can obtain the CRL.

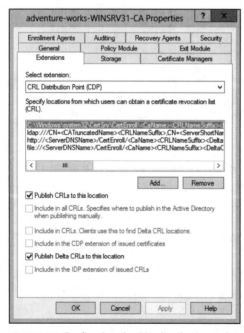

FIGURE 4-8 Configuring the CRL distribution point

From here, another configuration item includes publishing the CRL to the shared URL that you created previously. This can be accomplished by choosing Publish from the Revoked Certificates action items or by using the certutil -CRL command.

Taking the CA offline can be accomplished in one of several ways, including powering down the host, disconnecting the network cable, or simply stopping the CA service.

> **MORE INFO** **OFFLINE ROOT CA**
>
> See *http://social.technet.microsoft.com/wiki/contents/articles/2900.offline-root-certification-authority-ca.aspx* for additional details on creating an offline CA.

Configuring and managing Certificate Enrollment Web Services and Certificate Enrollment Policy Web Services

Certificate Enrollment Web Services (CES) and Certificate Enrollment Policy Web Services are added as service roles of the Active Directory Certificate Services role in Windows Server 2012 R2. Once installed, configuration steps are required for each role service.

In the case of CES, configuration items include choosing a computer or CA name for the CA, as shown in Figure 4-9. On this same screen, you can also configure Certificate Enrollment Web Services to operate in renewal-only mode.

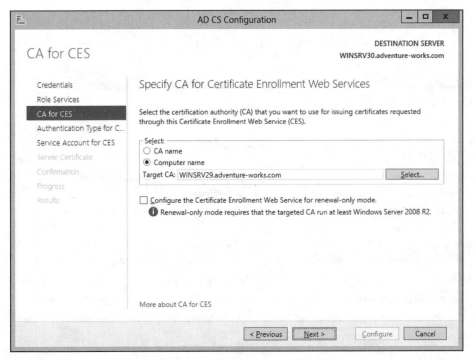

FIGURE 4-9 Configuring Certificate Enrollment Web Services

The CES authentication type is configured next from among the options:

- Windows integration authentication
- Client certificate authentication
- User name and password

Finally, the service account is configured, as shown in Figure 4-10.

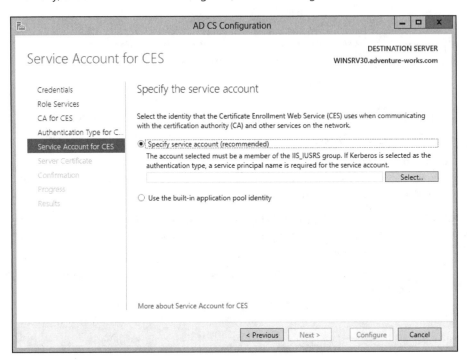

FIGURE 4-10 Specifying a service account

MORE INFO CES

See *http://technet.microsoft.com/en-us/library/hh831822.aspx* for additional configuration options and *http://social.technet.microsoft.com/wiki/contents/articles/7734.certificate-enrollment-web-services-in-active-directory-certificate-services.aspx* for an overview of CES.

Configuration of Certificate Enrollment Policy Web Services (CEP) is accomplished in the same manner as that of CES. When configuring CEP, you first choose the authentication type (Windows Integrated, Client Certificate, or User Name and Password), as shown in Figure 4-11.

Next, the certificate to be used for client communication is chosen. If a certificate isn't available, this choice can be skipped for now and configured later. Figure 4-12 shows this part of the wizard.

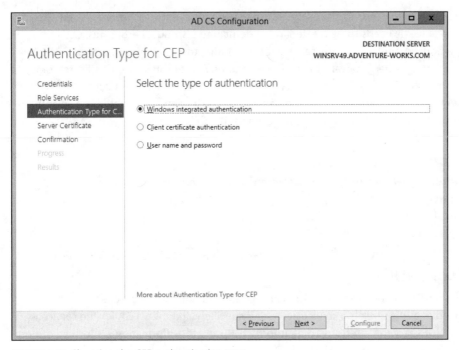

FIGURE 4-11 Choosing the CEP authentication type

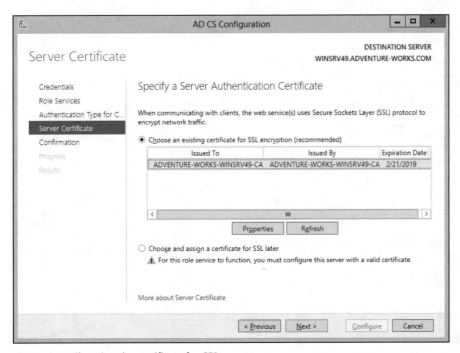

FIGURE 4-12 Choosing the certificate for CEP

Group Policy also needs to be configured so that clients use the CEP server. A new Group Policy Object (GPO) needs to be created in the domain to distribute certificates. CEP can distribute both computer and user certificates. Therefore, the location for the new GPO object will depend on whether you want to distribute computer certificates, user certificates, or both. In either case, the Configuration Model setting of the Certificate Services Client - Certificate Enrollment Policy object needs to be enabled and the policy server URI entered. The authentication type should match what was configured for the CEP server.

> **MORE INFO   CEP**
>
> See *http://technet.microsoft.com/en-us/library/hh831625.aspx* for more details on configuring CEP.

Configuring and managing Network Device Enrollment Services (NDES)

Configuring NDES follows the same overall process as configuring other role services in that it's installed as a role service, a service account is specified, and then a CA for the service is specified. NDES requires a registration authority (RA), and the information is specified during configuration time, as shown in Figure 4-13.

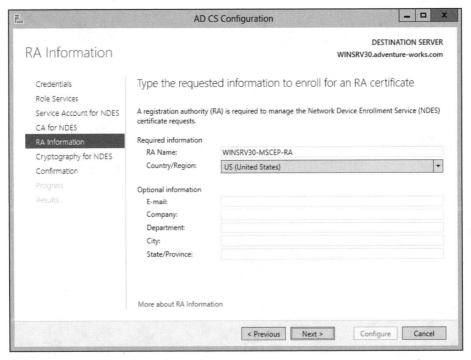

FIGURE 4-13 Providing RA details for NDES

Cryptographic service providers (CSPs) are specified for NDES, as shown in Figure 4-14.

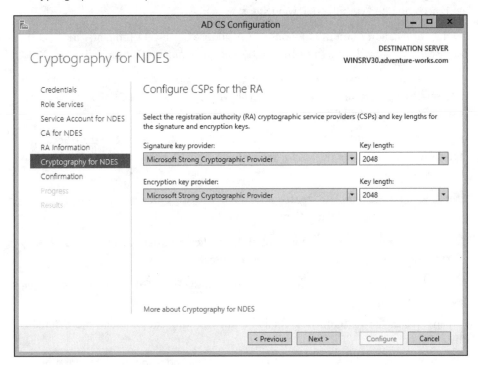

FIGURE 4-14 Configuring CSPs for NDES

NDES operates using service certificates. The CEP Encryption template provides the base for NDES. Objective 4.3, "Implement and manage certificates," later in this chapter contains information on creating certificate templates.

> **MORE INFO NDES**
>
> See *http://social.technet.microsoft.com/wiki/contents/articles/9063.network-device-enrollment-service-ndes-in-active-directory-certificate-services-ad-cs.aspx* for additional information on NDES.

Configuring Online Certificate Status Protocol (OCSP) responders

Online Certificate Status Protocol (OCSP) is implemented through the Online Responder service in Windows Server 2012. Unlike other role services, OCSP doesn't require much specific configuration through the Add Role Services Wizard.

The OCSP service requires a template for use with a revocation configuration. Creating the template is accomplished with the following steps:

1. In the Certification Authority tool on the CA, choose Certificate Templates, right-click, and select Manage. Doing so opens the Certificate Templates Console.

2. In the Certificate Templates Console, select OCSP Response Signing, then right-click and select Duplicate Template. Doing so will create a copy of the OCSP template that can be used by the OCSP service.

3. If you'll use the Auto-Enroll function for the OCSP, then you need to use the Security tab to add the Enroll permission for the computer object on which the OCSP service is running.

4. With the duplicate template created and (optionally) the Enroll permission added, close the Certificate Templates Console.

5. In the Certification Authority tool, right-click Certificate Templates and select Certificate Template To Issue from the New context menu.

6. Select the OCSP template that you created previously. The OCSP template will now be available for use.

The "Managing certificate templates" section of the next objective contains more details on certificate templates.

The Online Responder Manager is used to manage the online responder configuration. Within the manager you can add a revocation configuration. Doing so reveals the Add Revocation Configuration Wizard. Within the Add Revocation Configuration Wizard, you enter a name and then select the location of the CA to associate with the revocation configuration, as shown in Figure 4-15.

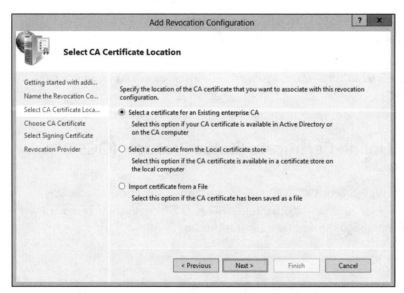

FIGURE 4-15 Selecting the certificate for the revocation configuration

Next, choose the CA certificate. You can auto-enroll using the certificate template created earlier, as shown in Figure 4-16.

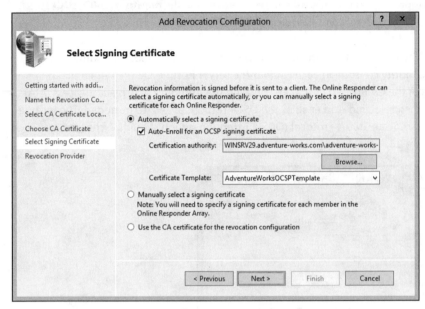

FIGURE 4-16 Choosing a signing certificate

The Revocation Provider Properties dialog box, shown in Figure 4-17, can be used to change details of the revocation for the configuration.

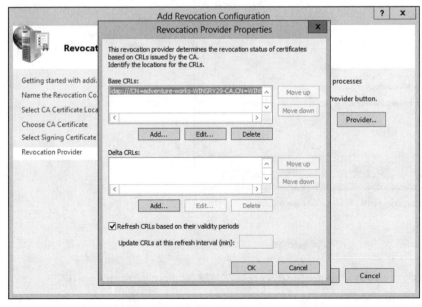

FIGURE 4-17 Configuring revocation provider details

CAs need to be made aware of the OSCP responder. This is accomplished within the
Certification Authority console on each CA (not the server hosting OCSP). Within the
Extensions tab of the CA Properties dialog, choosing the Authority Information Access (AIA)
extension and then selecting Add enables the OSCP responder URL to be added. The Include
In The Online Certificate Status Protocol (OCSP) Extension option should be checked, as
shown in Figure 4-18.

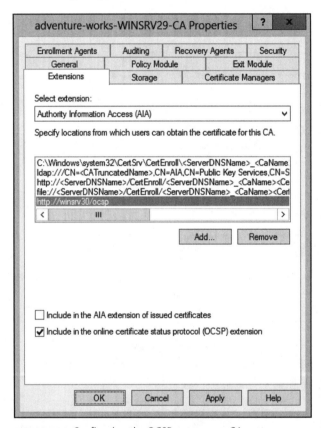

FIGURE 4-18 Configuring the OCSP server on a CA

Migrating the CA

Migrating the CA to a different server can involve various steps, depending on your configuration and migration needs. The basic steps include those described in Table 4-2.

TABLE 4-2 CA migration

Step	Description
Back up CA database and private key	In the Certification Authority tool, select Back Up CA from the All Tasks context menu of the CA. Ensure that Private Key and CA Certificate, as well as Certificate Database and Certificate Database Log, are selected. Enter a password. After backup, shut down the CA service.
Back up registry settings	Use the command reg export HKLM\SYSTEM\CurrentControlSet\Services\CertSvc\Configuration configuration.reg to back up the configuration details. Alternatively, you could also use regedit to export the configuration settings.
Back up CAPolicy.inf	If necessary, back up the CAPolicy.inf file typically found in %SYSTEMROOT%.
Remove the CA role service	Remove the CA role service from the CA. This step is necessary to prevent a conflict in Active Directory. Alternatively, you can disable the Certificate Services service and shut down the server.
Remove the CA from Active Directory	Use the netdom remove <CA-Server-Name> /d:<Domain Name> /ud:<Domain User Name> /pd:* to remove the CA from Active Directory. Ensure that the computer account has been deleted from Active Directory.
Join the new server to Active Directory	Join the new server to the domain with the same name as the old server.
Add the CA role service	Add the CA role service to the new computer.
Import the CA certificate	Use the Certificate MMC snap-in to import the CA certificate and private key created previously.
Restore the CA database	Use the Certification Authority tool to restore the certificate database and log.
Restore registry settings	Import the previously created backup of configuration settings to the new CA.

> **MORE INFO** **MIGRATE A CA**
>
> See *http://technet.microsoft.com/en-us/library/ee126140* for additional details on the steps discussed in Table 4-2.

Implementing administrator role separation

Several roles can be used to administer a certificate infrastructure, as discussed in Table 4-3.

TABLE 4-3 Certificate management roles

Role	Description
Auditor	Works with audit logs; not directly related to a certificate infrastructure role but can work with certificate-related logs.
Backup operator	Though not directly related to a certificate infrastructure, this role can perform backup of files related to a CA.
CA administrator	The primary role for management of a CA, this role can renew CA certificates and assign other CA roles.
Certificate manager	Approves enrollment and revocation requests.
Enrollees	Clients that can request certificates.

By default, the CA roles (CA administrator and Certificate manager) are granted to the local Administrators group as well as Enterprise Admins and Domain Admins as appropriate. However, on a standalone CA, only local Administrators are members of the CA administrators group, unless the standalone CA is joined to a domain, in which case Domain Admins are also CA administrators.

Numerous permissions can be assigned to implement further role separation. These are listed in Table 4-4, along with the specific roles to which they are assigned by default.

TABLE 4-4 Permissions and roles for a CA

Permission	Role(s)
Audit logs	Auditor
Back up the system	Backup operator
Configure audit parameters	Auditor
Configure certificate manager restrictions	CA administrator
Configure extensions	CA administrator
Configure policy and exit modules	CA administrator
Configure roles	CA administrator
Define key recovery agents	CA administrator
Delete a single row in the CA database	CA administrator
Delete multiple rows in the CA database	Must be CA administrator and Certificate manager, and role separation must not be enforced.
Deny certificates	Certificate manager

Permission	Role(s)
Enable, publish, or configure CRL schedules	CA administrator
Enable role separation	Local administrator
Install a CA	Local administrator
Issue and approve certificates	Certificate manager
Reactivate certificates	Certificate manager
Read CA configuration information	CA administrator, Certificate manager, Auditor, Backup operator
Read the CA database	CA administrator, Certificate manager, Auditor, Backup operator
Recover archived keys	Certificate manager
Renew CA keys	Local administrator
Renew certificates	Certificate manager
Restore the system	Backup operator
Revoke certificates	Certificate manager
Stop and start the AD CS service	Local administrator

Implementing administrator role separation involves assigning these permissions or using available groups to separate the tasks that a given user can perform. This is typically accomplished through the standard Active Directory Users and Computers tool within a domain environment. A best practice surrounding role-based administration for certificate infrastructure is to ensure that accounts are not members of both the local Administrators group and the CA administrator or Certificate manager group.

Implementing and managing trust between organizations

Cross-forest trust for certificates involves creating a trust between the two forests involved. Prior to that, a resource forest needs to be designated, as discussed in the first exam objective in this chapter.

The next step after designating a resource forest is to establish trust between the forests. A trust is created in Active Directory Domains and Trusts by choosing the domain to be trusted and then going into the Properties of the domain to be trusted and selecting New Trust from the Trusts tab. Doing so reveals the New Trust Wizard. In the New Trust Wizard, enter the name of the domain to be trusted, as shown in Figure 4-19.

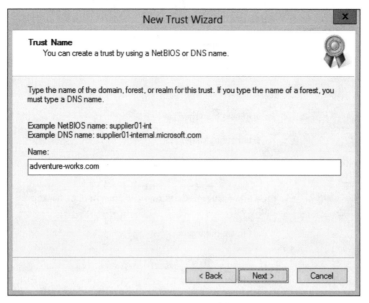

FIGURE 4-19 Entering the domain to be trusted in the New Trust Wizard

The remaining screens define the type, direction, and sides of the trust. The trust type should be selected as a Forest Trust, the direction should be Two-Way, and the sides should be Both This Domain And The Specified Domain option. You'll also be prompted for credentials that have administrative privileges in the external domain.

The scope of authentication is chosen next, with forest-wide allowing all authentication and selective authentication meaning that you need to grant access to resources individually. If the Selective Authentication option is chosen, then the Allow authenticate permission needs to be granted to various objects in both forests. Specifically, domain member computers in account forests need to be granted the Allow authenticate permission to enterprise CAs in the resource forest. Enterprise CAs need to be granted the Allow authenticate permission on domain controllers in account forests. Finally, administrators need the Allow authenticate permission to all domain controllers in all forests.

> **MORE INFO** **TWO-WAY TRUSTS**
>
> See *http://technet.microsoft.com/en-us/library/cc778851* for information on creating a two-way trust.

The next several steps to establish CA trust are as follows:

1. Enable LDAP referrals on enterprise CAs with the command:

    ```
    certutil -setreg Policy\EditFlags +EDIT_ENABLELDAPREFERRALS
    ```

2. Add enterprise CA computer accounts to the Cert Publishers group in the account forest.

3. Set the AIA and CRL distribution points within each enterprise CA or certificate template as necessary.

4. Publish the root CA certificate from the resource forest into the account forests using the commands:

```
certutil -config <Computer Name> | <Root CA Name> -ca.cert <root CA
   certificate file>
certutil -dspublish -f <root CA certificate file>
```

5. Publish enterprise CA certificates into the account forests. Specifically, publish the certificates into the NTAuthCertificates and AIA containers using the commands:

```
certutil -config <Computer Name> | <Enterprise CA Name> -ca.cert <enterprise
   CA certificate file>
certutil -dspublish -f <enterprise CA certificate file> NTAuthCA
certutil -dspublish -f <enterprise CA certificate file> SubCA
```

> **MORE INFO** **CROSS-FOREST CERTIFICATE ENROLLMENT**
>
> See *http://technet.microsoft.com/en-us/library/ff955845* for more information on creating certificate enrollment between forests.

CTLs can be created as part of Group Policy. Within the Group Policy Management Editor, selecting Computer Configuration, Policies, Windows Settings, Public Key Policies, and then Enterprise Trust enables a right-click context action to create a new Certificate Trust List. This invokes the Certificate Trust List Wizard, within which you can select parameters for the CTL, such as those shown in Figure 4-20. In Figure 4-20, a one-month duration has been selected, and the certificates found in the CTL will be valid for server authentication.

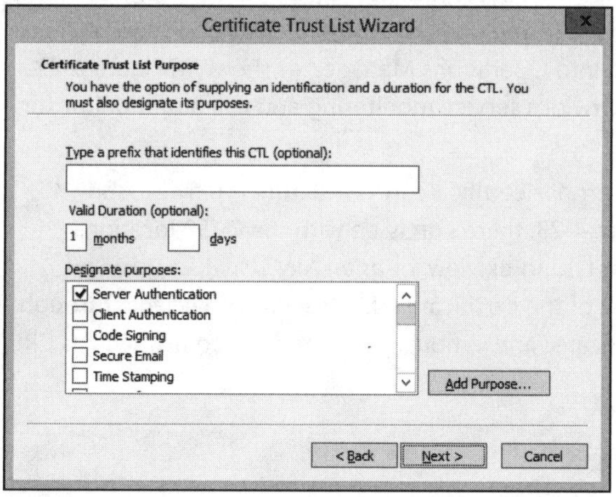

FIGURE 4-20 Choosing parameters for a CTL

The certificate or certificates to be included in the CTL are chosen next, as shown in Figure 4-21.

FIGURE 4-21 Choosing certificates for a CTL

> **MORE INFO CROSS-CERTIFICATION AND BRIDGE CA**
>
> See *http://technet.microsoft.com/en-us/library/cc759308* for information on cross-certification and bridge CA.

Monitoring CA health

Monitoring CA health can be accomplished with the Active Directory Certificate Services Monitoring Management Pack available for System Center Operations Manager. The management pack can be downloaded from *http://www.microsoft.com/en-us/download/details.aspx?id=34765* and then imported into Operations Manager, as shown in Figure 4-22. Once imported, the management pack provides service monitoring and can also monitor for various events.

Another option for monitoring an enterprise certificate infrastructure is pkiview, shown in Figure 4-23. As you can see from Figure 4-23, there's an issue with the OCSP location. Accessible from the command prompt by typing pkiview, or as an MMC snap-in, pkiview monitors the health of CAs. The hierarchy of the certificate infrastructure is available through pkiview. You can view the health of certificates and various CA-related endpoints, such as CRL distribution points, using pkiview.

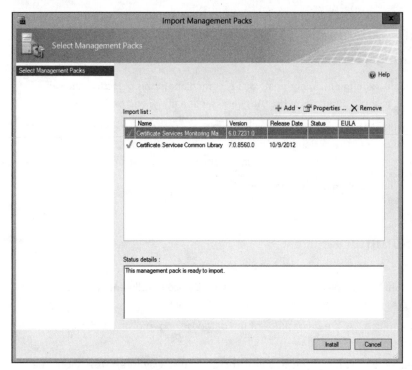

FIGURE 4-22 Importing certificate-related management packs into Operations Manager

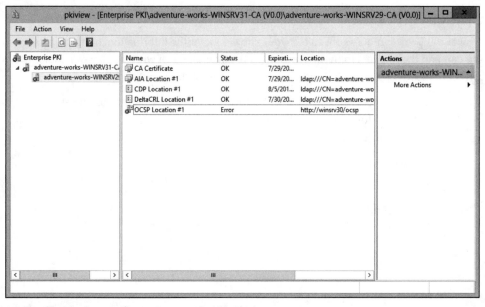

FIGURE 4-23 Viewing certificate server status with pkiview

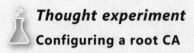

Thought experiment
Configuring a root CA

In this thought experiment, apply what you've learned about this objective. You can find answers to these questions in the "Answers" section at the end of this chapter.

You're assisting with the implementation of a certificate services infrastructure for a small organization. The design that's been chosen includes a root CA and a single subordinate enterprise CA. Your task is to install the root CA portion.

Discuss the configuration involved in a root CA.

Objective summary

- Offline root CA needs to be created as a standalone-type CA.
- Certificate Enrollment Web Services and Network Device Enrollment Services are both configured as role services within a certificate infrastructure.
- When migrating a CA, create backups of the database, log, registry, and other CA-related settings.
- When creating a trust for certificate infrastructure, a two-way forest trust should be created between the resource and account forest.

Objective review

Answer the following questions to test your knowledge of the information in this objective. You can find the answers to these questions and explanations of why each answer choice is correct or incorrect in the "Answers" section at the end of this chapter.

1. Which permission needs to be granted to various objects when choosing Selective Authentication for a forest trust?

   A. Allow Authenticate

   B. Allow Enroll

   C. Enterprise CA

   D. Certification Admin

2. Which role has the Install A CA permission by default?

    A. CA administrator

    B. Auditor

    C. Enterprise PKI

    D. Local administrator

3. When configuring an offline root CA, the request policy should be:

    A. Accept All

    B. Subordinate Enterprise CA

    C. Pending

    D. Designated

Objective 4.3: Implement and manage certificates

The previous two objectives looked at planning and then building the underlying certificate infrastructure for an enterprise. This objective examines managing the certificates themselves.

This objective covers how to:

- Manage certificate templates
- Implement and manage certificate deployment, validation, renewal, and revocation
- Manage certificate renewal, including Internet-based clients, CAs, and network devices
- Configure and manage key archive and recovery

Managing certificate templates

Certificate templates are managed through the the Certificate Templates Console in Windows Server 2012. Within the Certification Authority tool, selecting Certificate Templates and then selecting Manage reveals the Certificate Templates Console, as shown in Figure 4-24.

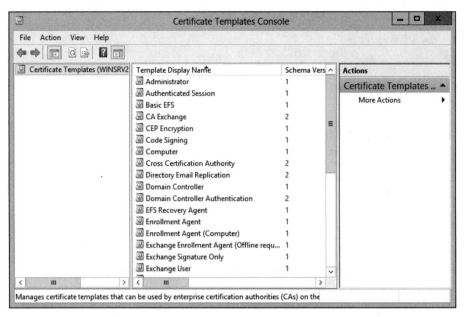

FIGURE 4-24 Viewing certificate templates in Windows Server 2012

Selecting any of the templates and then selecting Properties reveals the properties of the template, as shown in Figure 4-25.

FIGURE 4-25 Viewing properties of a certificate template

Table 4-5 discusses the properties found on the tabs of a certificate template's properties.

TABLE 4-5 Built-in certificate template properties

Tab	Description
General	Display name, CA support, validity period, renewal period, and whether to publish the certificate in Active Directory.
Request Handling	The purpose of the certificate along with cryptographic service providers from which requests are accepted.
Subject Name	Configures the allowed source of a certificate subject name as well as its type.
Extensions	The extensions included with a template.
Security	Groups and users that have access to a certificate template.

You can change these properties and others when creating a new template by selecting a template and then choosing Duplicate. When you do so, several tabs become available, as shown in Figure 4-26 and discussed in Table 4-6.

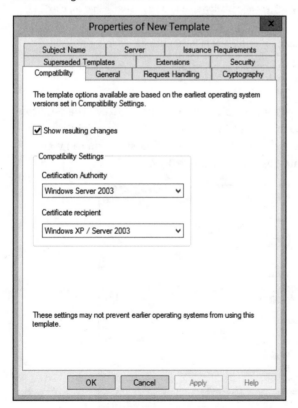

FIGURE 4-26 Configuring a duplicate template

TABLE 4-6 Certificate template settings

Tab	Description
Compatibility	Configures the operating systems that can use the resulting template.
General	The name of the template along with its validity period, renewal period, and whether certificates should be published in Active Directory.
Request Handling	The purpose of the certificate along with other cryptographic parameters, such as whether the private key can be exported and whether to include symmetric algorithms allowed by the subject. Also on this tab is whether the certificate should be enrolled if the private key is available and the subject is enrolled.
Cryptography	The minimum key size for certificates created with the template, along with cryptographic providers that can be used.
Superseded Templates	Whether certificates issued with the current template should supersede certificates issued by other templates, as designated on this tab.
Extensions	The extensions included with the template; these can be edited within this tab as well.
Security	Group and user permissions for the template.
Subject Name	The location from which subject information should be gathered, either supplied in the request or built from Active Directory information.
Server	Whether to stop the storage of certificates in the CA database.
Issuance Requirements	Whether to require CA certificate manager approval for enrollment along with requirements for reenrollment.

Once the settings have been configured for a template, the next step is to add the certificate template to the CA. This is accomplished in the Certification Authority tool by right-clicking Certificate Templates and then selecting New, Certificate Template to Issue. You can then select from among the available templates, as shown in Figure 4-27.

FIGURE 4-27 Choosing a template to add to the CA

MORE INFO **ADMINISTERING CERTIFICATE TEMPLATES**

See *http://technet.microsoft.com/en-us/library/cc725621* for additional details on the options available for a certificate template.

Implementing and managing certificate deployment, validation, renewal, and revocation

Deploying a certificate can be accomplished in several ways, the simplest of which is using the Certificates MMC snap-in to request a new certificate. The Certificate Enrollment Wizard steps through the process of obtaining a certificate within the enterprise. In the Certificate Enrollment Wizard, the policy is selected first, as shown in Figure 4-28.

FIGURE 4-28 Selecting the certificate enrollment policy

The available templates are shown, and the template from which the certificate request should be generated can be selected, as shown in Figure 4-29.

EXAM TIP

The templates that appear are dependent on the templates being published in Active Directory as well as your permissions to view them. Selecting the Show All Templates check box reveals additional templates.

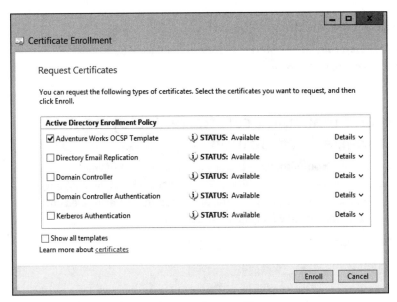

FIGURE 4-29 Choosing the template type for a certificate

There are also other methods for deploying certificates, including:

- **Configuration Manager**   You can use Microsoft System Center Configuration Manager to deploy certificates. See *http://technet.microsoft.com/en-us/library/gg682023.aspx* for details.

- **Group Policy**   See *http://technet.microsoft.com/en-us/library/cc770315(v=ws.10).aspx* for details.

Certificates can be validated through the Certificates MMC snap-in by selecting Open from the certificate's Actions menu. The Certification Path tab shows the status of the certificate, as shown in Figure 4-30.

OCSP through an online responder can be used for validation and revocation management. See the previous section for details on implementing OCSP.

Certificate revocation can be accomplished from the CA by selecting the certificate and choosing Revoke Certificate from the All Tasks menu of the certificate. When a certificate is revoked, a reason code can be given along with a date and time of revocation, as shown in Figure 4-31.

> **NOTE   DEPLOYING CERTIFICATES**
>
> Deploying certificates to clients can be accomplished by using Group Policy or through another push method.

FIGURE 4-30 Viewing the current status of a certificate

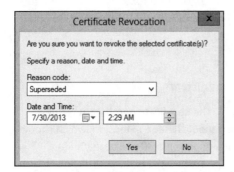

FIGURE 4-31 Revoking a certificate

Managing certificate renewal

Basic renewal of certificates takes place in the Certificates MMC snap-in. There are two
options for renewing a certificate:

- Renew Certificate With New Key
- Renew This Certificate With Same Key

The option chosen depends on the needs of the environment. Choosing to renew with a
new key can enhance security because you can strengthen the new key. Renewing certificates

is a standard operation, and more information can be obtained from *http://technet.microsoft.com/en-us/library/cc730605.aspx.*

EXAM TIP

Key-based renewal can be used as a means to achieve automatic renewal. Windows 8 and Windows Server 2012 are the minimum client requirements to use this feature. See *http://social.technet.microsoft.com/wiki/contents/articles/7734.certificate-enrollment-web-services-in-active-directory-certificate-services.aspx* for more information.

CES is used to provide certificate enrollment and renewal for clients, regardless of whether the client is part of the domain. CES uses HTTP and SSL (HTTPS) to provide the services. The section "Configuring and managing Certificate Enrollment Web Services and Certificate Enrollment Policy Web Services" earlier in this chapter discusses CES.

Managing certificate deployment and renewal to network devices

NDES can be used to provide certificate deployment and renewal to network devices. The CEP Encryption template is used as the basis for NDES, and you create a duplicate of the CEP Encryption template as you would when working with other templates. The basic process for enrollment is as follows:

1. Generate a key pair with the device. The key pair can be used for signing and signature verification, or decryption and encryption, or both signing/signature verification and decryption/encryption.

2. An administrator obtains a password from NDES.

3. Configure the device to trust the certificate infrastructure.

4. Submit a certificate enrollment request to NDES. The certificate enrollment request contains the password obtained earlier and also the KeyUsage extension, which should be defined as Key Encipherment (0x20), Digital Signature (0x80), or both (0xa0).

5. NDES then takes the enrollment request and submits it to the CA. The CA issues the certificate based on its policy.

Renewal is allowed as long as the device retains the same subject name.

MORE INFO NDES

See *http://social.technet.microsoft.com/wiki/contents/articles/9063.network-device-enrollment-service-ndes-in-active-directory-certificate-services-ad-cs.aspx* for more information on NDES.

Configuring and managing key archive and recovery

Key archival can be performed manually or automatically, depending on the configuration. If the certificate template requires key archival, then the process of archiving the key requires no manual intervention. However, key archival can also be performed manually if the private key is exported and then sent to an administrator for import into the CA database.

The Archive subject's Encryption Private Key setting on the Request Handling tab of a certificate template's Properties dialog box is where automatic key archival is configured, as shown in Figure 4-32.

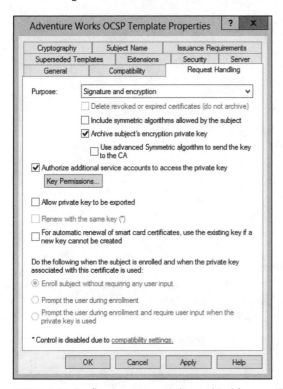

FIGURE 4-32 Configuring automatic key archival for a certificate template

There is also a Key Recovery Agent template that exists in the standard templates with Active Directory Certificate Services. The Key Recovery Agent template enables Domain Admins and Enterprise Admins to export private keys. Additionally, you can also add other accounts and groups to have the necessary permissions (Read and Enroll) through the Security tab of the template, shown in Figure 4-33.

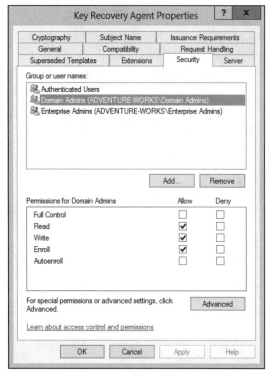

FIGURE 4-33 Configuring permissions for the Key Recovery Agent template

The Key Recovery Agent template also needs to be enabled, as with other certificate templates, through the Certification Authority tool by selecting Certificate Template To Issue. See the section titled "Managing certificate templates" earlier in this objective for more details on enabling a certificate template on a CA.

With the Key Recovery Agent template in place, the following process must take place for key archival and recovery:

1. Request a key recovery agent certificate using the Certificates snap-in.

2. Issue the key recovery agent certificate using the Certification Authority tool.

3. Retrieve the enrolled certificate using the Certificates snap-in.

4. Configure the CA for key archival and recovery.

The final step, configuring the CA for key archival and recovery, takes place in the Properties dialog box of each CA that will need to archive and recover keys. Specifically, the Recovery Agents tab shown in Figure 4-34 configures the behavior of the CA when a request includes key archival.

Each Key Recovery Agent certificate should be added using the Add button in the Recovery Agents tab.

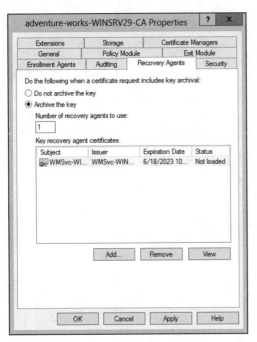

FIGURE 4-34 Configuring key archival settings for a CA

Thought experiment

Certificate templates

In this thought experiment, apply what you've learned about this objective. You can find answers to these questions in the "Answers" section at the end of this chapter.

Your certificate infrastructure consists of an offline root CA and two enterprise CAs. You have three websites that need internal SSL certificates. You'll be implementing certificate templates for SSL websites in your organization.

Describe the process for creating a certificate template and making it available for use.

Objective summary

- Certificate templates provide a means by which an organization can control the parameters for certificates.
- NDES provides certificate enrollment services for network devices.
- CES provides certificate services to Internet-based clients.
- Key archival and recovery can be automated through certificate templates or performed manually with key recovery agents.

Objective review

Answer the following questions to test your knowledge of the information in this objective. You can find the answers to these questions and explanations of why each answer choice is correct or incorrect in the "Answers" section at the end of this chapter.

1. On which tab of a certificate template Properties dialog box can the setting be found for automatic key archival?

   A. Server

   B. Request Handling

   C. Security

   D. Cryptography

2. To which setting should the KeyUsage parameter be set for an NDES request?

   A. Digital Signature (0x80)

   B. Key Change (0xF1)

   C. Key Archival (0x5150)

   D. Encrypt-Change (0x2a)

3. The online responder implements which protocol?

   A. Certificate Revocation Protocol

   B. Certificate Status Protocol

   C. Security Certificate Enrollment Protocol

   D. Online Certificate Status Protocol

Objective 4.4: Design and implement a federated identity solution

This section shifts away from certificates and into authentication and authorization, or at least a limited subset of authentication and authorization. This section examines federated identity and the exam objectives around the same.

This objective covers how to:

- Plan for and implement claims-based authentication, including planning and implementing relying party trusts
- Plan for and configure claims provider and relying party trust claim rules
- Plan for and configure attribute stores, including Active Directory Lightweight Directory Services (AD LDS)
- Plan for and manage Active Directory Federation Services (AD FS) certificates
- Plan for and implement Identity Integration with cloud services
- Integrate Web Application Proxy with AD FS

Planning for and implementing claims-based authentication

Claims-based authentication is provided through Active Directory Federation Services (AD FS). AD FS enables authentication and authorization for external resources, such as web-based applications. AD FS uses the concept of claims to provide authentication and authorization, and AD FS provides the means by which claims are exchanged between partners.

For example, when a user attempts to authenticate to a web application, a claim is generated and the organization hosting the web application, known as a relying party, processes the claim. The processing could be as simple as accessing the values in the claims and granting the user access to an application.

Claims-based authentication relies on trust between the organization making the claim and the organization accepting the claim. The organization that contains the user accounts is referred to as an *account partner*, while the organization that contains the application to be accessed is referred to as a *resource partner*.

AD FS uses rules to determine how to process claims and an attribute store to determine what values to place in a claim. This exam objective covers both trust rules and attribute stores later.

> **MORE INFO AD FS KEY CONCEPTS**
>
> This section doesn't provide exhaustive coverage of AD FS and the concepts of claims-based authentication. See *http://technet.microsoft.com/en-us/library/ee913566.aspx* for more details on the key concepts of AD FS.

The server on which AD FS is installed must be joined to a domain. Several items can be installed as part of an AD FS implementation, including:

- **Federation Service**   The main service to provide claims-based authentication.

- **Web Agents** Claims-aware or Windows token-based agents that process claims received from an AD FS 1.1 Federation Service.

- **Web Application Proxy** Gathers credentials from users and forwards them to the Federation Service. The Web Application Proxy cannot be installed on the same server as the Federation Service.

> **MORE INFO APPLICATION STRATEGY**
>
> The TechNet article "Determine Your Federated Application Strategy in a Resource Partner" contains several questions that can help frame the discussion when considering a federated identity implementation. The article is available at *http://technet.microsoft.com/en-us/library/dd807077.aspx*.

AD FS is configured through the AD FS Federation Server Configuration Wizard, in which you can create a new Federation Service or add the server to an existing Federation Service. When implementing the Federation Service, you can choose a federation server farm or a standalone federation server. For most enterprise environments, a server farm would be used to ensure fault tolerance.

The connection to AD DS is configured and then the Federation Service names and certificate are configured next in the wizard, shown in Figure 4-35.

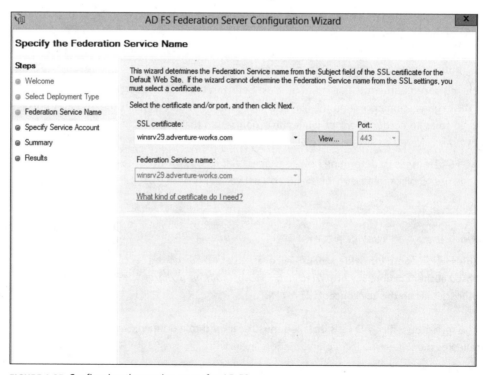

FIGURE 4-35 Configuring the service name for AD FS

The Federation Service name is derived from the SSL certificate used for AD FS. The SSL certificate can be based off of a template, and the common name for the certificate should be the name that will be contacted as part of the AD FS implementation. The SSL certificate needs to be enrolled and used by IIS.

EXAM TIP

For internal public key infrastructure, the computer on which the certificate will be enrolled should be granted the Enroll permission within the certificate template.

Once AD FS is installed and initial configuration is complete, the next step in setting up AD FS is to configure a relying-party trust. A relying-party trust can be configured using a URL obtained from the relying party. The URL contains federation metadata that can be used for the configuration. Alternatively, the relying party can also export the federation metadata to a file that can subsequently be imported. Finally, you can also configure a relying-party trust manually.

All three relying-party trust configuration options use the Add Relying Party Trust Wizard. Table 4-7 describes the information necessary to manually configure a relying-party trust.

TABLE 4-7 Relying-party trust manual configuration

Information	Description
Display Name	The friendly display name given to this relying-party trust.
Profile	Select AD FS profile for the standard Windows Server 2012 AD FS, or AD FS 1.0 and 1.1 profile for AD FS configurations that need to work with older versions of AD FS.
Certificate	The optional certificate file from the relying party for token encryption.
URL	The URL for the relying party. WS-Federation Passive protocol URL or SAML 2.0 WebSSO protocols are supported.
Identifiers	The unique identifier used for this trust.
Authorization Rules	Permit all users to access the relying party or deny all users access to the relying party, depending on the needs of this trust.

Other parameters can also be entered, such as a monitoring URL. These details can be added to the relying-party trust through its Properties dialog box, shown in Figure 4-36.

The relying party configures a claims provider trust that contains many of the same details and uses the token signing certificate from the claims provider's AD FS implementation.

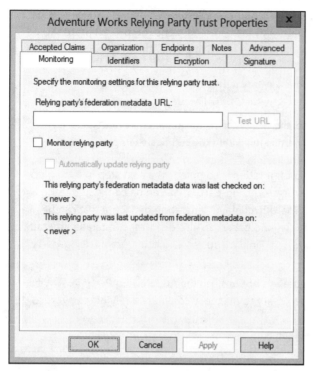

FIGURE 4-36 Properties of a relying-party trust in AD FS

MORE INFO CLAIMS PROVIDER TRUST

See *http://technet.microsoft.com/en-us/library/dd807064.aspx* for more information on creating a claims provider trust.

Planning for and configuring claims provider and relying-party trust claim rules

Claims provider trust rules are configured within the AD FS management console and are configured on a per-trust basis. Planning claims rules involves determining what claims are needed by the relying party to complete the authentication and authorization process and which users will need access to the relying-party trust. The relying party determines what claims need to be received and trusted from the claims provider.

MORE INFO CLAIMS RULES

See *http://technet.microsoft.com/en-us/library/ee913586.aspx* for more detail on the purpose of claims rules in AD FS.

Trust rules use templates as the basis for the rule. There are different types of claims templates depending on the type of rule being used. The claims rule templates for transforms are described in Table 4-8.

TABLE 4-8 Transform claims rule templates

Template	Description
Send LDAP Attributes as Claims	Attributes found in an LDAP directory (such as Active Directory) can be used as part of the claim.
Send Group Membership as Claim	The group memberships of the logged-in user are sent as part of the claim.
Transform an Incoming Claim	Used for configuring a rule to change an incoming claim. Changes include both the type and value of an incoming claim.
Pass Through or Filter an Incoming Claim	Perform an action such as pass through or filter on an incoming claim based on certain criteria, as defined in the rule.
Send Claims Using a Custom Rule	Create a rule that's not covered by a predefined template, such as an LDAP attribute generated with a custom LDAP filter.

The template is chosen as the first step of the Add Transform Claim Rule Wizard, shown in Figure 4-37.

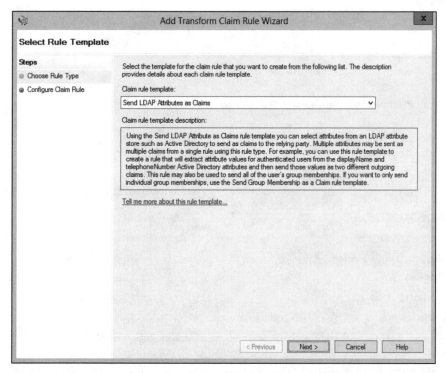

FIGURE 4-37 Creating a rule based on the Send LDAP Attributes As Claims template

The values and claim type are configured next in the rule. Note that multiple attributes can be sent as part of a single rule for most of the rule templates, as shown in Figure 4-38.

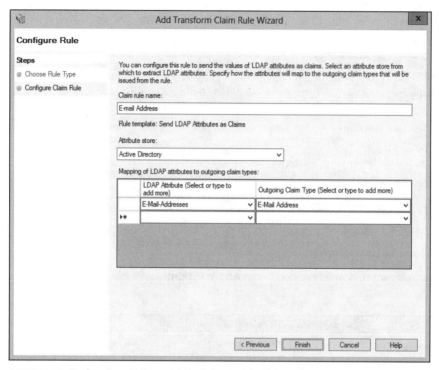

FIGURE 4-38 Configuring attributes to send as part of a claim rule

There are also templates for authorization, as described in Table 4-9.

TABLE 4-9 Authorization rule templates

Template	Description
Permit or Deny Users Based on an Incoming Claim	Defines whether users will be permitted or denied access to the relying party based on the contents of an incoming claim.
Permit All Users	Allows all users to access the relying party.

For example, creating a rule that denies access to Managers based on their group might look like Figure 4-39.

> **MORE INFO** USING AUTHORIZATION RULES
>
> There's a specific article with details about when to use an authorization rule. See *http://technet.microsoft.com/en-us/library/ee913560.aspx* for the article.

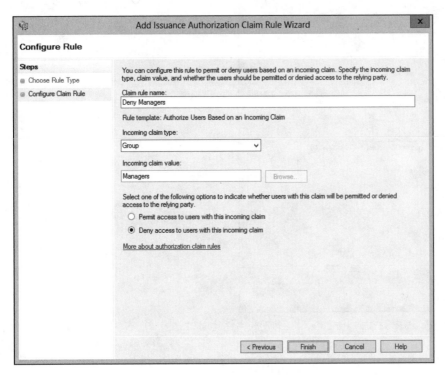

FIGURE 4-39 Creating a deny rule for a claim

Planning for and configuring attribute stores

Attribute stores are the directories from which claim values are obtained. AD FS supports Active Directory, including Active Directory Lightweight Directory Services (AD LDS) as an attribute store. AD FS also supports SQL Server and custom attribute stores.

You can use AD LDS in an environment that could benefit from directory services but doesn't have or need a domain or domain controllers available. AD LDS can be used as an attribute store in AD FS and is added within the Attribute Stores folder of AD FS Management.

When adding an attribute store, you can add a type of Active Directory, LDAP, or SQL. You also specify a connection string. For AD LDS, LDAP should be chosen as the Attribute Store Type, as shown in Figure 4-40.

FIGURE 4-40 Adding an AD LDS attribute store

The attribute store can then be chosen when specifying claims rules, as shown in Figure 4-41.

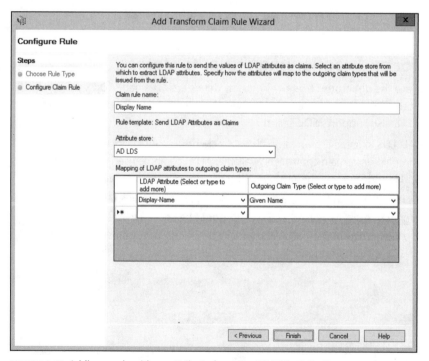

FIGURE 4-41 Adding a rule with an attribute from the AD LDS attribute store

Planning for and managing Active Directory Federation Services (AD FS) certificates

There are three types of certificates used by an AD FS implementation:

- Service communications
- Token decrypting
- Token signing

EXAM TIP

A single certificate can be used for all of the AD FS services.

The service communications certificate is used for communication with web clients over SSL and with Web Application Proxy services using Windows Communication Foundation (WCF). This certificate is configured in IIS and specified at configuration time for AD FS.

The token decrypting certificate is used to decrypt claims and tokens that are received by the federation service. The public key for the decrypting certificate is typically shared with relying parties and others as appropriate so they can encrypt the claims and tokens using the certificate.

The token signing certificate is used to sign all claims and tokens created by the server.

You can use multiple token encrypting and signing certificates as needed for an implementation, and new ones can be added within the AD FS Management tool, shown in Figure 4-42.

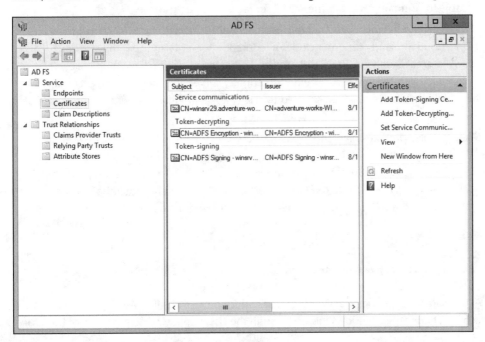

FIGURE 4-42 Certificates for an AD FS implementation

Management task for certificates in AD FS include adding an additional token signing or token encrypting certificate, changing the service communications certificate, or exporting the certificate. All of these tasks can be accomplished from within the AD FS Management tool. To add certificates, the certificates must exist in the certificate store for the AD FS server. However, to add a new token signing or encrypting certificate, automatic certificate rollover needs to be disabled. This is accomplished with the following Windows PowerShell command:

```
Set-ADFSProperties -AutoCertificateRollver $false
```

Once that command has been executed, a new certificate can be added.

Planning for and implementing Identity Integration with cloud services

AD FS is an excellent choice for integration with cloud services that can work with claims-based authentication, such as Office 365 and Windows Intune. The exam indicates that you should be aware of planning involved in such integration efforts. Therefore, at a high level you should be able to plan for and implement identity integration needed by a cloud service. This includes:

- **Directory synchronization**   Ensuring that changes to the local Active Directory are propagated to the cloud service.
- **Web Application Proxy**   Offsite users might have difficulty creating claims if they can't reach the AD FS federation server. A Web Application Proxy, configured to be able to communicate with the AD FS server, can solve this issue.

The recommended (*http://technet.microsoft.com/en-us/library/dn151324.aspx*) topology for AD FS cloud implementations includes a federation server farm using the standard Windows Internal Database (WID) and proxies. In this topology you have multiple servers hosting AD FS, with the first server being the primary server and others being secondary servers. Multiple proxies can then be used to relay information from external users to the AD FS servers.

Microsoft also provides planning guidance based on the number of users involved in the AD FS implementation. A Network Load Balancing server can be used to provide proxy services. For 1,000 to 15,000 users, there should be two dedicated AD FS servers and two dedicated proxies. When 15,000 to 60,000 users are involved, there should be between three and five dedicated AD FS servers and at least two dedicated proxies.

> **NOTE** **SERVERS**
>
> **WID supports up to five dedicated servers.**

Active Directory can be directly integrated with cloud services like Windows Intune. This is accomplished within Windows Intune through the Users area by activating Active Directory synchronization and then downloading and installing the Directory Synchronization tool (dirsync.exe), which can be downloaded from Windows Intune as well.

Integrating Web Application Proxy with AD FS

A new role service in Windows Server 2012 R2, Web Application Proxy enables a reverse proxy scenario that enables external users to access internal websites. Web Application Proxy can be integrated with AD FS to provide preauthentication for users. The preauthentication scenario then means that Windows Integrated authentication can be used for the internal websites published through the Web Application Proxy service.

Integrating Web Application Proxy means connecting it to the AD FS server. This is accomplished during configuration of the Web Application Proxy service. After it is integrated, you can add preauthentication through the Web Application Proxy console, a step called *publishing*. Adding a web application invokes the Publish New Application Wizard, in which you choose the preauthentication method, shown in Figure 4-43.

FIGURE 4-43 Adding a new application for Web Application Proxy

When using AD FS preauthentication, you'll next choose the relying party for the application, shown in Figure 4-44 (where Device Registration Service has been chosen).

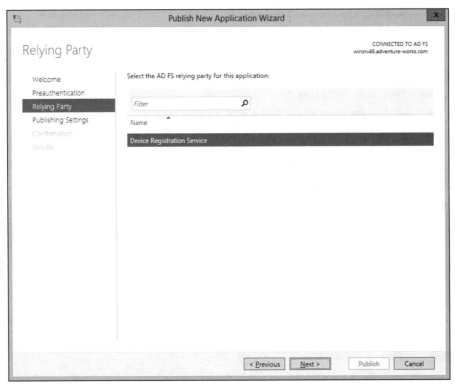

FIGURE 4-44 Choosing the AD FS relying party

MORE INFO **AD FS PREAUTHENTICATION CONFIGURATION**

See *http://technet.microsoft.com/en-us/library/dn383640.aspx* for more information on the steps described in this section.

 Thought experiment

Claims-based authorization

In this thought experiment, apply what you've learned about this objective. You can find answers to these questions in the "Answers" section at the end of this chapter.

You need to provide a claims-based authorization solution for users in your organization so that they can access a third-party web application without needing to provide credentials. This solution will be used by about 3,000 users, including those within the organization and several that gain access from remote locations.

Describe the infrastructure setup you'll use for this solution, including whether you'll be a claims provider or relying party.

Objective summary

- Claims-based authentication is implemented through AD FS in Windows Server 2012.
- AD FS works on the concept of claims providers and relying parties.
- Claims provider trust rules define the values sent within claims and can also transform claims.
- Attribute stores are the databases or directories of information used to provide claims values.
- AD FS uses several certificates, including a services certificate and signing and encrypting certificates, though the same certificate can be used for all of these use cases.
- AD FS can be used for identity integration with cloud services such as Windows Intune and Office 365.

Objective review

Answer the following questions to test your knowledge of the information in this objective. You can find the answers to these questions and explanations of why each answer choice is correct or incorrect in the "Answers" section at the end of this chapter.

1. Which of the following is an available option when configuring an attribute store type?

   A. HTTPS

   B. SSL

   C. WCF

   D. LDAP

2. Which of the following is an available template for configuring an authorization rule?

   A. Permit All Users

   B. Deny Computer

   C. Transform User

   D. Permit Claims

3. Supporting a Windows Server 2003 AD FS implementation requires which of the following?

   A. AD FS 1.0 or 1.1 support

   B. AD FS claims provider trust rule

   C. AD FS 2003 support

   D. AD FS down-level usage support

Objective 4.5: Design and implement Active Directory Rights Management Services (AD RMS)

The final objective in this chapter and for the exam looks at Active Directory Rights Management Services (AD RMS). AD RMS enables organizations to protect information regardless of the location where the information is accessed and whether the information is moved to a new location. AD RMS operates around the concept of usage rights and conditions that specify which trusted entities can access a given piece of information, such as a document. AD RMS also provides encryption of data and information.

> **This objective covers how to:**
> - Plan for highly available AD RMS deployment
> - Plan for AD RMS client deployment
> - Manage trusted user domains
> - Manage trusted publishing domains
> - Manage federated identity support
> - Upgrade or migrate AD RMS
> - Decommission AD RMS

Planning for highly available AD RMS deployment

Planning for a highly available AD RMS deployment means not only installing AD RMS in a highly available manner, but also ensuring that the AD RMS database is made highly available as well. AD RMS consists of the following:

- **AD RMS Certification Server Cluster**   The main servers used for providing AD RMS services.
- **SQL Servers**   The data store for AD RMS configuration and rights-management information.
- **AD RMS Client**   Software that runs on each client to enable the usage of AD RMS.
- **AD RMS Licensing-Only Cluster**   Optional servers that can be used to support external partners or special rights-management scenarios.

AD RMS is integrated with AD DS so that clients can find the AD RMS service. If there are multiple forests involved in an organization, then AD RMS needs to be installed in each forest. There are various means by which users in separate forests can consume protected content across forests, including:

- **Trusted user domains (TUD)**   A TUD enables AD RMS to work with rights certificates created by a different AD RMS cluster. TUD requires import of the server licensor certificate from the other AD RMS cluster.

- **Trusted publishing domains (TPD)**   A TPD enables AD RMS to issue use licenses using publishing licenses created by a different AD RMS cluster. TPD requires import of both the server licensor certificate and its private key.

- **AD RMS with AD FS**   You can create a trust using AD FS. This can be helpful if users from an external forest need to access rights-protected content in the AD RMS forest.

- **Microsoft account**   A Microsoft account, formerly known as a Windows Live ID, that's trusted with the Microsoft online RMS service can be used to access data.

A best practice when designing AD RMS services is to ensure that there's a DNS name for the cluster rather than addressing individual servers. This helps to alleviate any issues that might arise if one server becomes unavailable. If you'll be using a CNAME DNS record, then the SQL Server instances need to have a registry key changed in order to use the fully qualified domain name (FQDN). Specifically, the DisableStrictNameChecking setting needs to be changed from 0 to 1. This setting is found at HKEY_LOCAL_MACHINE\SYSTEM\CurrentControlSet\Services\lanmanserver\parameters.

The following protocols and ports need to be open for communication between AD RMS applications.

- **TCP/80 and/or TCP/443**   Open one or both of these ports for HTTP or HTTPS traffic to the AD RMS server from clients. This exception is created in Windows Firewall when AD RMS is installed.

- **TCP/445**   This port is opened on the SQL server for AD RMS. The port is used for SQL Server Named Pipes to provision the AD RMS server.

- **TCP/1433**   This port is opened on the SQL server for AD RMS for SQL communication.

- **TCP/3268**   This port is opened on the Global Catalog server from the AD RMS server.

There are new security groups created for AD RMS management, including:

- **AD RMS Enterprise Administrators**   This role enables AD RMS policy and settings management.

- **AD RMS Template Administrators**   This role enables AD RMS template management.

- **AD RMS Auditors**   This role enables the reading of logs and reports about the AD RMS cluster.

> **NOTE** **AD RMS SERVICE GROUP**
>
> There is also a group called AD RMS Service Group that enables members to run AD RMS services. The group isn't typically used for normal user accounts but rather for service accounts related to AD RMS.

Planning for the availability of SQL Server is an important step in an AD RMS design. Failover clustering and log shipping provide two primary means for ensuring availability of the SQL Server databases involved in delivering AD RMS. See *http://technet.microsoft.com/en-us/library/ee221084(v=ws.10).aspx* for more information on each of these options and *http://technet.microsoft.com/en-us/library/hh831554.aspx* for information on changes to AD RMS for Windows Server 2012.

Managing AD RMS Service Connection Point

The Service Connection Point (SCP) is used to store the URL of the AD RMS cluster. The SCP is stored as an object in Active Directory. The SCP can be configured when AD RMS is being installed or later, through the Active Directory Rights Management Services console.

Managing the SCP is accomplished on the SCP tab of the AD RMS cluster's Properties dialog box, shown in Figure 4-45.

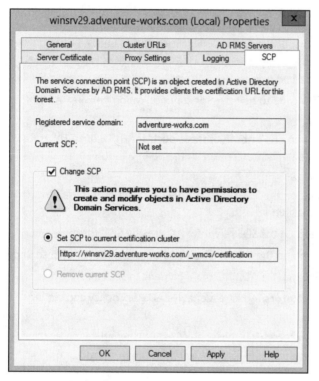

FIGURE 4-45 Setting the SCP in AD RMS

As you can see from Figure 4-45, changing the SCP requires permissions to create and modify objects in AD DS.

> **NOTE SCP**
>
> **The SCP has not yet been configured in Figure 4-45, but the process is the same regardless.**

Once set, you can view the current SCP properties through ADSIEdit on the domain controller, within the Configuration context in CN=Services,CN=RightsManagementServices,CN=SCP.

MORE INFO **WINDOWS POWERSHELL AND AD RMS**

See *http://technet.microsoft.com/en-us/library/ee221079(v=ws.10).aspx* for information on using Windows PowerShell with AD RMS.

Planning for and managing AD RMS client deployment

The AD RMS client is included as an optional download for Windows XP and is supported (and included) on the following operating systems:

- Windows Vista SP2
- Windows Server 2008 and Windows Server 2008 R2
- Windows 7 SP1
- Windows Server 2012 and Windows Server 2012 R2
- Windows 8 and Windows 8.1

There is a separate installer depending on the client computer architecture (x86 or x64), though the x64 setup program installs both the 32-bit runtime and the 64-bit runtime to maintain compatibility with 32-bit applications. There are two methods for installing the AD RMS client, and both require local Administrator privileges.

- **Silent mode** The /quiet switch to the setup program installs the client in silent mode, which would be useful for a scripted installation.
- **Interactive mode** A graphical installation of the client software.

Management of the AD RMS client can involve where files and licenses are stored. Table 4-10 describes the file and license locations for the AD RMS client.

TABLE 4-10 AD RMS client file and license locations

Location	Description
Program-related files	%ProgramFiles%\Active Directory Rights Management Services Client 2.x
License store	%localappdata%\Microsoft\MSIPC for client installations and %allusersprofile%\Microsoft\MSIPC\Server\<SID>\ for server installations.
Template store	%localappdata%\Microsoft\MSIPC\Templates for client installations and %allusersprofile%\Microsoft\MSIPC\Server\Templates\ for server installations.
Registry settings	HKEY_CURRENT_USER\Software\Classes\Local Settings\Software\Microsoft\MSIPC for clients and HKEY_CURRENT_USER\Software\Microsoft\MSIPC\Server\<SID> for server installations. The location HKEY_LOCAL_MACHINE\SOFTWARE\Microsoft\MSIPC can also be used to control certain aspects of AD RMS.
Unmanaged templates	%localappdata%\Microsoft\MSIPC\UnmanagedTemplates on a client installation and %allusersprofile%\Microsoft\MSIPC\Server\UnmanagedTemplates\<SID> on a server installation.

Several registry keys can be used to modify the behavior of the AD RMS client. Table 4-11 describes the management that can be done with registry settings.

TABLE 4-11 Registry management tasks for AD RMS

Registry Key	Description
HKLM\Software\Microsoft\MSIPC\TrustedServers	String values that define DNS names of trusted AD RMS servers.
HKLM\Software\Microsoft\MSIPC\TrustedServers\AllowTrustedServersOnly	If this value is non-zero, then the AD RMS client will use only the servers configured in the trusted list.
HKLM\SOFTWARE\Microsoft\MSIPC\ServiceLocation\EnterpriseCertification	Change the service location.
HKLM\SOFTWARE\Microsoft\MSIPC\ServiceLocation\EnterprisePublishing	Change the enterprise publishing location.
HKLM\SOFTWARE\Microsoft\MSIPC\Server\<SID>\TemplateUpdateFrequency	Change the template update frequency on a server installation (measured in days).
HKCU\Software\Classes\Local Settings\Software\Microsoft\MSIPC\TemplateUpdateFrequency	Change the template update frequency on a client installation (measured in days).
HKCU\Software\Classes\Local Settings\Software\Microsoft\MSIPC\<Server>\Template	Removal of this key causes the client to download templates at the next publishing request.
HKLM\Software\Microsoft\MSIPC\Federation\FederationHomeRealm	The URL of a federation service.
HKLM\Software\Microsoft\MSIPC\Federation\EnableBrowser	Enable support for forms-based federation.
HKCU\Software\Classes\Local Settings\Software\Microsoft\MSIPC\DisablePassportCertification	Disable ILS service consumption.
HKLM\SOFTWARE\Microsoft\MSIPC\Trace	Set to 1 to enable tracing.

One other registry entry worth noting is used if there isn't an SCP available. You can add a ServiceLocation subkey to HKLM\SOFTWARE\Microsoft\MSIPC and then, within that key, create an EnterpriseCertifications subkey that contains the URL of the AD RMS cluster name in the format *https://<AD RMS Cluster>/_wmcs/Certification*, as well as another subkey called EnterprisePublishing that contains the URL in the format *https://<AD RMS Cluster>/_wmcs/Licensing*.

Managing trusted user domains

TUDs enable trust between domains running AD RMS and are often used to connect users between forests. TUD management is accomplished in the AD RMS Management console. TUD information is exported to a .bin file and then subsequently imported using the Import Trusted User Domain dialog box shown in Figure 4-46.

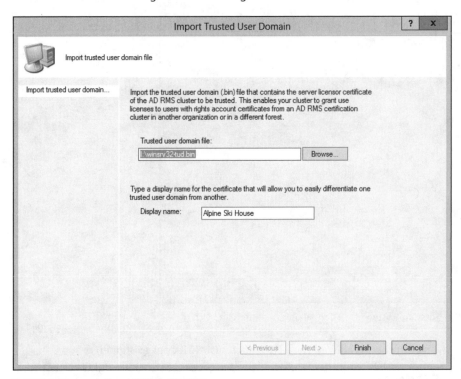

FIGURE 4-46   Importing a TUD in AD RMS

Once imported, you can manage the TUD through its Properties dialog box, in which you can choose whether to enable licensing SIDs and also specify trusted email domains, as shown in Figure 4-47.

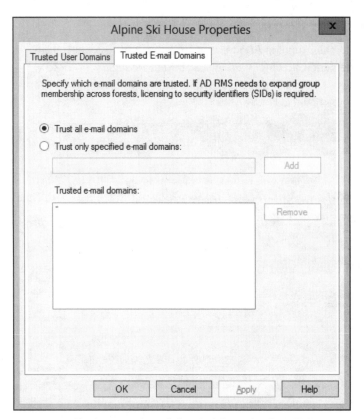

FIGURE 4-47 Viewing trusted email domain information for a TUD

While a forest trust isn't required for a TUD, if a forest trust does exist, then group expansion is also possible. Group expansion makes the process of granting rights easier. However, certain prerequisites need to be met for group expansion to work. First, the forest trust must exist. Next, the Service Account of the AD RMS cluster that trusts the authentication needs to be granted rights on the Group Expansion pages of the AD RMS cluster. Finally, a group contact should be created in the trusting AD RMS forest for each destination group so that the pointer will use the correct location. The email attribute of the group contact and the destination group, as well as the msExchOriginatingForest attribute, all need to be set to the FQDN of the destination forest for the group contact to work correctly.

> **MORE INFO** TUD
>
> See *http://technet.microsoft.com/en-us/library/dd983944(v=ws.10).aspx* for more information on TUD, including details on the trust.

Managing trusted publishing domains

Unlike a trusted user domain, a trusted publishing domain (TPD) enables an AD RMS cluster to issue licenses as if it was a different AD RMS cluster. To accomplish this, both the certificate and the private key need to be imported. This is different than a TUD scenario, where only the certificate is imported.

Importing a TPD is accomplished within the AD RMS Management console using the Import Trusted Publishing Domain dialog box, shown in Figure 4-48.

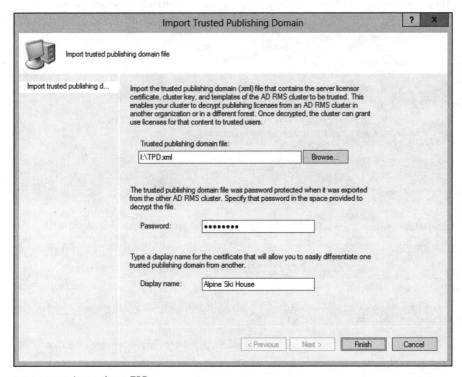

FIGURE 4-48 Importing a TPD

In addition to the import of the domain itself, clients need to be redirected to the trusted AD RMS cluster. This can be accomplished using registry settings or by adding a DNS alias.

> **MORE INFO TPD**
>
> See *http://technet.microsoft.com/en-us/library/dd996639(v=ws.10).aspx* for additional details on TPD.

Managing federated identity support

Federated identity support is provided through integration of AD FS and AD RMS when trust exists between organizations using AD FS. For federated identity to work with AD RMS, the AD FS service needs to be installed, the Identity Federation Support role needs to be added, and federated identity support needs to be enabled in AD RMS. This is accomplished by accessing Trust Policies and then the Federated Identity Support section of the AD RMS Management console. Once federated identity support is enabled, you can alter the validity period and URL, as well as whether to allow proxy email addresses, as shown in Figure 4-49.

FIGURE 4-49 Changing federated identity parameters in AD RMS

Managing distributed and archived rights policy templates

Rights policy templates are managed in the AD RMS Management console. This section focuses on management-related tasks for rights policy templates. Planning and overviews of rights policies are available at *http://technet.microsoft.com/en-us/library/ee221094* and *http://technet.microsoft.com/en-us/library/dd996658*.

You can specify a location for templates to be stored as well as whether the templates can be exported by using the Properties of the Rights Policy Templates node, shown in Figure 4-50.

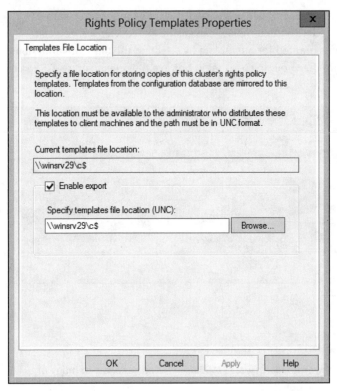

FIGURE 4-50 Configuring parameters for all rights policy templates

Rights policy templates have several properties that can be set on a per-template basis, including language support for clients, expiration policy, user rights, extended policy, and revocation policy, each of which has its own tab in a template's Properties dialog box. Table 4-12 describes the tabs for a rights policy.

TABLE 4-12 Rights policy template settings

Tab	Description
Identification Information	View and set client language support and view the template's Globally Unique Identifier (GUID).
User Rights	View and set rights for the template, including users, groups, and their rights. The rights request URL is set on this tab as well.
Expiration Policy	View and set expiration conditions for content and licenses that use the template.
Extended Policy	View and set parameters, such as whether a user can view content using a browser plug-in, whether to require a new license every time content is consumed, and additional information about the AD RMS application.
Revocation Policy	View and set whether revocation is required and parameters for revocation.

Templates can be archived. When a template is archived, it will no longer be available to clients; however, content protected with the template can still be issued licenses. You can view a summary of the user rights granted for a template by selecting the template and then selecting View Rights Summary. When you do so, a dialog box like the one in Figure 4-51 will be shown.

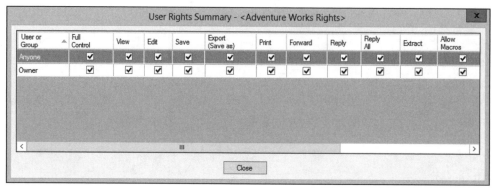

FIGURE 4-51 Viewing the rights summary for a template

MORE INFO **CONFIGURING RIGHTS POLICY TEMPLATES**

See *http://technet.microsoft.com/en-us/library/cc731599.aspx* for an overview of many of the same steps discussed in this section.

Configuring exclusion policies

Exclusion policies provide a means by which access to certificates and licenses can be prevented. Exclusion policies can be applied to user, application, and lockbox versions. Exclusion policies are enabled through the AD RMS Management console by selecting the appropriate exclusion policy to create. Prior to doing so, the exclusion policy typically needs to be enabled.

User exclusions can be done based on the user name or based on a public key string, which is helpful for users that don't have an AD DS account. The Exclude User dialog box is shown in Figure 4-52.

Application exclusion policies are configured based on the application name and version numbering, as shown in Figure 4-53.

It's worth noting that the minimum and maximum versions need to be specified in a four-digit format, such as 5.1.5.0 or 1.2.3.4.

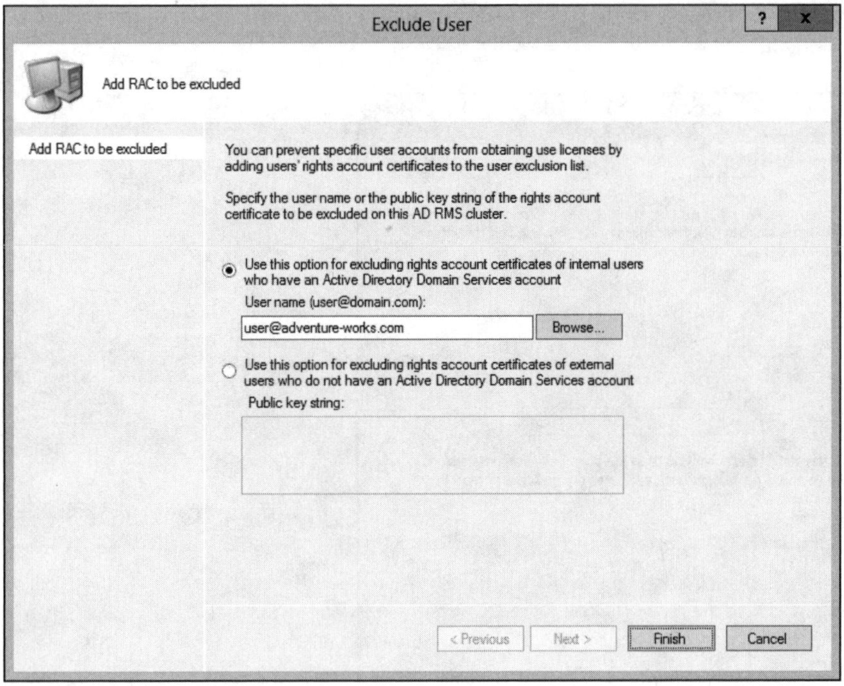

FIGURE 4-52 Creating an exclusion policy for a user

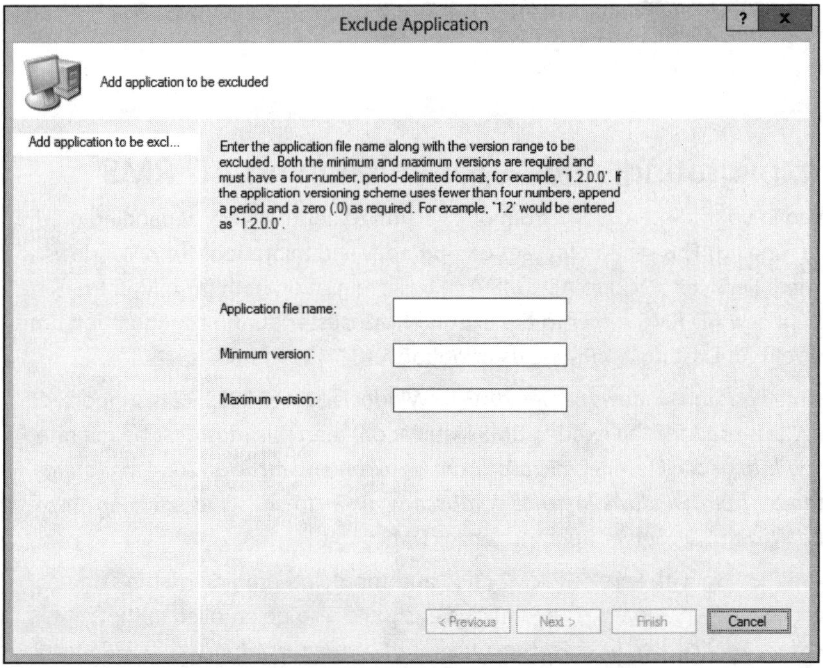

FIGURE 4-53 Creating an exclusion policy for an application

The Lockbox dialog box, shown in Figure 4-54, enables a minimum version of the lockbox that can be used with AD RMS.

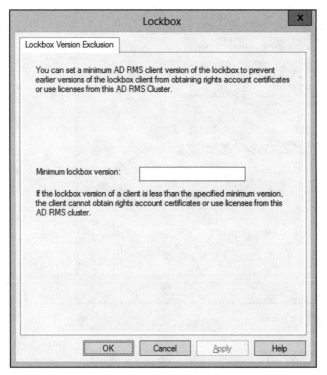

FIGURE 4-54 Configuring a lockbox exclusion policy

Upgrading, migrating, and decommissioning AD RMS

The tasks involved in upgrading AD RMS from one version to another vary depending on the version currently running. This section focuses on upgrades and migrations from Windows Rights Management Services (RMS) to AD RMS. The basic migration path from RMS to AD RMS is to join a new AD RMS server to the existing RMS cluster during configuration time by choosing the Join An Existing AD RMS Cluster option.

Upgrading directly from Windows Server 2003 to Windows Server 2012 R2 is supported. However, if the WID is used for the existing RMS installation, then this must first be migrated to SQL Server. See *http://social.technet.microsoft.com/wiki/contents/articles/1084.migrating-the-ad-rms-database-from-windows-internal-database-wyukon-to-sql-server-2005-sp2.aspx* for details on the WID to SQL Server upgrade for AD RMS.

RMS should be running with Service Pack 2 (SP2) and should be running on the same version across all legacy RMS servers. The RMS cluster should also be enrolled in the Microsoft Enrollment Service. See *http://technet.microsoft.com/en-us/library/cc730885* for details on checking enrollment status.

If the existing RMS installation is using CSP protection rather than RMS key protection, then the CSP private key needs to be imported into the new AD RMS server. See *http://technet.microsoft.com/en-us/library/cc753807* for details on this issue. Additionally, the server licensor certificate needs to be imported into the new AD RMS server by exporting the trust policies from within the Windows RMS Administration website.

Decommissioning AD RMS should be done in a specific order so that content protected by AD RMS can be unprotected. Additionally, once decommissioned, the server cannot be brought back to its previous state. Therefore, care should be taken before decommissioning AD RMS.

Decommissioning AD RMS means setting a property in AD RMS. Once decommissioned, users should unprotect their content. Only after these steps are complete should the AD RMS role be uninstalled. A special URL, *decommission.asmx*, is used to fulfill certificate requests while the AD RMS cluster is in decommissioned state. Therefore, permissions on the *decommission.asmx* file in IIS should be changed so that all users can access the file, and any AD RMS applications should also be reconfigured to send requests to the decommissioning web service URL.

Decommissioning is set in the Security Policies of the AD RMS Management console. Decommissioning itself, or the ability to select Decommission, is disabled by default. Once enabled, the Decommission button becomes available, as shown in Figure 4-55.

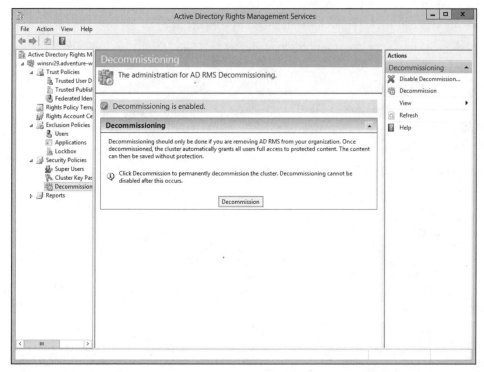

FIGURE 4-55 Getting ready to decommission AD RMS

Objective summary

- AD RMS is used to provide rights management for content within an organization.
- AD RMS should normally be set up in a fault-tolerant manner and uses SQL Server for its database, which should also be set up in a fault-tolerant manner.
- AD RMS uses trusted user domains and trusted publishing domains to enable cross-forest authentication.
- AD RMS can use AD FS for federated identity support.
- AD RMS uses templates for rights management.

Objective review

Answer the following questions to test your knowledge of the information in this objective. You can find the answers to these questions and explanations of why each answer choice is correct or incorrect in the "Answers" section at the end of this chapter.

1. Which protocol and port are used by AD RMS to contact the global catalog server?

    A. TCP/445

    B. TCP/1433

    C. TCP/22

    D. TCP/3268

2. Which of the following is a valid version number when creating an application exclusion policy?

   A. 1.0

   B. 5.3.7.2

   C. 1.4.3

   D. 1

3. Which user groups are allowed to make changes to AD RMS templates?

   A. Active Directory Rights Management Services Template Administrators

   B. Domain Admins

   C. Active Directory Rights Management Services Auditors

   D. Template Users

Answers

This section contains the solutions to the thought experiments and answers to the lesson review questions in this chapter.

Objective 4.1: Thought experiment

You can use a standard two-tier design with a root CA operated in the main data center and then multiple issuing CAs, one or more for each location. The root CA would likely be standalone, while the issuing CAs would be enterprise in order to take advantage of AD DS integration.

Objective 4.1: Review

1. **Correct answer:** B

    A. **Incorrect:** Enterprise cannot be operated in offline mode.

    B. **Correct:** Standalone can be operated in offline mode.

    C. **Incorrect:** Offline is not a valid option.

    D. **Incorrect:** On/off is not a valid option.

2. **Correct answer:** C

    A. **Incorrect:** Publishing interval defines how long between publications.

    B. **Incorrect:** Validation is not a valid option.

    C. **Correct:** Validity defines the amount of time a CRL is valid.

    D. **Incorrect:** Revocation interval is not a valid option.

3. **Correct answer:** A

    A. **Correct:** Standalone CA and NDES should exist on the same server.

    B. **Incorrect:** Enterprise CA should not exist on the same server.

    C. **Incorrect:** Multiforest is not a valid option.

    D. **Incorrect:** CA trust is not a valid option.

Objective 4.2: Thought experiment

The root CA is installed as a role in Windows Server 2012. Within the role, the CA role service is configured. A standalone CA should be chosen, because that's the only type that can be offline. A new private key will likely be created unless one already exists within the organization. The request handling should be set (verified) to pending for new requests, the CRL distribution point should be set to a server that will be online, and the server should be taken offline.

Objective 4.2: Review

1. **Correct answer:** A

   A. **Correct:** Allow Authenticate needs to be granted to Administrators, domain member computers, and enterprise CAs.

   B. **Incorrect:** Allow Enroll is not a valid permission.

   C. **Incorrect:** Enterprise CA is not a valid permission.

   D. **Incorrect:** Certification Admin is not a valid permission.

2. **Correct answer:** D

   A. **Incorrect:** CA administrator does not have the ability to install a new CA.

   B. **Incorrect:** Auditor does not have the ability to install a new CA.

   C. **Incorrect:** Enterprise PKI is not a real role.

   D. **Correct:** Local administrator has the permission to install a CA by default.

3. **Correct answer:** C

   A. **Incorrect:** Accept All is not a valid policy.

   B. **Incorrect:** Subordinate Enterprise CA is not a valid policy.

   C. **Correct:** Requests should be set to pending on a root CA.

   D. **Incorrect:** Designated is not a valid policy.

Objective 4.3: Thought experiment

The first task is to duplicate an existing certificate template, such as the Web Server template. With a duplicate template available, any settings specific to the environment can be changed. Once the template has been configured, it needs to be made available on each CA by selecting the Certificate Template to Issue option from the Certificate Templates folder context menu in the Certification Authority tool.

Objective 4.3: Review

1. **Correct answer:** B

   A. **Incorrect:** The Server tab does not contain this information.

   B. **Correct:** Request Handling contains the archive subject's encryption private key setting.

   C. **Incorrect:** The Security tab contains permission information for users and groups.

   D. **Incorrect:** The Cryptography tab does not contain this information.

2. **Correct answer:** A

   A. **Correct:** Digital Signature (0x80) is one of the allowed KeyUsage parameter settings.

   B. **Incorrect:** Key Change (0xF1) is not a valid parameter setting.

   C. **Incorrect:** Key Archival (0x5150) is not a valid parameter setting.

   D. **Incorrect:** Encrypt-Change (0x2a) is not a valid parameter setting.

3. **Correct answer:** D

   A. **Incorrect:** Certificate Revocation Protocol is not a valid protocol.

   B. **Incorrect:** Certificate Status Protocol is not a valid protocol.

   C. **Incorrect:** Security Certificate Enrollment Protocol is not a valid protocol.

   D. **Correct:** Online Certificate Status Protocol is the protocol implemented by the online responder.

Objective 4.4: Thought experiment

You'll need to set up at least two AD FS federation servers and at least two AD FS Web Application Proxy servers for this solution to maintain fault tolerance. Your company is the claims provider and will provide claims based on whatever the third-party web application needs for authentication and authorization.

Objective 4.4: Review

1. **Correct answer:** D

   A. **Incorrect:** HTTPS is not one of the options for an attribute store type.

   B. **Incorrect:** SSL is not one of the options for an attribute store type.

   C. **Incorrect:** WCF is not one of the options for an attribute store type.

   D. **Correct:** LDAP, along with SQL and Active Directory, are the options for an attribute store type.

2. **Correct answer:** A

   A. **Correct:** Permit All Users is one of the available authorization templates.

   B. **Incorrect:** Deny Computer is not a template.

   C. **Incorrect:** Transform User is not a valid template.

   D. **Incorrect:** Permit Claims is not a valid template.

3. **Correct answer:** A

   A. **Correct:** AD FS 1.0 or 1.1 support is needed to support Windows Server 2003 AD FS.

   B. **Incorrect:** AD FS claims provider trust rule is not needed to support Windows Server 2003 AD FS.

   C. **Incorrect:** AD FS 2003 support is not a valid option.

   D. **Incorrect:** AD FS down-level usage support is not a valid option.

Objective 4.5: Thought experiment

The AD RMS design includes two AD RMS servers and two SQL servers to provide fault tolerance. The AD RMS elements include those servers along with an AD RMS client on each computer that will need to access the AD RMS–protected content. TCP/445 and TCP/1433 will need to be open between the AD RMS servers and the SQL servers. The AD RMS server should be allowed to communicate on TCP/3268 to the AD DS servers to obtain global catalog information. Finally, TCP/443 should be allowed from clients to the AD RMS servers.

Objective 4.5: Review

1. **Correct answer:** D

   A. **Incorrect:** TCP/445 is not used for global catalog traffic.

   B. **Incorrect:** TCP/1433 is typically used for SQL Server traffic.

   C. **Incorrect:** TCP/22 is typically used for Secure Shell (SSH) traffic.

   D. **Correct:** TCP/3268 is the protocol and port used for global catalog traffic.

2. **Correct answer:** B

   A. **Incorrect:** 1.0 is not a valid version-numbering scheme for an application exclusion policy.

   B. **Correct:** Application exclusion policies require four-digit version numbers, so 5.3.7.2 is valid.

   C. **Incorrect:** 1.4.3 is not a valid version-numbering scheme for an application exclusion policy.

   D. **Incorrect:** 1 is not a valid version-numbering scheme for an application exclusion policy.

3. **Correct answers:** A, B

   A. **Correct:** Active Directory Rights Management Services Template Administrators can make changes to templates in AD RMS.

   B. **Correct:** Domain Admins can make changes to templates.

   C. **Incorrect:** Active Directory Rights Management Services Auditors cannot make changes to templates.

   D. **Incorrect:** Template Users is not a valid group.

Index

A

access-based enumeration settings, 83–84

access solutions

AD RMS, 242–255

client deployment, 245–246

federated identity support, 250–254

highly available deployment, 242–245

TPDs (trusted publishing domains), 249

TUDs (trusted user domains), 247–248

upgrading, migrating, and
decommissioning, 254–255

certificates

deployment, validation, and revocation, 221–223

key archival and recovery, 225–227

renewal, 223–224

templates, 217–221

certificate services infrastructure, 189–215

administrator role separation, 209–211

CA migration, 209

Certificate Enrollment Policy Web
Services, 201–204

Certificate Enrollment Web Services, 192–193,
201–204

configuring NDES, 204–205

configuring offline root CA, 196–201

disaster recovery, 194

monitoring CA health, 214–215

multi-forest CA deployment and trust, 192

multi-tier certification authority
hierarchy, 190–191

NDES (Network Device Enrollment Services), 193

planning for validation and revocation, 193–194

trust between organizations, 211–214

ACS (Audit Collection Services), 22–25

ACS Collectors, 22

ACS Database, 22

ACS Forwarders, 22

actions allowed, Tenant Administrator (VMM user role
profile), 123

Active/Active option, 96

Active Directory. *See* AD (Active Directory)

Active Directory database monitoring (AD monitoring
scenario), 30

Active Directory Federation Services. *See* AD FS

Active Directory Rights Management
Services. *See* AD RMS

Active/Passive option, 96

AD (Active Directory)

monitoring, 27

recovering domains and forests, 102–103

restoring objects and containers, 103–104

Add/Edit Port Rule dialog box, 69–70

/AddGroup parameter (AdtAdmin), 24

Add IP Address dialog box, 66–67

Add Load Balancer button, 73

Add Operations Manager Wizard, 41–42

Add Physical Disk dialog box, 78–79

Add Relying Party Trust Wizard, 231

Add Revocation Configuration Wizard, 206

Add-SCCustomPlacementRule cmdlet, 140

Add-SCStorageProvider cmdlet, 160, 163

Add Storage Devices Wizard, 160–162

Add Transform Claim Rule Wizard, 233

Add-VMHardDiskDrive cmdlet, 136

Add VM Network button, 73

Add-WindowsFeature fs-iscsitarget-server
command, 90

W

About the author

STEVE SUEHRING is a technical architect with significant hands-on experience in system administration, networking, and computer security. Steve has written on numerous subjects, including Windows, Linux, development, and networking. You can follow him on Twitter at @stevesuehring.

From technical overviews to drilldowns on special topics, get
free ebooks from Microsoft Press at:

www.microsoftvirtualacademy.com/ebooks

Download your free ebooks in PDF, EPUB, and/or Mobi for
Kindle formats.

Look for other great resources at Microsoft Virtual Academy,
where you can learn new skills and help advance your career
with free Microsoft training delivered by experts.

Microsoft Press

Now that you've read the book...

Tell us what you think!

Was it useful?
Did it teach you what you wanted to learn?
Was there room for improvement?

Let us know at http://aka.ms/tellpress

Your feedback goes directly to the staff at Microsoft Press,
and we read every one of your responses. Thanks in advance!